BASKETBALL

A Guide to Skills, Techniques and Tactics

BASKETBALL
A Guide to Skills, Techniques and Tactics

ALEXANDRU RADU

THE CROWOOD PRESS

First published in 2010 by
The Crowood Press Ltd
Ramsbury, Marlborough
Wiltshire SN8 2HR

www.crowood.com

British Library Cataloguing-in-Publication Data
A catalogue record for this book is available from the British Library.

ISBN 978 1 84797 187 6

Disclaimer
Please note that the author and the publisher of this book are not responsible, or liable, in any manner whatsoever, for any damage, adverse outcome, or injury of any kind, that may result from practising or applying the techniques and methods and/or following the instructions described in this publication. Since the exercises and other physical activities described in this book may be too strenuous in nature for some readers to engage in safely, it is essential that a doctor be consulted before undertaking such exercises and activities.

Illustration credits
Jane Haslam Photography – Figs 6, 7, 8, 14, 25, 29, 33, 44, 45, 46, 71, 72, 73, 74, 75, 76, 80, 81, 82, 100, 114, 115, 116, 142, 143, 144, 193, 194, 198, 229, 230, 231, 236, 237, 238, 250, 253, 260, 309, 311 and 320; and pages 2, 9, 35, 107 and 135.

Mark Pritchard – Figs 15, 16, 20, 21, 22, 26, 27, 28, 30, 31, 32, 34, 35, 36, 47, 48, 49, 50, 51, 52, 53, 54, 55, 56, 57, 58, 59, 60, 61, 62, 63, 83, 84, 85, 86, 87, 88, 89, 90, 91, 92, 97, 98, 99, 108, 109, 110, 111, 117, 118, 119, 120, 122, 123, 124, 125, 126, 127, 128, 130, 131, 132, 133, 134, 135, 136, 137, 138, 139, 140, 145, 146, 149, 150, 151, 152, 154, 155, 156, 157, 158, 159, 160, 161, 162, 166, 167, 168, 169, 170, 171, 172, 173, 174, 183, 190, 232, 233, 234, 241, 242, 244, 245, 246, 247, 248, 249, 251, 252, 254, 255, 256, 258, 275, 276, 278, 280, 282, 284, 297, 298, 299, 300, 301, 302, 303, 305, 306, 308, 310, 312, 313, 314, 315, 316, 317, 318, 319.

FIBA – Figs 1, 2, 3, 4, 12, 321, 322.

Line illustrations by Keith Field

Typeset by Bookcraft, Stroud, Gloucestershire

Printed and bound in Singapore by Craft Print International Ltd

CONTENTS

ACKNOWLEDGEMENTS

A text of this nature could not be written without the support and assistance of a number of people.

My deepest gratitude and my special thanks go to Dan Pavelescu, my first basketball coach and my role model. He is the person who inspired me and who planted the seeds for a love of this beautiful game. A big 'thank you' for everything you taught me.

I would also like to say 'thank you' to several other people, including my players from North Shields All Stars and North Shields Rockets teams (John Walker, Paul Lynn, Lee Mains, Serge Mitrofanov, Alex Richardson, Ross Doolan, David Neal, Ben Richardson, Nathan Boyd, Scott Brewis, Liam Chaplin), who, along with Sabra Wrice and Abi Scott (from Northumbria University) very kindly agreed to appear in the photographs; Mark Pritchard and Jane Haslam, the photographers who provided me with the lovely pictures that highlight the points I am trying to present in my book; The Crowood Press, who provided me with constant feedback and helped me through the process of writing the book; my reviewers Karl Wharton (Senior Lecturer in Sports Coaching at Northumbria University and GB International Gymnastics Coach) and Ian McLeod (Newcastle Eagles U16 Head Coach), who took the time to read the manuscript and provided some useful comments; to Lubomir Kotleba and FIBA for kindly giving me permission to use the FIBA and FIBA Europe logos, together with some information from the fiba.com website; Chris Brown and England Basketball for allowing me to reproduce some copyrighted material from England Basketball publications, *Basketball. Manual for Table Officials* (2007) and *Basketball Level 1 Coach Award. Candidate Manual* (2001).

And, finally, a big 'thank you' to my wife Lidia and my two boys Alexandru and Richard, who gave me the constant love and the support that I needed to see this project through to the finish line.

Key to Diagrams

○-	ATTACKING PLAYER (facing towards right)
○-	PLAYER WITH A BALL
□	DEFENDER
⊐	DEFENDER WITH ARMS OUT (facing towards right)
∿∿∿→	DRIBBLING
- - - - - - →	PASS
⎯⎯⎯→	PLAYER MOVEMENT (WITHOUT BALL)
⇨	LAY-UP (OR JUMP SHOT)
→‖	OFFENSIVE PLAYER SETTING A SCREEN
⊋‖	SCREEN AND ROLL
△	PLAYER WAITING TO JOIN A DRILL (as an attacker)
⤻	PLAYER FAKES A MOVE TO THE LEFT AND CHANGES DIRECTION TO THE RIGHT
⊗	CONES
C	COACH
○	BASKET

PREFACE

Basketball is a fast-moving, high-scoring indoor (and, sometimes, outdoor) game that demands of the individual player extreme qualities of skill, precision, control and agility as well as the physical pre requisites vital for athletic excellence. Being a team sport, it needs players to understand and cooperate with each other, constantly making choices and decisions within a limited time frame.

This book is intended as a practical, instructional guide and was written with you, the basketball enthusiast – whether you be coach or player (active or aspiring) – in mind. It should also be very useful for Physical Education teachers who would like to know more about the game and will be able to use it when teaching, for students who are studying for a sports sciences/coaching degree, and for parents and volunteers wishing to become coaches. I hope the drills, practices, technical and tactical advice it presents will help those who would like to get involved in coaching basketball for the first time, as well as more experienced coaches who are subject to a continuous process of self-appraisal.

The book is based not only on my experience as a player and as a coach at all levels of the game in two different countries – Romania and England (mini-basketball, junior, senior, professional level) – but also on my study of numerous publications about coaching and playing the game (books, journal articles, specialized coaching magazines, and so on), on my attendance at various national and international coaching clinics and on my lecturing Sports Coaching modules to Higher Education students.

The main aim of the book is to contribute to the process of improving your ability, performance and knowledge of this fast-paced game. In order to achieve this, there are several objectives. First, I wanted to emphasize the paramount importance of learning/teaching the fundamentals of the game in a proper manner and this is reflected in the description of different skills, technical and tactical solutions offered via several drills/exercises for different levels of ability. Second, I have tried to provide complete information for coaching/teaching individual and team skills for both offence and defence. Third, by highlighting the growing importance of coaching as an academic discipline, I have presented the coaching of basketball as a 'process' that incorporates several components and areas of knowledge.

The book has a simple structure that is easy to follow. The first part provides an introduction to basketball, and includes an overview of the rules of the game, a brief history, ways in which to develop a coaching philosophy and communicate it to players, and the best ways to run a basketball programme. The second and third parts examine the fundamental skills, techniques and tactics needed to play offensively and defensively as an individual and as a team. Alongside the description of each skill, several drills/practices are provided, supported by photos and diagrams for a better understanding. The fourth part concerns itself with the 'total training' concept and refers to all the aspects that provide the building blocks for modern coaching: technical, physical, tactical, psychological, theoretic-methodical, biological and artistical training.

Basketball is a challenging sport. The ultimate experience for any player and coach is to play well and win. If you play well, you have a great chance to win. And you play well when you master all the fundamentals and when you apply them in match situations. This book offers unlimited opportunities to perfect your game.

Alexandru Radu

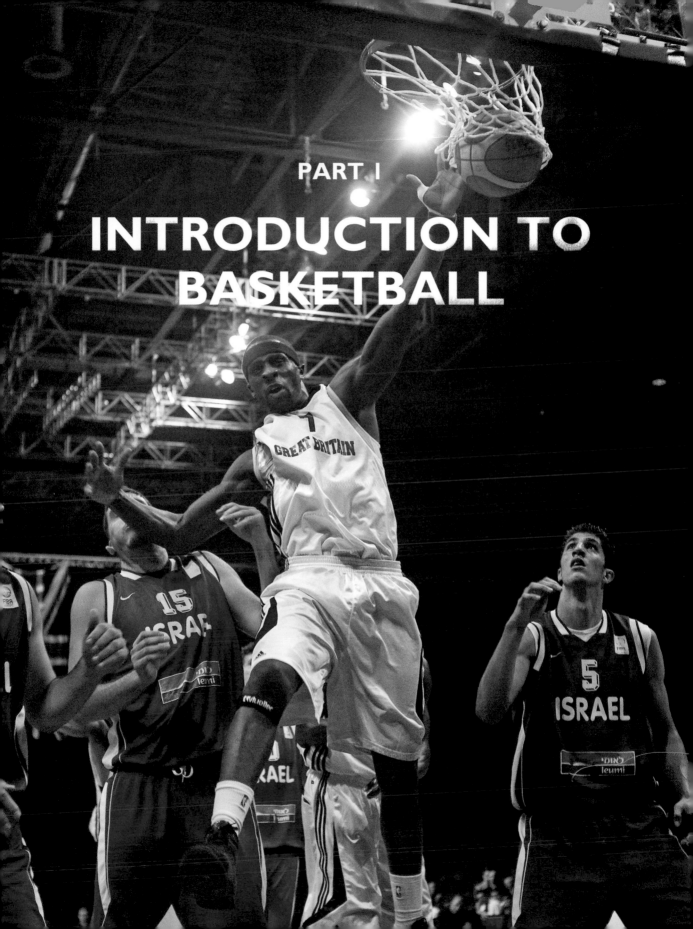

PART I

INTRODUCTION TO BASKETBALL

CHAPTER 1

LAWS OF THE GAME – OVERVIEW

Short History of the Game

It all started over 100 years ago, in 1891, when Dr James Naismith, an American Canadian-born lecturer, created a game for his students at Springfield College (International Young Men's Christian Association – YMCA Training School) in Massachusetts (USA). Devised initially as an indoor activity or sport for students during the cold winter season, the game involved throwing a ball into peach baskets suspended above the ground, fixed to the balcony at each end of the gymnasium. The seven original rules evolved and were developed during the years into what basketball is today – a fast-paced, complex and very dynamic game played by both boys and girls, men and women, at local, national, European and international level.

Some very important milestones are presented below, highlighting several stages through which basketball has passed, up to today, when it is one of the most popular sports worldwide. FIBA (the International Basketball Federation, the world governing body for basketball) has 213 affiliated national federations distributed across all continents within the FIBA family: FIBA Europe, FIBA Oceania, FIBA Americas, FIBA Africa and FIBA Asia.

- 1891: Dr James Naismith invents basketball as an indoor sporting activity for students during the winter season.
- 11 March 1892: the first official basketball game is played between teachers and students of the YMCA in Springfield, Massachusetts, in front of a crowd of 200 people. The students win 5–1.

- 22 March 1893: the first women's game takes place at Smith College, Northampton (Massachusetts). No men are allowed to watch the game.
- 1904, 1924 and 1928: basketball is an exhibition sport at the St Louis, Paris and Amsterdam Olympic Games, respectively, and American teams play exhibition matches. 1936: the game of basketball is officially introduced at the Berlin Olympic Games; 22 countries enter the competition and the creator of the game, Dr James Naismith, is a guest of honour during the Olympic tournament.
- 18 June 1932: the International Basketball Federation, more commonly known by the French acronym FIBA (Fédération Internationale de Basketball), is created in Geneva, with eight founding nations (Argentina, Czechoslovakia, Greece, Italy, Latvia, Portugal, Romania and Switzerland). Nowadays, it comprises 213 affiliated countries.
- 1936: the Amateur Basketball Association of England and Wales (ABBA) is founded. Its first National Championship is staged in Birmingham on 6 June in the same year, won by Hoylake YMCA, who beat London Polytechnic 32–31.
- 1956: the Welsh Association becomes autonomous.
- 1974: the Amateur Basketball Association of England and Wales (ABBA) changes its name to the English Basketball Association (EBBA).
- 1979: EBBA becomes a Company Limited by Guarantee.
- 1994: EBBA amends its name again and is now called England Basketball (EB).

- 1992: as a result of cooperation between FIBA and NBA (the National Basketball Association), and with International Olympic Committee (IOC) agreement, NBA professional basketball players play for the first time in the Olympic basketball tournament at the Barcelona Olympic Games.

Currently the World Championships, the Olympic tournaments and the European Championships are the major basketball events (tournaments for men and women) at international level. In Europe there are also European Championships for Under 20, Under 18 and Under 16 teams (for both boys and girls).

FIBA has organized a FIBA World Championship for men since 1950 (when it took place in Buenos Aires, Argentina) and a World Championship for women since 1953 (Santiago, Chile). Both events are now held every four years, alternating with the Olympics.

Today basketball has become one of the most popular sports on the planet, rivalling football for worldwide popularity

---

FIBA FAMILY

The FIBA Family comprises all affiliated National Federations, which are grouped in 5 zones:

- FIBA Africa (www.fiba-afrique.org) = 53 member National Federations
- FIBA Americas (www. fibaamerica. com) (incorporating North, Central and South American Zones) = 44 members
- FIBA Asia (www. fibaasia.net) = 44 members
- FIBA Europe (www. fibaeurope.com) = 51 members
- FIBA Oceania (www. fibaoceania.com) = 21 members

and trailing only volleyball and track and field/athletics in terms of number of affiliated member federations (213 federations in August 2006). It is estimated by FIBA (in March 2003) that 450 million people are playing basketball worldwide.

The Game

Basketball is a team sport that can be played indoors or outdoors by two teams of five players each on court at any one time. A basketball team roster consists of up to twelve players who can be entered in the official match score sheet. Substitutions are unlimited but may only be made when play is stopped by any of the two (or three, in major competitions) referees or match officials. When on court, all players on both teams attempt to score more points than their opponents by handling and manoeuvring the ball under organized rules. Points are scored by shooting the ball through the basket so that the ball goes through the net from the top, in a downward direction. The team with more points at the end of the game wins.

The ball can be advanced on the court by bouncing (dribbling) or passing between teammates. Disruptive physical contact (a foul) is not permitted and there are restrictions on how the ball can be handled (violations).

All teams have a Head Coach who oversees the development and strategies of the team. Other team personnel and followers might include assistant coaches, statisticians, a team manager, doctors and trainers.

While competitive basketball is primarily an indoor sport, less regulated, outdoor variations have become also very popular. One form frequently encountered in inner cities is streetball, which is basketball usually played three against three, or sometimes two against two.

Court, Kit and Equipment

Essentially, basketball requires a ball and a court. Apart from this, a range of other equipment is generally used at all competitive levels, including score sheets, a scoreboard, alternating possession arrow, whistle-operated stop-clock systems, 24-second clocks, team foul markers (indicators) and player foul markers (numbered 1 to 4 on white background and number 5 on red background).

A regulation basketball court is a flat, rectangular surface, free from any obstructions, 28m long by 15m wide, usually made

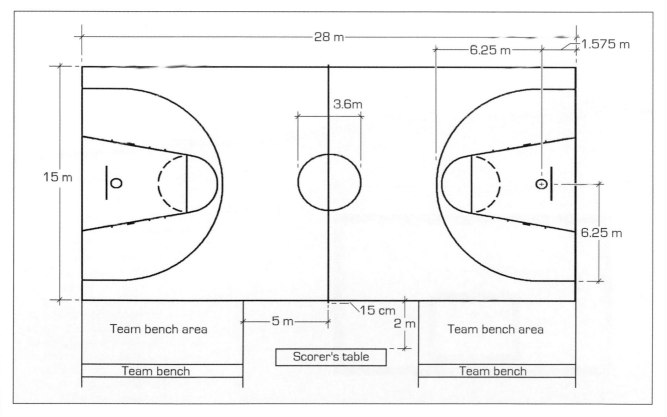

Fig 1 The full-size basketball court.

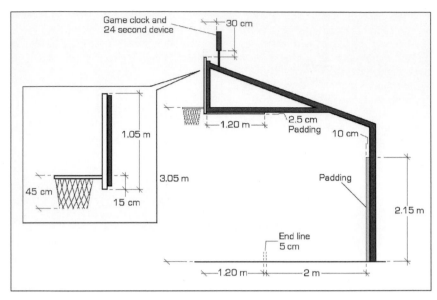

Fig 2 The backstop unit with ring, net and basket support structure.

out of wooden parquet, with baskets at opposite ends (see Fig 1).

The steel basket unit that hangs over each end of the court comprises a ring, net and support structure (Fig 2), and a backboard (the rigid rectangular board behind the rim – Fig 3). At all levels of competition the top edge of the ring is exactly 3.05m above the court and 1.2m inside the baseline.

The size of the ball is also governed by regulations. It is an inflated sphere (usually made of leather) with an outer covering. The rules say that the ball shall be not less than 74.9cm and not more than 78cm in circumference and that it shall weigh no less than 567 grams and no more than 650 grams for all men's competitions (a Size 7 ball). For all women's competitions, the circumference of the ball shall be no less

than 72.4cm and no more than 73.7cm and the ball shall weigh no less than 510 grams and no more than 567 grams (a Size 6 ball).

A standard basketball uniform consists of a pair of shorts and a jersey with a clearly visible number (from 4 to 15) printed on both the front and back, for both men's and women's teams. Players wear basketball shoes rather than simple trainers, providing extra ankle support and comfort, and providing a firm grip on the court surface.

Starting the Game

The game officially begins at the beginning of first quarter with a jump ball at the centre circle. One player from each team – usually the tallest or the best jumper – will jump when the referee throws the ball between them and will try to tip the ball to one of their teammates, who are waiting outside the circle. The ball may be tapped with the hands only *after* it has reached its highest point.

RULES

Neither jumper may catch the ball or touch/tap it more than twice until it has touched one of the non-jumpers or the floor.

The jump ball occurs only at the beginning of the game. Afterwards, all jump-ball situations (when two players from different teams hold the ball, when the ball goes out of bounds and referees are in doubt about who touched the ball last, or when the ball is stuck between the ring and the board) will be resolved using an alternating arrow possession. This causes the ball to become live with a throw-in (sideline possession), which is taken at the place nearest to where the jump-ball situation occurred. The team that does not gain control of the live ball on the playing court after the jump ball that begins the first period will start the alternating possession,

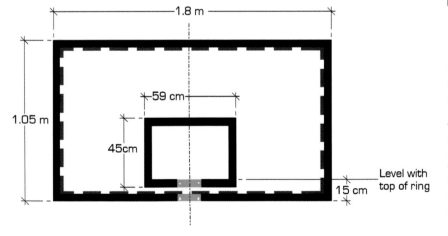

Fig 3 The backboard (front view).

with an arrow indicating which team will have possession next.

The game is controlled by two referees (three referees at major competitions), match officials (who are also called table officials) and a commissioner (who is usually present at major competitions). The table officials are responsible for keeping the score (for both teams), for keeping and indicating the time (both playing time and the shot clock time), and keeping a record of individual and team fouls, player substitutions and the team possession arrow.

Time Limits

Basketball games are played in four quarters (or periods) of 10 minutes effective playing time (or 12 minutes in NBA games). Up to 15 minutes are allowed for a half-time break (between the second and third quarter) and 2 minutes are allowed between the first and second period and between the third and fourth period (and also before each extra period). Teams exchange baskets before the third quarter. The clock is stopped while the play is not active so the time allowed is actual playing time.

There are a number of other important time limits:

- 3-seconds rule: an attacking player is not allowed to remain for more than 3 seconds in the rectangle-shaped area at the end of the court where the basket at which he is shooting is situated.
- 5-seconds rule: when a team has to put the ball back in play from a side-line possession, it must be passed into the court within 5 seconds. Also, a closely guarded player must pass, shoot or dribble the ball within 5 seconds, otherwise a violation is deemed to have occurred and the opposition will obtain possession of the ball at the nearest point on side-line.
- 8-seconds rule: after receiving a basket, a team has 8 seconds to move the ball over the half-way line from the back court to the front court.
- 24-seconds rule: once a team has secured the possession of the ball, that team has 24 seconds in which to take a shot.
- 1 minute: a limited number of time-outs (1 minute each) can be requested by a coach for a quick meeting with the players, discussion of the tactical plan or even for rest purposes.

Scoring System

The main aim of the game is for the team to outscore its opponents by throwing the ball through the opponents' basket (travelling in a downward direction), while at the same time preventing them from doing the same in its own basket. An attempt

to score in this way is called a *shot*. A successful shot is worth 1, 2 or 3 points: 1 point for a free throw, when the player who is shooting has a completely free shot at the basket from behind the free-throws line, which is 4.60m from the basket; 2 points for a normal shot, taken from inside the 3-points semicircle; and 3 points for a long-range shot taken from beyond the 3-points arc, which is 6.25m from the ring (for NBA games this distance is 7.24m).

Fouls

Offensive and Defensive Fouls
Basketball is generally said to be a non-contact sport, a game in which, in theory, physical contact between players is illegal. In practice, with ten players moving so quickly in such a small area, contact does occur. A foul is an illegal action perpetrated by a player from one team on a player from the opposing team. There are two types of foul: *defensive fouls* occur when the attacking player is being fouled by the defender (defenders may not block, push, trip, strike or hold the player in possession, or not, of the ball); an *offensive foul* is committed, for example, when an attacking player is charging into a stationary defender.

Personal Fouls
When unfair contact occurs and one (or both) of the two referees calls a foul, the player charged with the foul must raise his hand. Every player may commit up to five fouls, called *personal fouls*; after a fifth personal foul, the player must leave the court and may not play again in that game. However, a replacement (substitution) player can be sent on court.

The principle of the 'cylinder' (with each player occupying a space within an imaginary cylinder between the floor and the roof, with a base roughly equivalent to his body dimensions – see Fig 4) is useful in interpreting contact situations. When a player runs or reaches into an opponent's 'cylinder' and causes contact, then he is responsible for that contact and is duly penalized.

Team Fouls

During any of the four quarters, when a team has accumulated four fouls as a consequence of its players 'acquiring' personal fouls, every further foul will result in the other team shooting two free throws (bonus shots). At the end of each quarter the four team fouls are cancelled and the team fouls count starts from zero for the next period of play. The only exception is when there is overtime being played; in this case, the team fouls get carried away in the extra period. All personal fouls remain against the individual players when playing extra period(s).

Other Sanctions

Apart from personal fouls, referees can sanction players for unsportsmanlike fouls, technical fouls and/or disqualifying fouls.

An *unsportsmanlike foul* is a personal foul that is deliberately committed, usually with

Fig 4 The cylinder principle.

no intention and no effort to play/steal the ball. It may be committed by either an attacking or a defensive player. The penalty for this type of foul is a free throw(s) plus possession from the half-way line. The number of free throws will be decided according to the following criteria:

* If the player being fouled is not in the act of shooting: two free throws will be awarded.
* If the foul is committed on a player in the act of shooting: the goal, if made, shall count and, in addition, one free throw will be awarded.
* If the foul is committed on a player in the act of shooting who fails to score: two or three free throws will be awarded.

Any player who is charged with a second unsportsmanlike foul is automatically disqualified.

A *technical foul* is committed when there is deliberate or repeated non-cooperation or non-compliance with the spirit of the rules of conduct. Each team may do its best to secure victory but this must be done in a spirit of sportsmanship and fair play. Any player committing acts of violence or flagrant acts of aggression against opponents and/or officials will be disqualified. The penalty in this situation is two free throws followed by possession from the sideline.

A *disqualifying foul* is deemed to have been committed when a player conducts himself in a violent or flagrantly unsportsmanlike fashion. Following disqualification for this kind of foul, a player may take no further part in the match. This type of foul is a player foul and the penalty is the same as for an unsportsmanlike foul.

Playing Positions

Each player is assigned a position when playing basketball. The basic three positions are *center* (or post or pivot), *forward* and *guard*, and they are usually determined by the area of court taken up by a player when playing in attack and also by the height of the player. Height is not the only

RULES

A technical foul is a non-contact foul of a behavioural nature, including but not limited to:

* disregarding warnings by officials;
* communicating disrespectfully with the match officials (referees, table officials, commissioner);
* using language or gestures likely to offend or incite the spectators;
* excessive swinging of elbows.

factor to take into account when selecting a player to play in a particular position; the coach also needs to consider each player's skills level, as well as team tactics. However, as a general rule, the tallest person plays 'center' or 'position 5', while the medium-sized ones play 'forwards' or 'position 3 and 4', and the shortest play 'guards' or 'positions 1 and 2'. (See Fig 5 for a diagrammatic representation of the playing positions while on court.)

Guards

Usually, the guards (also called 'playmakers' or 'play callers') are the smaller and faster players on the team. They are the team leaders – as well as being good safe passers and competent ball handlers, they also organize the team's offensive moments by bringing the ball up the

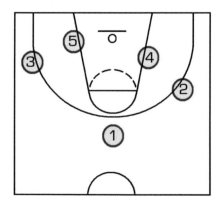

Fig 5 Playing positions: ① point guard; ② shooting guard; ③ small forward; ④ power forward; ⑤ center.

court, running set-up plays (play calls) and making sure the ball gets to the right player at the right time. They also dictate defensive movements. Generally, they play away from the basket (in the area of court between the half-way line and the free-throws line) and quite frequently they shoot from long distance (for a 3-points shot).

There are two types of guard. *Point guards* act as described above but, in addition, their contribution to the game is often measured by the number of assists (passes that lead to an easy 2- or 3-points shot) that they deliver. They may also be referred to as 'playmaker' or '#1 player'. *Shooting guards* create a high volume of shots on offence and they have a good ability to drive to the basket. They are also referred to as '#2 player' or 'position 2 player'.

Forwards

Because they are taller (generally) than the guards, the forwards play mainly in the area of the court at either side of the key (the 3-seconds space, in other words, the painted space) up to the sidelines. In terms of skills they are mainly good rebounders, capable of shooting well from the corners and from the sides of the key, they are good drivers and they are competent at passing to the centers.

There are two types. The *small forwards* are usually tasked with scoring points after cuts to the basket and dribble penetration. Defensively, they aim to get as many rebounds and steals as possible. Many small forwards (also called 'the three', or 'position 3 player', or '#3 player') can play shooting guard too and, because they can switch between the two positions, may also be referred to as 'wings' or 'swing men'.

The *power forward* plays offensively, often with his back to the basket. It is a similar role to that of a center, especially in situations in which a team lacks a tall player. Usually, these players (also known as '#4 player' or 'position 4 player') are expected to be aggressive when rebounding and they score most of their points on the low post (very close to the basket, that is, 2–3m away from it).

Fig 6 Great Britain (GB) guard Nate Reinking (1.83m, in white jersey, number 12).

Centers

The tallest players on the team are very active close to the basket (in and around the key). Centers may also be called pivots or post players (or '#5 player' or 'position 5 player'). Their main ability is to get open to receive a pass and to shoot from close to the basket. Good rebounders, both defensively and offensively, they use their size to score and defend from a position close to the basket. Blocking shots is another skill they need to master. A tall player who possesses athleticism and skill constitutes a very valuable member in the line-up.

Captain's Role

The basketball captain's role is similar to that of the captain of any other sport: to provide much-needed leadership on and off the court. The selection of the captain is an important decision for the coach of a basketball team. He is often one of the older or more experienced members of the squad, or a player who can heavily influence a game, and is expected to

Fig 7 GB forward Luol Deng (2.06m, in white jersey, number 9).

be the coach's correspondent on the court. The team captain needs to display a number of attributes: he must have a positive attitude and a significant knowledge of the game, as well as great listening and decision-making skills; he needs to be a good motivator of his teammates and someone who can manage those on the floor; he should be someone who puts the team before himself; and he may need to be able constructively to confront undisciplined teammates and hold them accountable. Interestingly, even if the captain is one of the most skilful and reliable players, he still may not take part in a game in which he is in foul trouble. The captain may, however, act as coach in the absence of any other coach for the team.

Fig 8 GB centre Pops Mensah-Bonsu (2.06m).

CHAPTER 2

DEVELOPING A BASKETBALL COACHING PHILOSOPHY

One major influence on the coaching process is the philosophy of the individual coach involved – ideally, every coach should develop his own basketball coaching philosophy. There are several great basketball coaches who argue that the first and most important step towards becoming a successful coach is developing their own philosophy. Without a philosophy, a coach will lack the road map necessary to achieve the goals set up at the beginning of the season. A coaching philosophy will enable any coach to command a clear view of where he has come from and where he is going with his coaching.

A coaching philosophy that is well thought through clarifies many aspects of the coach's delivery and, most importantly, presents a consistent and positive message to the athletes being coached. It can also be communicated to others, such as parents, colleagues/fellow coaches, volunteers, club officials, and so on. Coaching is all about helping athletes achieve their dreams, and for this reason alone the development of a coaching philosophy is essential for all coaches.

In summary, a coaching philosophy encompasses the following:

- a set of values and behaviours that serve to guide the actions of a coach;
- a comprehensive statement based on the beliefs and values that characterize and direct a coach's practice;
- a mission statement (the coach's reasons for coaching), that is to say, five to ten key points about his approach to coaching.

Motivation for Coaches

Broadly speaking, a coaching philosophy will reflect what the coach most values in his coaching role – his attitudes, beliefs and (equally important) his reasons for coaching. Researchers have examined the reasons why coaches get involved with coaching, and found that the most frequently expressed motives include the following:

- a desire to contribute to the psychological, social and physical development of young people;
- the pleasure they derive from the athletes having fun and enjoying their own participation; and
- the desire to develop a winning or otherwise successful team.

These are just three possible reasons why a coach may involve himself in the role. Every day (indeed, every match, every training session) brings new experiences, new challenges, new thoughts, new outcomes, each of which influences the individual as a coach and brings adjustments to his philosophy and ways of doing things. Clearly, it is an ongoing process and it is worthwhile for a coach to examine and reflect constantly on his main motives for coaching. In this way, he will be able clearly to identify his priorities when it comes to coaching practice.

Coach Development

A coaching philosophy can be established in many ways, usually over a number of years. It begins with your personal experiences as a player (from the moment you first step on to a basketball court and pick up the ball), and develops with your ever-increasing knowledge of the game – which grows as you watch games on TV or in person at sport centres and arenas. Learning about the game (history, rules, recent developments and changes in the game, how the sport is organized at local, national and international level, and so on), and working with players of different ages will clearly benefit and have a positive influence on your philosophy.

In developing a coaching philosophy, there are a number of useful measures that will help you to build a strong foundation. First, carefully analyse and examine the different approaches taken by successful coaches. Read their books and articles in specialized coaching magazines, seek out their interviews in different types of media (TV, newspapers, newsletters, websites, and so on), or – even better (if you have access to them) – talk to them direct, and ask how and why they did it. Second, attending coaching clinics is of paramount importance. You will hear what top coaches think about the game and how they approached different aspects and different parts of the game. The most recent ideas and the modern way of playing and coaching basketball are usually delivered during these clinics. Apart from networking with other coaches, you might have a chance to chat privately with elite coaches and share with them your opinions, and hopefully receive some sort of feedback in relation to what you have done and what you intend to do. Third, keep up to date with all developments within coaching as a discipline and attend coaching conferences and even sport sciences conferences. This will enable you to learn about the support that is available, which can give you and your team that extra edge on the way to being successful. Fourth, observe other coaches (not only basketball coaches, but those involved in other sports too) while they coach, during training sessions and also during matches (both friendly games and more important encounters). This will give you an accurate picture of different ways of dealing with athletes in different situations.

Three Key Issues

In developing a coaching philosophy, it is important to consider the following three key issues: know yourself; know what you are up against; and understand your athletes. You can use this information to the best of your ability to formulate a coaching philosophy document. Your aim should be to be a better coach, to improve coach/athlete satisfaction and to achieve superior athletic results.

Know Yourself

An understanding of your own personality traits and habits is very important and is usually a good starting point. Knowing yourself well will enable you to use your strengths, to minimize weaknesses and to identify areas requiring improvement. Asking yourself some of the following

questions might help: What do I value? What do I know about myself? Why do I want to be a coach? What are my priorities? What do I want the team to accomplish? What are my priorities regarding the development of athletes as players and people?

Know What You Are Up Against

If your coaching philosophy is able to adapt to reflect the coaching situation in which you find yourself, your chances of becoming a more effective and productive coach will increase. Once again, several questions need very specific and detailed answers:

- Do you have a good understanding of the characteristics of age, gender and training level of the athletes you coach?
- What are your goals/objectives (short, medium and long term) for the athletes you work with?
- How much time do you and your athletes have available to train and compete?
- What funding, facilities, equipment, additional services are at your disposal?
- What is your development programme based upon? Can it be enhanced if you incorporate support from sport sciences such as psychology, physiology, nutrition, match analysis techniques?
- Are you aware of all policies regarding safe practice and child protection?

- How frequently do you communicate with the parents of your performers?
- How do you find out information about all the other teams playing in the same competition/division/conference with your team?
- Are you aware of other external pressures such as other sports, school rules, parental pressure and influences?

Understand Your Athletes

People are more likely to derive enjoyment and remain involved in a sport if it fulfils their needs. This means you as a coach have to know your participants and their needs, which might change as time goes on. One of the vital elements in the relationship between coach-athlete is *communication* (how, when, and its quality). It is important to talk to your players to find out why are they playing the game and to make yourself familiar with their goals (in the sport, but also on the academic and social fronts). Knowing your athletes, their personalities and their abilities well will help you to guide and motivate them to achieve their objectives and fulfil their potential, to cope with success and failure, and to enjoy competing. Developing a *team* philosophy that is realistic and rewarding in terms of improved performance, alongside your personal coaching philosophy could be another important step towards success.

CHAPTER 3

COMMUNICATING YOUR APPROACH AND MOTIVATING PLAYERS

Communication is one of the many valuable skills that a coach should possess. To coach well and to be an effective coach you must be able to communicate effectively, not only with your players but also with other people who have an interest in your coaching and in your involvement in sport – parents, referees and match officials, your own team support staff, mass media, supporters, and so on (see Fig 9 for a detailed overview).

Often, good coaches are excellent communicators who, using verbal (talking) and non-verbal communication methods (eye contact, facial expression, posture, arm movements, smiles, head nods,

laughter, and so on), pass their message to the receiving end. Such coaches may not know more than anyone else, but they organize their thoughts better. Sometimes, some coaches feel that, because they have the knowledge and skill, they must spend all their coaching time giving information and sharing their experiences. However, good listening is just as important as talking, and is a key part – often forgotten – of effective communication. At the same time as giving verbal instructions/explanations, a coach can also ask questions, use demonstrations to convey his thoughts and observe what performers say and do.

Communication with Players

When communicating with your players, you need to consider the way in which your instructions are given and received – try to be clear, brief and straight to the point, and deliver messages immediately. Always avoid hidden agendas and be consistent with your non-verbal messages. It is preferable to give all your athletes equal attention and to communicate in a fashion that is appropriate to their age, ability, level of understanding and learning style. Use your voice as a tool, by changing the tone, pace and emphasis. If you impose the simple rule of 'no dribbling the basketball while the coach is talking', everyone should be able to hear and understand what is being communicated (instruction, explanation, feedback, and so on).

When giving out instructions, remember two simple acronyms: KISS ('Keep It Simple') and TOTAT ('Teach One Thing At a Time'). Generally, it is advisable to attempt to get across no more than two or three coaching points. Remember the old saying 'demonstration is worth a thousand words'. When using demonstration, make sure all players can see what you are doing. The full attention of the players is the key to the communication working, and you need to find your own ways of gaining it instantly (for example, a whistle can be very effective). It is good practice after demonstrations to invite questions and check for understanding.

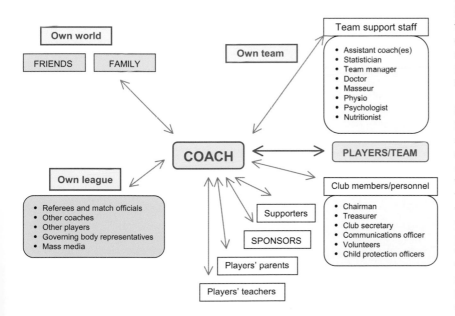

Fig 9 People with whom a coach can communicate.

On-Court Communication

During friendly or official matches and training sessions, the on-court communication is as important as the off-court communication. For the on-court situation, which can be a very loud environment (with noise from spectators, fans and the opposite team), players and coach(es) should develop a simple set of signals and codes to facilitate communication between them. In crucial moments during close games (for example, in the last seconds/minutes of the game, or during overtime), effective communication may be the decisive factor in the final outcome of that match. The way players react to what is transmitted to them needs to lead to a 'doing' approach rather than to a 'questioning' one.

Off-Court Communication

Before and after training sessions and/or matches during the season, and during the off-season, off-court communication is about building a rapport with your players. In order to achieve this, you need to show interest in and respect for each participant. A simple 'Hello!' followed by the use of the other person's first name, and a 'How are things?' is a very effective way to build relationships. Try to smile and make eye contact, too. Remember to coach the person rather than just the sport – talk with your players about their home life and family, and their academic progress (if that is relevant), and ask about any problems they might have and help them where possible.

Clearly state your expectations of the players, preferably at the beginning of the season or whenever you start working with a new group of players. Rules about attendance at practices, being on time for all activities (training, matches, meetings, and so on), what to do when hearing the coach's whistle, behaviour on and off the court – all of these kind of things need to be communicated. They also need to be enforced each time someone steps out of line. It is a good idea to have a written 'Code of Conduct for Players' in place for your team/club. When using praise

and punishment coaches must constantly exercise their judgement and must make a realistic assessment of each player's efforts. Punishment, for example, should never be administered in a humiliating or degrading manner if it is to be effective (see below, 'Motivating Your Players', for more about rewards and punishments).

Communicating with Referees and Match Officials

Referees and match officials are an essential part of the basketball game and it is therefore important for the coach (as well as the players and other coaching staff) to establish effective communication with them. When dealing with referees it is about building a rapport – if you treat them with respect, hopefully they will do the same to you. There are several moments at which a coach can build a good relationship with match officials: 'meet and greet' them on their arrival at the venue; during the warm-up, take the opportunity to have a chat and maybe to get a point across to them about your playing system; during the actual game, you are entitled to ask – in a polite manner – for clarification on any decisions; talk to them at the half-time break and during intervals (between quarters), as well as after the game.

As with the players, try to compliment the officials every time you consider they deserve it, no matter whether your team is winning or losing the game. Remember that your players will usually copy the way you treat the officials and communicate with them, so always act in a professional manner and set a good example.

Communicating with Assistant Coaches and Your Support Team

No matter what level you are coaching, good communication with your coaching staff (assistant coaches) and any support team (team doctor, physio, psycholo-

gist, and so on) is vital and can have a significant impact on your team's day-to-day well-being and performance. The head coach should promote a climate of teamwork and cooperation; he should make it clear to his assistants that he welcomes new ideas, constructive suggestions and solutions, and endeavour to make them feel comfortable with their roles. The coaching staff should agree a common plan of action (usually at the beginning of the season) and deliver it, so that all coaches are 'singing from the same hymn sheet'.

Communicating with Parents

Dealing with parents is a very important part of your life as a coach, especially (and not only) if you coach youngsters. Every coach has a duty to inform parents and keep them updated about the progress and development of their child. This can be done in a variety of ways: face to face, or via mail, email, club meetings or newsletters.

It takes tact and diplomacy to handle and manage this relationship. You may encounter a situation in which parents are shouting advice from the sidelines and distracting players' attention away from what the coach has to say. As a coach you need to deal immediately with such issues, otherwise the situation can only get worse. Coaches also need to deal with parents' unrealistic views of their child's playing ability. This can create extra pressures for the player involved and this is clearly something that coaches do not want.

Good communication and clarification of the roles is the secret, and setting clear boundaries – perhaps in a 'Code of Behaviour for Parents' – is clearly necessary in any serious basketball programme.

Communicating with Mass Media

Coaching at higher levels of the game means that the coach may come into contact with mass media. The general advice is for the coach to make himself available as much as possible to communicate with the media representatives. He should be positive in his comments, aiming to promote the team and his players (and not himself). The communication can take the form of interviews or stories about your team. Another option is for a coach (or a Communications Manager, if the club has someone with this job within its structure) to write a press release or article about recent performances and submit it to be published. Being easily accessible to the media will lead to more coverage for your team/basketball programme.

Communicating with Sponsors

Whatever the level at which you and your team play the game, financial support from sponsors is always welcome. This support can come in different forms – from cash sums to a team kit, new basketballs, rings and boards, and so on. It is common sense to show your (and your team's) appreciation to the sponsors and to communicate constantly with them as a way of saying 'Thank you'. Apart from advertising their name/brand/product on playing equipment and in various publicity materials (press releases, the club's website, leaflets, newsletters, and so on), simple gestures such as 'Thank you' letters or a Christmas card (signed by all players) will enhance the relationship. They may even lead to further material support.

Communicating with Teachers and Others

Constant contact with the teachers of your players is desirable. In this way, their academic progress can be monitored and

kept on track and any potential problems can be identified early. Teachers can help the team not only by dealing with academic issues but also by being part of the coaching staff (keeping the statistics, for example), or by creating posters for home matches or perhaps writing articles about the team's performances.

The coach may also have to communicate with the wider student population (colleagues of your players) and members of the local community (for example, kit providers, transport companies, local businesses, and other potential sponsors).

Barriers to Communication

Breakdowns can occur during the communication process, and may happen at both ends of the spectrum. They may be the result of sender failures (the message may be poorly transmitted, ambiguous, or inconsistent), but they may also be due to receiver failures (for example, because of a failure to listen carefully or misinterpretation). Other barriers to communication include the receiver (player) not paying attention to the sender (coach); lack of trust between the individuals attempting to communicate; the athlete lacking the knowledge required to understand what the coach is trying to communicate; and a lack of a common language. Sometimes, a coach working with players who do not share his native language may have difficulty in expressing himself. This problem can also work the other way, with the players unable to understand the language used by the coach.

Motivating Your Players

Apart from persuasion, evaluation, information and problem-solving, motivation is another important purpose of communica-

tion. Motivational skills are closely linked to a mastery of communication. Effective coaches will use their communication skills to find out what motivates their participants to play the game.

Do you know why your participants take part in your sport and what motivates them to stay involved? The answers may include any of the following: to have fun; to meet people and make friends; to keep fit and healthy; for the challenge of the competition; to please others (for example, parents or friends); to gain a reward such as a title, a gold medal, a trophy or even money; a desire and determination to succeed; the feeling of achievement from perfecting a skill and acknowledgement from peers, coaches and family; pride; role models; to prove a point; the desire to learn a new skill; a determination to succeed; celebrity status; fame; and inspiration from parents or coaches.

People are more likely to derive enjoyment from and remain involved in sport if it fulfils their needs. As a coach, you must know your players and understand their needs, which may change as time passes. Understanding what motivates people to be involved in sport will help the coach to select the most appropriate approach and to provide a fun, enjoyable and supportive training environment. The right approach means that, at times, you will be called upon to praise, discipline or encourage your participants. It is good to bear in mind the fact that your players are not all the same. Some of them need more of a push, while others are self-starters.

CHAPTER 4

RUNNING A BASKETBALL PROGRAMME

Successful coaching depends on coaches' understanding of planning at all levels. The modern coach must organize each phase of the basketball season in order to obtain optimum results. Methodical planning is required for a well-coordinated basketball programme.

Planning

Planning involves considering all the aspects of performance improvement and then developing a programme that takes performers/athletes and the team from where they are to where they want to be. The planning function and the delivery of quality programmes must be a systematic process, which should be based on objective facts and the performers themselves. This process is based on a number of components

- a clear and accurate picture of your players – knowing where they are now and where they want to be (individual and team targets);
- a timescale (knowing how much time you and your team have available to achieve the aims and objectives);
- your knowledge as a coach (of your sport, of your own team and of the opposition);
- planning ability (including the use of relevant information on which to base your training programme); and
- constant monitoring and evaluation of your plans.

It is important to remember that the *performance factors* (technical, physical, tactical, psychological, theoretic-methodical and biological) cannot be developed in isolation. Instead, they are building blocks that must be supported by each other.

All these factors need to be considered and planning is the bedrock of the entire process of preparation for performance, whether it is for a single session, a week of training, a 2- to 3-month period, a year or a season, four years (an Olympic cycle), or longer.

When planning, a coach must also recognize that a coaching programme needs to be flexible; in reality, a number of different factors – personal issues (injuries, school commitments, and so on), facilities and equipment problems, players' reactions to the programme that is imposed – can come into play and affect any plan. Similarly, in team sports, coaches need to plan at two levels: individual and team. The performance of the team depends on the performance of the individuals within it and that is why individual training programmes need to be incorporated into the master plan. The challenge for any coach is to balance the needs of the individual with the needs of the team, and that is where detailed planning is the key.

Annual/Season Planning

When planning for a season, the whole year will be split into different phases: preparation (also called pre-season), competition (season) and rest/recovery (post-season). The pre-season phase itself is normally broken down into a general and then a specific phase, as the competitive phase gets closer. This phasing of the year is known as *periodization*. Periodization also has certain cycles that help the planning process:

- a macrocyle – a phase of considerable length aimed at achieving peak performance in competition. It includes all three phases – pre-

season (general and specific preparation), season and rest/recovery.
- a mesocycle – usually a period of 1 to 6 weeks within any phase of the plan.
- a microcycle – normally a training period of 2–7 days (several microcycles are included in a mesocycle).

The coach should draw up a master pre-season schedule, listing the goals that he hopes to accomplish in defence and attack before the first game. He then works within this programme of operation to make up weekly and daily schedules and to determine the drills he wishes to incorporate. When planning the whole season, the coach should take into consideration all the relevant factors, such as the players/team (their strengths, weaknesses, experience, numbers, age), the details of the schedule (official matches, any friendlies, and so on), the opponents, training times available, facility (size of sports hall) and equipment available (number of hoops, number of balls, bibs, stopwatch, whistle, and so on). The coach will prioritize the performance components on the basis of the performer's/team's strengths and weaknesses and the time of the year. He will then balance the time spent on the different components, to ensure that young participants develop the right skills at the right time.

Session Planning

The most detailed level of planning is the *single session*. Each practice session should have specific goals (what do you hope to accomplish on that particular day) and ideally should be linked to the previous session(s) and to the one that follows. The sessions should always meet the needs of the participants. The session aims must be progressive and attainable, leading to the overall goal for the season, and participants need to know precisely what is expected of them. Some coaches give players a copy of the practice schedule for the week to come, so that they all know what time practice is scheduled for and what they will be practising.

Having planned a session, the coach must conduct it in such a way that all participants benefit from taking part. The division of practice time is very important in order to make sure all players are properly warmed up and ready to take part actively in the drills that are planned. The most frequently used procedure is as follows:

1 *Introduction*: the coach will take a register and then give a very brief overview of the session's aims and objectives. Players may also be reminded of safety considerations and standards of behaviour.
2 *Warm-up*: it should consist of a series of gentle and general body movements including jogging, and running at different speeds and intensities, followed by a period of stretching (see Part IV) and more sport-specific exercises.
3 *Main part*: after the warm-up period, sessions should normally include a period devoted to learning or developing skills or techniques. Plan and organize your drills very carefully, considering the number of players participating. When running a drill, explain its purpose and emphasize the coaching points. It is useful to use competitive drills and to imitate game conditions as much as possible. Individual/fundamental drills should be alternated with team drills. Similarly, defence and attack must be practised too.
4 *Conditioned games*: playing the game is very important for all players, whether they be beginners, improvers or advanced, and the opportunity for game play should be included in any training session. This will give players a chance to learn more about the game and to apply what they

have been working on during a training session. The coach can condition the game to focus attention on one particular aspect. For example, if a main part of the training session had been devoted to passing, then during a game the coach may want to impose a restriction on dribbling, such as no dribbling at all or only one dribble allowed.

5 *Games*: since all players probably like to scrimmage better than anything else, it is important that a coach gives this phase of the coaching session considerable thought. It is a chance for the whole team to rehearse play calls and set-up tactics.
6 *Warm-down and summary*: the aim of this final phase of the training session is to bring the body gradually back to a pre-exercise condition, to help prevent muscle stiffness. Various gentle activities can be used, such as jogging or walking, taking free throws and stretching.

During the session, water breaks and short rest periods also need to be included.

Coaching Games

The coach has a number of duties and obligations in all three phases – before, during and after the game.

Before the Game

Before the game a coach needs to consider several factors: using scouting reports; choosing the team; planning for the game and conducting the pre-game practice; organization for the game and pre-game team talk; game warm-up; and selecting the starting five.

Using Scouting Reports
Scouting is useful to the coach for the purposes of talent-spotting and appraising the strengths and weaknesses of opponents, at both individual and team level. Objective data (for example, match statistics), along with subjective impressions obtained

through scouting, can help a coach to prepare his team for an upcoming match. This information can be collated by any of the members of the coaching team and can include previous seasons' scouting reports, press releases from newspapers, material from publicity brochures and match programmes, opinions and comments from coaches of other teams, and even the comments of the spectators who are watching the match/team being scouted. After the scouting takes place, the coach reviews the report together with the member of staff who did the scouting in order to clarify all the ideas that will be included in the game plan.

Choosing the Team
A coach must do everything possible to maximize the strengths of his players and to get the most out of his team as a unit. A proper playing system (in both attack and defence) needs to be selected according to the characteristics of the opposite team. This is where adaptability is essential. One of the most difficult tasks for a coach is to determine which ten (or maximum twelve) players should be listed on the match official score sheet. Selecting the team involves an insight into each candidate and several factors can be taken into account when analysing players: basic physical factors (fitness, speed and agility, good balance, coordination, height, jumping ability), good mental attributes, enthusiasm, competitiveness and determination, sound emotional background, all-round abilities, and so on. Similarly, choosing the captain is one of the most important decisions to make as a coach. There are two usual methods: either the coach nominates the captain for the coming game or the squad members elect the person for this role. Ideally, this person must be an extremely stable individual, mentally, morally and emotionally. He should get along well with all the players on the team and must have their confidence at all times. He will need to be a calm and confident leader on and off the court.

Planning for the Game and Conducting the Pre-Game Practice
Each new game means a new challenge to the coach. His plan for the game needs to

be very structured; it should include the attacking patterns that are most likely to be successful against a particular opponent, arrangements for defensive moments, and take into account the strengths and weaknesses of the opposition. And it should be clearly explained to all players.

Any practice session before the match needs to be devoted to the game plan and to the scouting report. If there is time during or after practices, film of previous games could be shown and analysed. In all cases, a team must start preparing a game in the proper frame of mind if it is going to come close to doing its best. Apart from the activities designed to prepare the players and the team for a particular game, the daily practice sessions should still contain drills to maintain the physical condition of the players, to rehearse shooting jump shots and free throws, and to look after their mental and moral condition. A regular routine as much as possible is needed, without placing any unnatural or artificial stress on the playing of the game.

Organization for the Game and Pre-Game Team Talk
It is advisable for both home and away games to have all your players in the changing room at least one hour before the scheduled tip-off. This will enable them to get changed, to take care of any physiological needs and to be ready for the team talk before getting the warming-up under way. The players should eat their pre-game meal at least 3–4 hours before the start and should get a little rest. When travelling is required for away matches, all details about the trip – departure time and place, duration of travel, means of transport, destination, opposition, estimated arrival time back at the departure point – should be communicated, in writing, to all selected players and also to their parents. They should also be told what the players need to bring in terms of equipment and food. Punctuality is vital in all situations (home or away) and all players must be on time for buses, meals, team meetings and all other occasions.

About 10 minutes before the team gets ready for the warm-up, the coach reviews the overall game plan during his team talk. Once again, defensive and offensive arrangements are highlighted, together with the strengths and weaknesses of the opposite team and how to take advantage of them. The coach will also provide individual players with instructions as to their role in the overall plan.

Game Warm-Up
It is extremely important for players to get used to the different features of the location, especially on away matches. Does the court have glass or wooden backboards, rigid or flexible rings, a wooden or rubber floor? What is the lighting like, where are the substitute benches area and the spectators' seating, and so on? A good warm-up (including 5 to 10 minutes of static and dynamic stretches) will facilitate a good performance in the game to follow.

In order to eliminate confusion when the team goes on court for the warm-up drills, these drills should have been discussed and integrated into the training sessions before the first game takes place. The chosen drills should allow all players to practise shooting from their normal positions and then, individually, to take several free throws. Dribbling, passing and cutting should also be incorporated, together with some drills for attacking and defending moments. It is common, also, for coaches to allow for 2 vs. 1 or 3 vs. 2 situations to be rehearsed.

Selecting the Starting Five
In order to select the starting five, the coach and his assistants must exchange ideas well before the game takes place. During the warm-up, they also need to look at the preparation of the other team and, after identifying from the score sheet the opponents' starting five, need to closely monitor them in order to identify relevant characteristics – preferred dribbling hand, favourite side or area of court when shooting, and so on. With 1–2 minutes before the tip-off, it is good to call the team in and very briefly to go through the major points you want to emphasize (which will be in the game plan that you have prepared, discussed and agreed). This is the time to highlight any special instructions you might have and to assign an appropriate defensive player to each opposite team player, based on position, height and ability. A team cheer before entering the court indicates that the players are ready to start the game.

During the Game

There are a number of factors that must be taken into consideration during the progress of a game if the team is to perform as efficiently as possible (and accordingly to their ability). The coach plays an important role during the game.

Coach's Conduct
During the game the coach needs to keep track of several things: his own players and the execution of the agreed plan; the members of the opposing team and their strategies (offensive and defensive); personal fouls and team fouls; time-outs; communication with referees and table officials, and so on. He needs to remain alert, in order to make any criticism or corrections necessary to improve the play of his team. Constant encouragement of his team by word and action is a must – keeping his self-control, he leads the team by example, showing that he is there fighting for them at all times. That does not necessarily mean shouting or making personal remarks to referees or the opponents – match officials will not give you anything if you continually question and complain about their calls/decisions.

First Half and Game Plan Adjustment
The coach must exchange ideas frequently with his assistants. Ideally, one of them should be in charge of keeping the statistics and a record of essential information such as team and individual fouls for both teams, time-outs taken, opponent substitutions and other commentaries. The coaching staff should also assess the level of execution of the initial game plan. If things are not going according to the plan then adjustments are vital to ensure a positive outcome of the first half and, consequently, of the match. These adjustments are communicated to players on the court either during time-outs or by

using a substitute player who will inform all other players on the court about the changes required.

Substitutions

A coach should use substitutions purposefully. By carefully monitoring what is happening in the game, he can strategically substitute to obtain a tactical advantage, to rest a player or even to keep a player away from fouls trouble too early in the game. There are a number of situations in which a coach could consider using substitutions:

- Coaches often bench players depending on the course of action in the game – if, for example, the opposition's coach has changed the offensive patterns to a quick offence that does not involve his big man, you can give a rest to your own center while a reasonably tall (and good jumper) substitute can play important minutes in the game.
- You might want to rest the starters or the players who are doing well. When players get overtired, they are no longer effective on the court – fatigue is easily recognized by a player showing a diminished reaction time, or not hustling as much. Introducing a fresh player even for just a couple of minutes can be beneficial to both the individual and the team.
- Players who are in danger of being fouled out can be given a few minutes on the bench when they need to be reminded about the important role that they (especially starters) have to play in the whole match. (The coach also needs to be aware of the number of fouls that each player on the opponent team has. He should instruct his own players to play against those defenders who have three or four fouls, because they cannot play 100 per cent defence.)

Before a player enters the court as a substitute, the coach should briefly reinforce some of the tactical instructions presented in the team talk, and give him some encouragement to play to the best of his ability. Too much talk and too many instructions at that moment will confuse the player and add unnecessary stress. When a player comes off the court, the coach should provide some feedback in relation to his performance and give him some constructive advice. This will make its greatest impact when it is given immediately, during the first minutes after the substitution has occurred.

A coach might request a substitution in a number of other situations:

- when an injury occurs;
- in order to discipline a player (who is, for example, not concentrating on the game or making remarks to the referees);
- to provide instructions to a specific individual;
- to develop team morale and to give all players a chance to perform (especially when the outcome of the game is reasonably certain); or
- to replace a player who is not doing well.

Time-Outs

A time-out is a good strategic move for a coach and consequently it should be used wisely. The most frequent reason for asking for a time-out is to stop the other team when it is on a scoring run (5–10 unanswered points). The time-out is a very important asset, which in this situation can be used to interrupt the momentum of an opponent who has scored several quick successive baskets. It might also be used in one of the following situations:

- when the opponents have used a strategy that you have not been prepared to meet, giving you a chance to adjust the game plan;
- when you need to rest your players;
- in case of injury; or
- in the late stages of the game when an opposite team player is about to shoot a crucial free throw.

The coach(es) and the players should always be aware of the number of

time-outs that each team has remaining. During the time-out it is paramount that all players (on the court and substitutions) give 100 per cent attention to what is being said to them, usually by the head coach. If time permits, before the end of the time-out, the coach can quickly answer one or two questions that players might have.

Different coaches organize their players differently during time-outs. One possibility is to seat on the bench the five players who are on the court, while the remaining players stand forming a semicircle in front of them, with the coach in the middle facing the people on the bench.

Players on the Bench

All substitute players should be reminded of the fact that they are not there just to spectate the game. They should be encouraged to study the game and pay attention to such factors as the player they are most likely to guard and the player who is most likely to be guarding them. They need to be aware of all situations in which they can pick up information that will enable them to do a good job when they are required to take part in the game. Players on the bench must be taught to cheer, encourage, warn and advise their teammates on occasions, but they must remain seated. In the official rules the coach is the only person allowed to stand up, and a technical foul is given to the team bench if there are other people standing. At the same time, they must refrain from making any comments to the officials, opposing players or coaching staff or spectators.

Half-Time

When half-time starts, all players need to go quickly straight into the changing room (taking care of any toilet needs). They are allowed to spend a couple of minutes talking to each other, constructively, while the head coach confers with his assistants in order to obtain the statistics and any points of view regarding alternative options and strategies. The half-time talk should be a short, straight-to-the-point analysis of the flow of the game. The coach should point out what patterns have worked best for his own team (both offensively and defensively) and indicate various solutions to counteract the opposition's way of playing. Depending on the outcome of the first half, constructive criticism and/or praise for the good things (and scorers) should be heard by all in the changing room.

After they have been hydrated and checked for any injuries (and any first aid has been administered), the players will be asked by the coach to return to the playing area. By shooting free throws or taking lay-ups, they can then prepare themselves for the second half.

After the Game

Whether his team has won or lost, the coach has several post-game responsibilities. First, he needs to see the opposing coach and either congratulate him for a win, or graciously accept congratulations.

Players should be encouraged to go and shake hands with their opponents, whatever the final result. The coach should also thank the referees and match officials and then should gather his players round him for a cheer — one for the opposition and one for their own team.

Back in the changing room, the coach might like to give a 2- to 3-minute talk to his players, perhaps reminding them about the programme for the coming days/week. At higher levels of the game, coaches will also have a duty to talk to the press/media. They should be objective and positive in their comments, without criticizing their own players, opponents, referees or match officials.

Evaluation

Evaluation is a very important process that is often overlooked by coaches, however, it is essential in coaching and should form the basis of future planning. The procedure might include analysing and evaluating the programme that the coach has delivered (looking at each training session and match, and at the season overall), evaluating the players and also the performance of the coach himself, and of his coaching staff.

Programme Evaluation

In order to evaluate the effects of any basketball programme, every coach should keep a record of what has been done in each coaching session, along with a few comments about how he feels each practice went. The session planner must include some space (either a column or a row) entitled 'Evaluation' (or 'Post-session analysis' or 'Session review'), answering the following questions:

- Have the aims and objectives of the session been achieved?
- Are there any organizational (group numbers, composition, equipment, playing area, and so on) and/or safety factors which may need changing next time so that the session runs better?

- What worked best and how could the practices be adapted for future coaching?
- Are there any disciplinary issues?
- Are there any injuries?
- Are there any problems related to the coach himself (for example, time management, group management, spending too much time on a particular drill, voice projection, and so on)?

Ideally, these notes need to be written down as soon as the session finishes, while it is still fresh in the mind. It is good practice to keep the session plans, together with all notes and comments, on file, readily available for consultation by the coach to identify the technical and skills progress of the participants. As with planning, the time spent by a coach in evaluating his own sessions is an investment in improving the effectiveness of his coaching.

A post-season evaluation could contain numerical data about winning and losing games, about the number of participants (number at the beginning of the season and at the end of it), number of players promoted to regional or national squads, and number of injuries during the season. It could also contain qualitative aspects (comments): changes in players' relationships with others; when and why they depend on you as coach for support; growth and maturation indicators (recording the physical changes in the participants); observation of whether or not the participants still enjoy taking part.

As well as the the coaching sessions, all the official and friendly matches played during a season need to be evaluated too. A match is reviewed via a system of analysis to identify areas of performance, strengths and weaknesses in the team. During and after a game, the coach will usually be affected emotionally and for this reason it is better to wait a couple of days before attempting to analyse the performance. Alongside an analysis of the extent to which strategic goals were achieved, match reviews will often highlight training priorities that can be agreed by the whole team. Outcomes of the match reviews, which ideally should be based on very objective information – for example, match statistics – can be integrated into the subsequent preparation strategy of the team and can assist the coach in identifying priorities for specific players to focus on.

Player Evaluation

Evaluation is an ongoing task for the coach – from the first training session of the season until the summer holidays, the coach needs constantly to evaluate the players he is working with and assess their progress throughout the season (not only during training sessions and matches but also on and off the court).

Player evaluation may be objective or subjective, depending on the information collected. Generally speaking, objective assessments are those that are based on empirical evidence – time played, points scored, shots taken, shots made (shooting percentages), and so on. Subjective assessments depend on the coach's impression of the performance. For example, the coach may believe that the playmaker's hustling, constant encouragement and overall positioning play led to the team finding a winning way, but he has no actual figures to prove it. In basketball, one of the most objective ways of evaluating a player's performance during a game is to use match statistics – a detailed description of everything a player is doing from the moment he enters the court until he leaves it (or until the match is over). The statistics might relate to minutes played, points scored, free throws made or attempted, defensive and offensive rebounds, interceptions and steals, wrong passes, weak control, assists, and so on. The match statistics form may also be used in training sessions in order to evaluate players.

Gathering the information is sometimes the easy part of evaluating performance. The information must then be interpreted and a judgement made on the performer or team. Although the process of analysing and interpreting the results of valid, reliable and objective assessments may appear fairly straightforward, subjective judgements often need to be made on the basis of the information collected.

Systematic attempts to analyse sport performance require the coach to consider in advance of the interpretation stage the nature of the priority information that is going to be gathered, and *how* it is to be collected and organized. But *why* should the coach monitor and evaluate players, *which* performance indicators should he use and *when* might he monitor those indicators?

There are a number of reasons why coaches test and evaluate or monitor their players:

- To assess athletes in terms of strengths and weaknesses in order to establish priorities for training.
- To isolate and assess individual components that cannot be measured in a competitive situation.
- To assess the players' progress, providing feedback for the performer and the coach.
- To prescribe the optimal training programme (in terms of intensity and volume).
- To provide baseline data for individual training programmes.

During the selection of a squad, basketball skills (such as dribbling, passing, shooting, playing in 3 vs. 3 and 5 vs. 5 games) need to be tested, along with athletic skills/ability. The basic physical attributes that should be sought are coordination, vertical and lateral speed and quickness, balance, aggressiveness, reflexes, good hands, and height (both actual height and playing height). Other desirable characteristics are the ability to learn, desire, good mental attributes, enthusiasm, sound emotional background, and competitive instinct. All fundamental passing and dribbling drills may be evaluated on a merit scale – for example, from 1 to 5 or from 1 to 10 (1 for poor, 5 or 10 for excellent). The coach should be on the look-out for players with ability in one area as well as those with all-round abilities. Good athletes tend to learn more quickly and they play at a higher level than those with less physical ability.

When players are very close in ability, moral, emotional and academic factors may be taken into account when choosing players.

The coach should always be on the alert to identify as early as possible any players who may cause friction. All players on a team must be compatible, in order to work together for the common objective. Players who are difficult to get along with or who show emotional, mental or social instability will make poor squad members. Other players may be affected by their behaviour too.

Several forms may be used by coaches for evaluation purposes during the season:

- *Teammate evaluation sheet* –players fill in (anonymously) a form, highlighting the positive and negative aspects of other players in the team. For example, they may be asked to identify the three best rebounders, three best shooters, three best defensive players, three poorest defenders, three poorest hustlers, and so on. The coach will then assess the results against his own evaluations.
- *Self-evaluation sheet* – encouraging players to contribute constructively to post-match evaluation of their own performance involves them in an active manner in the coaching process. This approach is likely to produce an effective coaching programme and a better-motivated athlete. Qualities that need to be assessed in any self-assessment form are basketball instinct, attention, ability to follow the coach's instructions, alertness, aggressiveness, coordination, team defensive abilities, individual defensive abilities, team offensive abilities and individual offensive ability.

When monitoring and evaluating players, a coach can create an *individual player profile* for each of the team members. Key elements within each of the performance factors and individual characteristics must be included – these may vary according to your system of play, but the following are always important:

- quickness and speed in relation to those who will be playing the same position;
- size and jumping ability – it is not how tall you are, but how tall you play;
- coordination and balance;
- experience;
- fight, determination, courage and desire;
- ball-handling and shooting ability;
- enthusiasm;
- cooperation and team attitude;
- self-control and the ability to play well under pressure;
- alertness; and
- remaining years of eligibility – you must prepare for the future without sacrificing the present.

The coach should analyse each practice session and each game and evaluate each player's progress (or lack of it), attentiveness and attitude. A record of such an analysis/evaluation should be kept for the duration of the whole season.

Any evaluation a coach makes is preceded by an analysis of the information available (and is influenced by the original objectives of the performance observation). Evaluation is the endpoint of a coach's interpretations, which puts them in the context of the overall plan and will lead the coach to the next stage of the coaching process. A coach may decide to formulate a new coaching plan or modify the existing one based on his evaluation of individual and team performance. Ultimately, an evaluation is still a personal judgement. However, the combination of intuitive and systematic analysis should help coaches to make a more accurate and reliable evaluation of performance. This is because it should provide a more complete picture of what occurred and some ideas as to why.

Once you have identified indicators that you will use to monitor your athletes' progress, using these indicators will produce data that must be analysed and recorded. Attendance records and results in competitions will complement the data recorded in different ways.

Working with a big squad (twelve to fifteen players), it is difficult to keep regular and accurate records of each member. However, it is vital if progress is to be monitored and evaluated successfully and objectively. Information about players could include any or all of the following:

- individual contact details (name, address, phone number, email, parents, school attended, and so on);
- growth and development records (height, weight, shoe size, arms wing span);
- attendance record;
- competition results sheet and match statistics;
- testing results (data): fitness, mental skills, tactical and technical skills, bio-mechanical assessments, nutritional assessments, medical screening;
- injuries report sheet;
- annual periodization plan;
- session plans;
- goal-setting form.

Obviously, recording all the data required for a proper evaluation is difficult and time-consuming. This is when the head coach can cooperate efficiently with other members of the coaching staff and assign duties in relation to these essential aspects of the coaching process – monitoring and evaluation.

And finally a piece of advice – conduct all of your evaluations and make any resulting adjustments within the framework of your own personality and coaching philosophy. There are no magic coaching formulas that you can apply to a group of players for guaranteed success.

Coach Evaluation

In the same way as you evaluate your players and the programme that you deliver, you should also monitor and evaluate your own performance as a coach. *Self-reflection* is a process whereby coaches analyse and compare their current practice against an ideal set of practices (ideal model) using a systematic procedure to make comparisons between real life (what happened) and the ideal (what should have happened ideally). Coaches should ask themselves whether the things they do and say as a coach make a difference, and whether their coaching behaviours are effective and lead to an improvement in the performance of their athletes. It is very important for coaches to take control of their own learning; those who fail to learn from their mistakes are doomed to repeat them.

When reflecting on his own performance, a coach could make notes on the following:

- his coaching style in delivering the session;
- whether his instructions were clear, concise and appropriate;
- whether appropriate coaching methods were being used in developing each athlete;
- whether explanations and demonstrations were clear enough and appropriate for the age and level of participants;
- his own body language and tone of voice;
- whether he has made appropriate use of existing resources;
- whether he has provided enough feedback to players to help their learning process;
- whether he has achieved his objectives for the session;
- whether he had control of the group and the ways in which he was able to deal with any behaviour problems;
- whether he included and spent an equal time with all players; and so on.

The external help available for a coach during the reflection process includes video analysis and using another coach as a mentor.

Video analysis is a useful tool in the self-reflection process, since it provides permanent images that can help with in-depth analysis and evaluation. Looking back at the tape may help you to spot things that could have been done differently.

A mentor acts as an 'auditor' of the coach's interpretation of his own coaching practice, listening to the coach's analysis of his own coaching performance and confirming (or otherwise) the accuracy of his comments. The mentor guides the coach towards a deeper understanding of his work. Any mentoring coach must be someone whom the subject respects. He could be a coach who is an expert in the same field (or, indeed, in another sport) and who is prepared to share his opinions and ideas.

Committed coaches certainly need an ongoing self-development programme. Once a coach decides to make that commitment, he must then find the time to improve. There is an abundance of resources available today, to support the self-directed programme of an aspiring coach, including coaching websites, DVDs, videos, coaching positions (voluntary or paid) at all levels of the game, clinics, seminars and workshops. If a coach manages his own self-paced training programme effectively and efficiently, he is more likely to achieve the best results on and off the court.

Organizing Basketball Events

Generally speaking, basketball games can be organized serving two main purposes: they can be either 'friendly' matches (between different teams during different stages/parts of the competitional year, that is to say, pre-season, in-season or post-season), or they may be 'official' games (part of a competition recognized by and played under the rules of England Basketball, including regular season encounters, play-off matches, cup games, tournaments, and so on). All types of match can be played as part of age-group competitions (Minibasketball, for 8- to 12-year-olds, Under 13s, U14s, U15s, U16s, U18s and U20s), or at senior level in a local, regional, national, European or international context.

Three of the most common types of playing system are the *elimination system*,

a *tournament-type competition* (home and away championship) and the *mixt* format.

Elimination System

This system is usually used when there is a significant number of participating teams and the time available for organizing the event is relatively short, as with Cup or with Streetball competitions. All the names of the teams are drawn and placed next to a number (see Figs 10 and 11). Within this system, each team that has lost one game is eliminated from the competition. A single elimination tournament is completed in a short time with a winner quickly emerging, which is why it is good for a large number of entries.

Tournament System

This system allows each team to play against all the others that are eligible and registered to take part. Either each team plays every other team twice, on a 'home and away' basis (like most National League competitions), or every team plays every team only once (as with group stages of

all age-group European Championships, or friendly tournaments, for example). According to FIBA rules, each team is awarded 2 points for a win and 1 point for losing a game (with no point being given for forfeited games). The team that accumulates the highest number of points is declared the winning team (or champion).

This type of competition is played over a long period. If there are, for example, seven teams participating, there will be a total of twelve games to be played (in the home and away system). With eight teams participating, there will be a total of fourteen games to be played. A few examples are provided in the tables overleaf to illustrate the situation for tournaments with five and six teams.

This type of competition (tournament) is also known as a 'round robin'. It can be run as a single round robin (with each team playing every other team only once) or a double round robin (each team playing two games with every other team). The formula for determining the total number of games to be played in a round-robin tournament is $N \times (N - 1)$ divided by 2, with N representing the number of teams or participating units in the tournament. A round robin with six entries

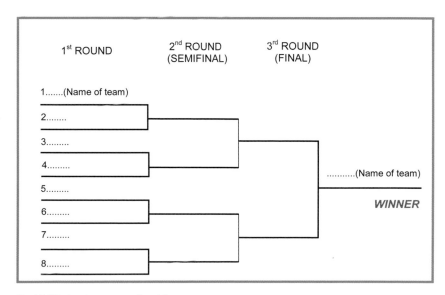

Fig 10 Elimination system for eight teams.

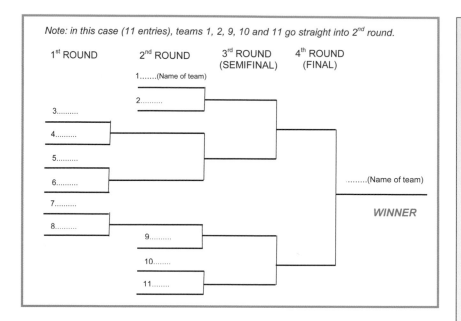

Fig 11 Elimination system for eleven teams.

TOURNAMENT PLAYING SYSTEM FOR FIVE TEAMS

Round 1	Round 2	Round 3	Round 4	Round 5
1 vs. 4	5 vs. 3	4 vs. 2	3 vs. 1	2 vs. 5
2 vs. 3	1 vs. 2	5 vs. 1	4 vs. 5	3 vs. 4
5 – no game	4 – no game	3 – no game	2 – no game	1 – no game

TOURNAMENT PLAYING SYSTEM FOR SIX TEAMS

Round 1	Round 2	Round 3	Round 4	Round 5
1 vs. 6	1 vs. 5	1 vs. 4	1 vs. 3	1 vs. 2
2 vs. 5	6 vs. 4	5 vs. 3	4 vs. 2	3 vs. 6
3 vs. 4	2 vs. 3	6 vs. 2	5 vs. 6	4 vs. 5

BASKETBALL EVENT CHECKLIST

No matter what playing system is in place, the following equipment should be available for use by Table Officials at any game:

- official scorebook (score sheet) – one copy;
- player foul markers (five in total) – used by the scorer to indicate the number of fouls committed by the players on the court;
- team foul markers (two) – to indicate when a team has committed four fouls in a quarter;
- team fouls indicator – a suitable device to indicate the accumulative number of team fouls;
- a device for producing distinct signals – to be used by Table Officials when indicating or communicating with the referees;
- clocks (two) – one of these clocks is designated as the 'game clock' and approved by the referee. It should be large enough to be seen by the players, coaches, officials and spectators. The second clock/watch will be used as the 'time-out clock';
- a device for administering the 24-second rule;
- a scoreboard (electronic or manual one);
- one alternating possession arrow;
- two pens for scorer's use (either black and red or blue and red);
- one table and four chairs – one for scorer and one for timekeeper and two for players who request substitutions.

Apart from this equipment, the following items are very useful for basketball events, depending on the level of play (junior, senior, national, international):

- first aid box;
- banners for sponsors and own club;
- chairs/seating area for spectators;
- team benches;
- match programme;
- changing room signs – one each for home team, visiting team, referees' room;
- certificates/awards/medals/trophies.

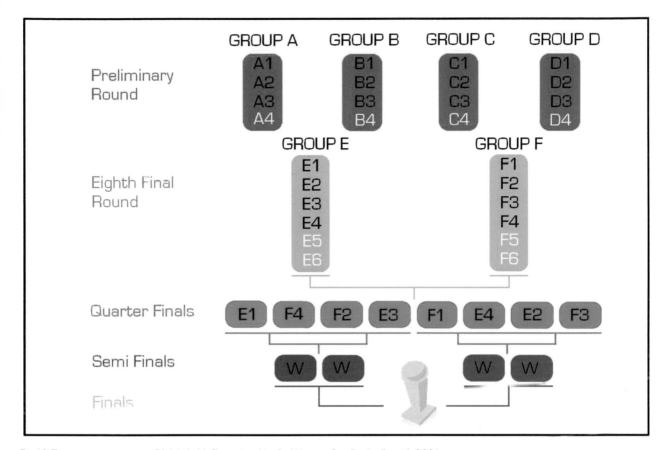

Fig 12 Tournament system – FIBA World Championship for Women Sao Paolo (Brazil) 2006.

therefore requires 6 × (6 − 1) divided by 2 = 6 × 5 divided by 2 = 15 games. This formula can be used with any number of entries.

This playing system selects a true winner and is more representative of a team's ability than the single elimination system, in which the eventual winner is not always the best entrant. Another advantage is the fact that it ranks all competitors. The main disadvantage is that it takes a longer time to complete.

For a simplified example of a top competition (the FIBA World Championship for Women 2006) organized using the tournament system (round robin), see Fig 12.

Mixt System

For this type of competition both elimination and round-robin systems are used. It is very useful when there are many participating teams, spread out throughout a country in different geographical areas.

As an example, thirty-two teams are divided into four groups of eight teams in each group; they play using the elimination system. The top two teams (finalists) in each group will take part in a single round-robin tournament to establish the final classification from first to eighth placed team.

Another option is to use the 'play-off' system, a very modern way of organizing the last stages of a competition (quarter-finals, semi-finals and finals). It is very popular, not only in NBA championship, but also in numerous European countries (including England) because of the way in which it selects a final winner.

The example given here is for a competition with twelve teams. After the regular season is finished (all teams having played

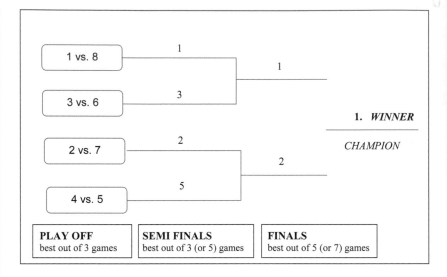

Fig 13 Play-off system.

each other twice on a 'home and away' basis – a double round-robin tournament), the teams will enter into the 'play-off' phase: Team 1 vs. Team 8, Team 2 vs. 7, Team 3 vs. 6 and Team 4 vs. 5. At the same time, in the 'play-out' group, Team 9 will play Team 12 and Team 10 will play Team 11. The 'play-off' will decide the champion team while the 'play-out' will indicate the last two teams in the classification, which will be relegated to a lower division.

At this stage ('play-off' and 'play-out'), all the games can be played using the 'best out of three' (or five) system, with two games on the home court of the better-placed team at the end of the regular season (or three games in case of the 'best out of five' system). The winner in each game will qualify for the semi-finals, which can also be played using the 'best of three (five)' system (see Fig 13). The final will be played by the winning teams while the losing semi-finalists will compete for the third and fourth places. The losing teams after the first round of play-offs can play in a fifth- to eighth-place classification tournament following a similar pattern.

POSSIBLE BASKETBALL EVENTS AND TARGET AUDIENCE

Name and type of event	Target audience
Mini-Basketball Festival	Children (beginners) grouped in two categories: 8–10 and 10–12 years old.
Streetball (3 vs. 3 basketball games at one basket)	All ages (usually over 12 years old), divided by age group (U14s, U16s, U18s, Seniors, Open).
'Children's Day' Trophy – two- to three-day event	Children playing as part of their school or club team.
Central Venue League (CVL)	Club (or schools) teams in age-group divisions (U12, U14, U16 and U18) – usually a development league.
Golden Basket (free-throws competition)	All ages – university students, schoolchildren.
School Championship – inter-class competition	Schoolchildren, in year groups.
University Championship – inter-faculties competition	University students.
British Universities and Colleges Sport (BUCS) Basketball Tournament – inter-universities competition	Students at British universities.
National League – inter-clubs competition	Registered players within basketball clubs across the UK, divided by age group (U13, U14, U15, U16, U18, U20 and Seniors).
European Championship	Senior players representing their country and competing at European level (Division A, B and C) – final tournament takes place every two years. Youth competitions are organized for U16, U18, U20 (Division A and B) on a yearly basis.
World Championship	Senior players representing their country and competing at world level – final tournament takes place every four years (two years after the Olympic Games). Competition organized by FIBA.
Olympic Games Basketball Tournament	Senior players representing the countries that have qualified to the Olympic Games. Tournament organized under FIBA patronage every four years as part of the Olympic Games.
Euroleague	Competition for top European professional clubs/teams playing against each other for a season.
EuroChallenge (Euro Cup)	Competition for top European professional clubs/teams playing against each other for a season.

PART II

ATTACK – SKILLS, TECHNIQUES AND TACTICS

CHAPTER 5

INDIVIDUAL PLAYER ATTACK

Passing the Ball

Basketball is a team game, which means that all players are involved in the process of playing the game and should function as one. *Passing* is one of the primary/basic skills required to accomplish this and is one of the best ways of keeping possession of the ball. It also helps to get the ball up the court towards the opponents' basket faster than dribbling.

There are many types of pass that a player must master, using one or two hands, and direct or using the floor. The majority of passes in the modern game of basketball are sent from one moving player to another moving player, which means that quick judgement as to what type of pass to use is vital. A team that passes well will have fewer turnovers and will create more scoring opportunities.

The different types of pass are the chest pass, bounce pass, overhead pass, javelin (or baseball) pass, and behind-the-back pass.

Fig 14 GB International Stefanie Collins holding the ball in front of the chest, just below shoulder level.

Chest Pass

Description and Use
This is probably the most frequently used pass in basketball. Ideally, the ball moves from the passing player's chest to where the receiver is signalling, either to his hand or to where he is pointing. If the receiver does not send any signals, the ball should be passed to his chest.

The ball is held between the finger pads (all fingers spread comfortably on the ball) in front of the chest (just below shoulder level); the palms are not touching the ball – see Fig 14. The pass starts as the player holding the ball steps forward; moving his body in the direction of the pass gives more power and balance while

Fig 15 The player steps forwards before sending a chest pass.

Fig 16 The arms remain extended after the chest pass (after a vigorous snap of the wrists), with fingers pointing towards the receiver and thumbs pointing downwards.

releasing the ball (see Fig 15). While the step forward is being taken, the player should extend his arms away from the chest; when they are straight, the wrists are snapped out simultaneously. After the ball leaves the hands of the passer, the fingers should end up pointing towards the receiver, with the thumbs pointing downwards (towards the floor) and the palms pointing outwards (see Fig 16). The snap of the wrists is important as it makes the pass crisp and firm.

The chest pass should travel in a straight line towards the receiver, who will take a step forward to meet and catch the ball with both hands.

Coaching Points

- Step into the pass to give more power and balance.
- Leave your arms extended after the pass and parallel between themselves (with fingers pointing towards the receiver and thumbs pointing towards the floor).
- The ball should travel in a straight line towards the receiver.

Drills

Chest Passes in Pairs
In pairs, one ball between two players. Players stand 3–4m apart, spread out along the court (see Fig 17). Alternately, they send a chest pass towards their partner (hold the ball with fingers spread out on the ball, step forward, extend arms and snap wrists, finish with arms extended and fingers pointing towards the pass), then get ready to receive the ball, arms out in front of the chest.

Passing Game – 'Ball at the Captain'
In groups of five to six players, one is the 'Captain' and the others are the 'soldiers' (see Fig 18). The Captain has the ball and stays 3–4m away from his soldiers, who will line up in single file. The Captain passes the ball (using a chest pass) to the first soldier (Moment A on Fig 18), who returns the ball in the same manner to the Captain (Moment B) and then joins the end of queue (Moment C). After he has passed to all his soldiers, the Captain

will be replaced by the first soldier in the queue and the Captain will join the back of the queue. All the soldiers have a chance to be captain and to repeat the chest pass. Once the chest pass has been learnt, this game can be played as a competition between several groups.

Chest Passes in a Triangle Formation
Groups of players stand in a triangle formation. Player 1 sends a chest pass towards his left to Player 2 (Moment A on Fig 19 overleaf) and then joins the back of his own queue (Moment B). Player 2 will do the same: chest pass to his left to Player 3 (Moment C) and then join the queue of the group where he belongs (Moment D) and so on.

There are a number of alternative options: players can pass towards the

player situated on their right-hand side and join the same queue; after the pass, the player can follow his pass and join the queue that he passed to; the player can pass to the left and join the queue on the right.

Bounce Pass

Description
The bounce pass is very similar in execution to the chest pass; the only difference is that the ball is sent powerfully on to the floor towards a teammate – see, overleaf, Fig 20 (step into the pass), Fig 21 (extending arms and sending the ball on to the floor with a wrist action) and Fig 22 (arms left extended after the pass, with fingers pointing towards the place where the ball hits the floor).

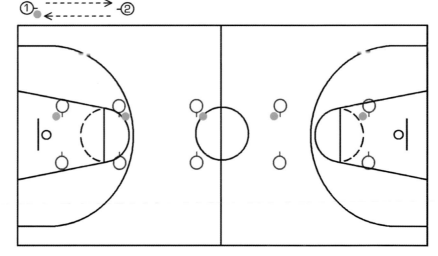

Fig 17 Display of players on court for chest passes in pairs.

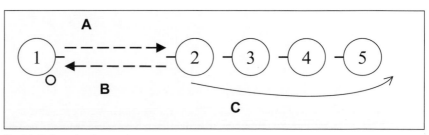

Fig 18 'Ball at the Captain.'

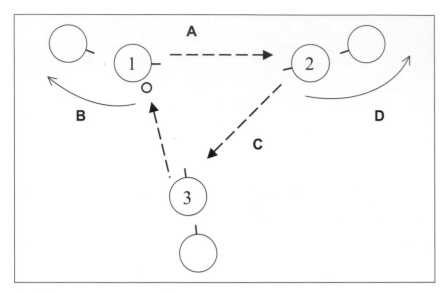

Fig 19 Chest passes in a triangle formation.

Coaching Points

- Step into the pass and push the ball powerfully on to the floor, at about two-thirds of the distance between you and the receiver.
- Leave your arms extended after the pass, with the fingers pointing towards the floor (at the point where the ball hits the floor).
- Aim for optimum speed, to enable safe catching.

Common Mistakes

- The sender pushes the ball too slowly or too hard on to the floor.
- The sender sends the ball on to the floor too close to himself (causing it to bounce over the receiver's head) or too close to the receiver (causing it to hit his legs below knee height).
- There is no step into the pass and the arms are not left extended after the pass.

Normally the ball should strike the floor about two-thirds of the way between the passer and the receiver and should bounce high enough to reach and to be caught by the receiver at waist height.

Use

The bounce pass is very effective when there is a defender between the passer and the receiver, especially when the opponent is a tall player and has his arms up. It may also be used as a pass to a cutter breaking for the basket on a fast-break situation, into and from a post man and as a pass for an out-of-bounds play. This is a slow type of pass, which takes longer to complete. It can be made using two hands or one only (one-handed push). In the second situation, instead of stepping forward, the sender will use a crossover step, at the same time adding an extended lateral movement (arm extended to the side) to get the ball around the obstacle (the defender).

Drills

All the drills and formations for the chest pass (see page 37) are useful for the bounce pass, too, as well as the following.

'Pig in the Middle'

In this simple passing game, two attacking players attempt to pass the ball to each other without the defender in between them touching or intercepting the ball. The game is played in any of the three circles on the basketball court and the

Fig 20 The player steps into the pass before sending a bounce pass.

Fig 21 The player extends his arms when sending the ball on to the floor together with a powerful wrist snap.

Fig 22 The arms remain extended after the pass with fingers pointing towards the point at which the ball hits the floor.

attackers are required always to have one foot on the circle; they are allowed to pivot, to open the passing angle. The defender's mission is to intercept the ball using a variety of quick moves (sideways, backward, forward) or fakes (pretending he is attacking the ball in order to cause the player to catch the ball, and then quickly moving in the opposite direction to anticipate and eventually intercept the pass) (see Fig 23).

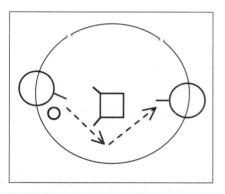

Fig 23 'Pig in the Middle' – 2 vs. 1.

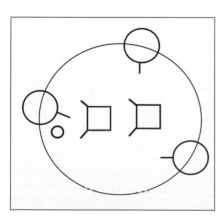

Fig 24 'Pig in the Middle' – 3 vs. 2.

As an alternative, this game may be played 3 vs. 2, with three attackers on the circle and two defenders in the middle (see Fig 24). The defender closest to the ball is attacking the ball, trying to determine the player to catch it, while the other defender is trying to anticipate where the pass will go.

Keeping Possession

There are two teams with an equal number of players. One team has possession and the players on offence are trying to pass the ball to each other, with the aim of making ten or fifteen consecutive passes without the opponents intercepting it. There is no dribbling and no shooting, only passing (using bounce passes) and pivoting. All the other rules of basketball – in relation to travelling, out of bounds, and so on – apply. Depending on the number of players in each team, the game can be played on the half-court or full court. After the required number of consecutive passes are achieved, the losing team can receive a punishment.

This drill may be progressed by imposing the use of all types of pass at different intervals (2 to 3 minutes for each type). Then, the rules may be changed slightly, with players not allowed to return the ball to the player who has just passed it to them.

Overhead Pass

Description

Holding the ball with two hands, relaxed, in front of his chest, as for the chest pass, the player extends his arms straight up over his head in preparation for the overhead pass (see Fig 25). The pass is initiated by a quick, short step in the direction of the receiver (see Fig 26 overleaf), and then the ball is released by extending the arms and using a vigorous snap of wrists and fingers (see Fig 27 overleaf). After the pass, the fingers point towards the receiver with the palms facing the floor (see Fig 28 overleaf). Ideally, the ball should travel in a straight line towards the receiver's chest area or to the point where he indicates he wants to receive it.

Use

This pass is very effective in feeding the ball in to a player in the post position (a pass to the pivot). It is also quite frequently used when a rebounder makes an 'outlet' pass to a teammate to initiate a fastbreak or when a forward hits a guard cutting to the basket.

Coaching Points

- Step into the pass and, extending your arms over your head, press and push the ball with your fingers from its back towards the front.
- Leave your arms extended after the pass.
- The ball should travel in a flat line towards your teammate's chest.

Common Mistakes

- The ball is thrown to the partner in a high arch shape (inverted U shape), giving the defender time to move and intercept.

Fig 25 GB International Rosalee Mason has her hands extended straight over her head ready for an overhead pass.

Fig 26 Before sending an overhead pass, the player steps forwards.

Fig 27 The player releases the ball by extending the arms and executing a powerful wrist action.

Fig 28 The arms remain extended (with fingers pointing towards the receiver and palms facing the floor) after the overhead pass.

- There is no step in to the pass and the arms are not left extended after the pass (no follow-through).
- There is no proper snap of the wrists and fingers.

Drills

All the drills relating to the chest pass and bounce pass can be employed to teach and improve the overhead pass.

Javelin Pass

Description

The javelin pass is also called the baseball pass or the shoulder pass.

From a normal, well-balanced stance (feet shoulder-width apart, weight evenly distributed), the right-handed player brings the ball with both hands up to a point above his right shoulder and just behind the right ear (see Fig 29). In this passing position, the right hand is behind the ball, with the fingers pointing upwards and the palm towards the receiver, while the left hand is semi-flexed on the front side. When he

is ready to pass, the passer will reach back with the ball (see Fig 30), shift his weight from his rear foot to the foot in front and then release the ball by stepping forwards on the opposite foot (Fig 31). The throwing movement is accompanied by a quick snap of the elbow, wrist and fingers (see Fig 32). The passing player needs to end up facing the receiver, with the arm extended and the palm facing the floor (see Fig 33).

Use

This pass is often used to inbound the ball quickly after the opposite team has scored or to initiate a fastbreak. It is also very useful as a long pass from any position on the court.

Coaching Points

- Keep two hands on the ball for as long as possible.
- Shift your body weight towards the front (when you step into the pass) and have the right hand with opposite foot (left) in front when passing.
- Leave your arm extended after the pass, with the palm facing the floor.

Common Mistakes

- The ball is pushed instead of being thrown.
- There is not enough action from the wrist and fingers.
- The passer has the same foot in front as the throwing hand.
- The ball does not travel in a flat line.

Drills

All drills and formations described above are applicable to learn the javelin pass.

Behind-the-Back Pass

Description

Generally, the behind-the-back pass is used by skilful players who also possess good awareness and peripheral vision. The passing player carries the ball from the front (chest area) towards his back (as in Fig 34) and, cupping the ball in his passing hand, releases it with a quick back-hand flip of his wrist (see Fig 35). The passer will finish the action with his fingers pointing at the receiver (Fig 36) and his body will

LEFT: Fig 29 GB International Kimberly Butler brings the ball above her shoulder getting ready to send a shoulder pass.

CLOCKWISE FROM ABOVE: Fig 30 The player reaches back with the ball before the shoulder pass is sent. Fig 31 The player releases the ball while stepping forwards on the opposite foot. Fig 32 The player releases the ball for a shoulder pass with a snap of the elbow, wrist and fingers.

pivot on the right foot (for a right-hand pass) away from the path of the pass.

Use

The behind-the-back pass could be used either as a straight pass or a bounce pass to a teammate coming behind for a screen or as a solution to pass to a free cutter in a 2 vs. 1 fastbreak situation, for example.

Coaching Points

- Have your elbow bent and the passing hand cupping the ball.
- Release the ball with a move of your arm from the shoulder and using a quick wrist and finger snap.

Fig 33 GB International Lisa Hutchinson (number 12 in white jersey) leaves her arm extended, facing teammate Sarah McKay (number 15), after sending a shoulder pass.

Fig 34 The player brings the ball from the front to the back ready for a behind-the-back pass.

Fig 35 The player is cupping the ball and releasing it with a quick back-hand flip of the wrist.

Fig 36 Passing-hand fingers are pointing towards the receiver.

Common Mistakes
- Beginners will roll the ball on to their front and back of the body.
- Beginners will lift the ball upwards instead of releasing it sideways.

Drills

Passes between Two (Stationary)
The players are in pairs, 3–4m apart, with a ball for each pair. The players have their left shoulder facing their partner for a right-hand behind-the-back pass (see Fig 37). After they have mastered the right-hand pass, each player will turn around 180 degrees, so that their right shoulder is facing their partner's right shoulder, and they will practise left-hand passes.

Passes in a Circle
All players are grouped in a circle formation (all facing inside the circle), with one holding a ball. To start the drill, the player with the ball will send a behind-the-back pass with his right hand to the player on his left; the next player will do the same and the drill continues with the ball going around the circle (see Fig 38).

As a progression, the coach will introduce a second and then a third ball.

Passes between Two on the Move
The players are in pairs, one ball for each pair. The partners are 3–4m apart, on the same level. The first pair at each end of the court will start the drill by passing the ball between them (using behind-the-back passes), while running along the court towards the opposite basket, without dropping the ball on the floor (see Fig 39). When they have finished, they join the queue at the other end of the court. Once the first pair has gone over the half-way line the next pair starts.

Coaching Points
- Pass ahead of the receiver (towards the front in relation to his movement).
- Turn the upper body only (arms, shoulders) towards the receiver and run properly facing the front.

Other Types of Pass

One-Hand Tap Pass (or Tip Pass)
This is a controlled deflection of a ball in flight to a teammate who is in a better position to control it and, potentially, to score. The palm of the passer is facing the ball (with fingers well spread) and then, once ball contact is made, will turn towards the receiver with a quick flip of

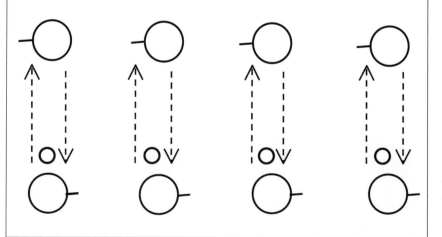

Fig 37 Positions of the players for a behind-the-back pass drill (using their right hand to pass).

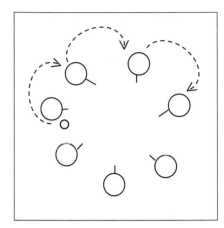

Fig 38 Behind-the-back passes in a circle formation.

the wrist and fingers. It can be executed with one or both hands (the latter gives better control). This pass is very similar to a tip-in shot.

Hook Pass

This is a very effective pass when the passer is being defended and pressured on the side. It can also be used by the pivots and also by the forwards. When starting the passing action, the player will take a cross-over step to get away from pressure, jump, turn, hook, pass using the hand furthest from the defender, and land, facing squarely in the direction in which the pass was made. He should land on both feet (shoulder-width apart), knees bent and ready to move quickly. The ball is released with an arm-extended hook and a flick of the wrist and fingers. The technique is essentially the same as that for a hook shot.

Hip Pass

For this pass, the ball is held close to the hip with the elbows flexed, with fingers spread wide and pointing downwards, and is released with a quick wrist and finger snap. The ball does not get behind the

Fig 39 Behind-the-back passes on the move (in pairs).

line of the body and each hand is equally important, regardless of whether the ball is released using one or two hands.

Flip or Hand-Off Pass

The passer releases the ball with a quick flip, directly into the hands of the receiver. He should not make the receiver take it off his hand, but should flip it and get his hand out of the way. His off hand and arm help protect the ball. The wrist and fingers follow through, but usually the arm will not be extended. The passer must be holding the ball firmly and must not release it too soon, as he may want to fake the pass if a defensive man is pressuring him, and then needs to be prepared to give the cutter a delayed pass.

Passing and Catching Drills

Passing on the Move in Threes (Without Changing Places)

Players wait in groups of three outside the court (see Fig 40 overleaf), with the player in the middle holding the ball. The player with the ball will pass either right or left, run forward to receive the ball back, and then pass it to the other side, to the third player. For example, Player 2 in Fig 40 will pass to Player 3, 3 will pass back to 2, who will then pass to Player 1 and so on, until the group arrives at the other end of the court, under the opposite basket. All players need to follow the 'man ahead of the ball' principle: if a player does not have

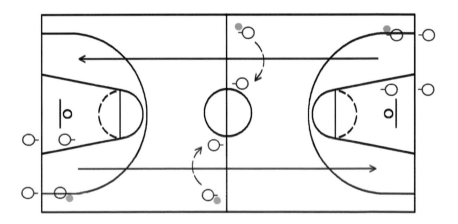

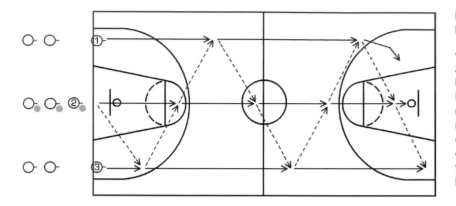

Fig 40 Passing on the move in threes drill (without changing places).

the ball he needs to move (run) forward to be ahead of the ball line (an imaginary line that is drawn from where the ball is towards the side lines, parallel with the two end lines of the court). As soon as the first group has passed over the half-way line, the next group starts its turn.

The drill may be taught at walking speed, then jogging, then progressed to running. Shooting a lay-up could be added at the end (with the other two players going to get the rebound).

Coaching points

- Always use two hands for catching and passing the ball.
- Run straight forward and turn the upper body only (arms, shoulders) towards your teammate when passing and/or receiving.
- If you do not have the ball, run forward and be ahead of the ball line.

TOP TIP

The 'man ahead of the ball' principle: if a player does not have the ball, he needs to move (run) forward to be ahead of the ball line (an imaginary line that is drawn from where the ball is towards the side lines, parallel with the two end lines of the court), so that he will be in an advantageous position (close to the basket) when receiving the ball.

Three-Man Weave

Exactly as in previous drill, three players are passing to each other but this time, after the pass, the player who passes the ball has to follow his pass and run around behind the receiver. The player receiving the ball should change his direction and cut towards the middle of the court, being ready to pass to the third man in the group, who will repeat the same moves (see Fig 41). To simplify things each player is running inside a channel along the court (three players = three channels) and, once a player has left his channel, somebody else needs to fill that channel. The drill demands accurate passing and develops the ability of

players to pass, watch and anticipate other people's moves while running.

Beginners can be taught the drill at walking speed then increase to jogging and running. The drill can be progressed by combining it with shooting a lay-up. For advanced players, there may be a restriction on the number of passes that may be sent while running one length of court (five, four or even three passes only). Alternatively, the number of lengths that need to be run (consecutively) may be increased.

Coaching points

- Keep the head up and turn the upper body only when passing or receiving the ball.
- If you do not have the ball, run forward so that you are always ahead of the ball.
- Pass and follow your pass.

Two-Man Two-Ball Drill

Players stand in pairs, 3–4m apart, each with a ball. Both players pass at the same time – Player 1 with a bounce pass and Player 2 with a chest pass (see Fig 42). After a couple of minutes they change, with Player 2 bounce passing and Player 1 chest passing. This excellent drill requires good ball handling (since a player must get rid of one ball quickly, in time to receive the other ball), concentration and quick thinking.

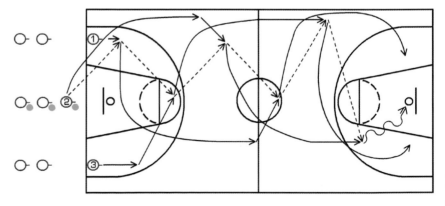

Fig 41 Three-man weave drill.

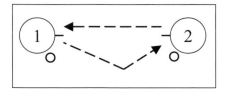

Fig 42 Two-man two-ball drill.

The drill may be progressed by using other types of pass, such as the overhead pass, chest pass, one-hand hip pass and javelin pass. It may also be performed on the move, at walking speed, then jogging, then running. Players may be asked to change over the type of pass they are sending once they go over the half-way line (see Fig 43).

Dribbling

Together with passing and shooting, dribbling is one of the fundamental skills in the game of basketball. It is one of the three methods used to advance the ball on the court and it is the only way of moving *with* the ball. It is a skill that has always been overused by some players who have a tendency to dribble too much.

A player should be able to use both hands and be capable of changing direction and rhythm/pace while moving and dribbling around the court. The rules of the game impose certain restrictions with regards to the dribble: it must be executed with one hand at a time; if the player catches the ball in two hands after dribbling it, he has to either pass to a teammate or shoot – he is not allowed to dribble again.

Description

Dribbling (exactly like passing and shooting) involves the use of the wrist and fingers to control the ball by pushing it towards the floor. The ball is dribbled and controlled with the finger pads, fingertips or the top part of the fingers, which are spread out comfortably 'over the top of the ball'. In order to dribble efficiently, the player needs to keep the ball at waist height (some coaches recommend a height between the waist and the knee), and keep his head up so that he is aware of teammates and opponents, allowing him to make a quick pass. The dribbling hand needs to be kept on the top of the ball for accurate control. For best control, the dribbler actually touches the ball with his fingers while it is on the upward move. Touching the ball late in the dribble, when it is on the way down, is more like slapping it than dribbling it and could result in a loss of control.

When dribbling, the body needs to maintain a crouched position, with knees bent, hips lowered slightly and the back almost straight. The non-dribbling hand is

extended in front of the body, protecting the ball from being stolen. The opposite foot also creates the barrier (see Fig 44 overleaf).

Types of Dribbling

High Dribble (or Speed Dribble)
The high (or speed) dribble is mainly used when leading a fastbreak, when driving to the basket, when bringing the ball to the opposite court, and generally when getting from one point on the floor to another. The body is in an upright position (leaning slightly forwards for better balance) and the player is pushing the ball further away from him (one arm extended or one arm and a half away from him) to create more speed in a forward direction (see Fig 45 overleaf).

Fig 43 Two-man two-ball drill on the move.

Fig 44 GB guard Jarrett Hart (number 4 in white jersey) dribbles the ball (while protecting it) towards the Israeli basket.

The ball is continually pushed on the floor with a pumping motion, forward and slightly to the dribbling side, the ball bouncing at a height of between above waist level and below the shoulders, depending on the individual player. If the ball is allowed to come too high or too low it slows down the player or leads to a dribbling violation.

Low Dribble (or Protective Dribble)

The low dribble is used mainly when trying to clear and to get the ball away from a crowded area; when driving past a defensive man on a move towards the basket; and even when dribbling to protect the ball in order to keep this option alive (instead of catching the ball).

The player who is dribbling low should have his knees and hips bent and his body

Fig 45 GB guard Nate Reinking advances on the court using a high (speed) dribble.

Fig 46 Very low (protective) dribble performed by GB forward Nick George.

Fig 47 The player on the left is using her left arm and left foot to protect the ball while dribbling it low.

in a crouched position, but should try to keep his head up (see Fig 46). He will push the ball away using the wrist and fingers and will try to control it when the ball is bouncing off the floor no higher than knee height ('half-way up to the knee' is what some coaches recommend). This is the main reason why this type of dribble is also called a 'control dribble'.

The non-dribbling arm is used mainly for protection (together with the foot opposite to the dribbling hand) but also for maintaining a good balance (see Fig 47). The dribbling arm is held close to the body, with the elbow almost touching it. The dribbler can use a combination of head, body and/or shoulder fakes, together with continuous pivoting (around the foot closest to the defender), especially against extreme defensive pressure. This is also when the ball is dribbled and controlled at an even lower height.

Behind-the-Back Dribble

Every complete player (that is to say, someone who possesses a wide repertoire of skills and has a good technique) is able to perform the behind-the-back dribble, which is slightly harder to execute than dribbling in a straight line. This type of dribble requires the player to bounce the ball behind him (see Fig 48), so that the ball will bounce up under his left hand when the right hand is used to dribble. The ball is flicked close behind the back by a quick flip above the back of the knee and across the back of the thigh as the opposite leg moves forward (see Fig 49). This will enable the opposite foot and leg to stay out of the way as the ball hits the floor and allows the ball to come up under the opposite hand for a continuation of the dribble (as in Fig 50). This dribble can be used very efficiently when changing direction and also when trying to avoid a close defender.

Cross-Over Dribble

The cross-over dribble is particularly useful when changing pace and direction of movement with the main purpose of evading a defensive man or getting to a better position for a pass or a shot. With the ball on the right side, the dribbling hand (right) flicks the ball to the opposite side by pushing it on to the floor from slightly outside the ball (as in Figs 51 and 52 overleaf); the ball will go into the player's left hand, which will pick it up and will continue the dribbling (Figs 53 and 54 overleaf). The feet play an important role too: as the foot on the dribbling side makes contact with the floor, a hard push-off is initiated towards the opposite foot.

Fig 48 The player starts bouncing the ball behind her.

Fig 49 The ball is flicked close behind the back, across the back of the thighs.

Fig 50 The ball bounces up under the player's left hand and the player continues to dribble in the new direction.

Fig 51 The dribbling hand (right) flicks the ball towards the opposite side by pushing it into the floor.

Fig 52 The dribbling hand (right) finishes off the flicking action.

Fig 53 The left hand picks up the ball after it bounces off the floor.

Fig 54 The player regains control of the ball using her left hand and continues to dribble the ball in the new direction.

Extra care should be taken by the player using cross-over dribbling if the defender is close and moving quickly.

360-Degree Dribble (or Pivot Dribble or Spin Dribble)

Extremely efficient especially in a one-on-one drive or when changing direction, this type of dribble requires some extra skill from the player, together with good balance and quick change of hands. While the player is dribbling with his right hand, he has a quick stationary moment (dribbling on the spot), left foot in front and right one behind his body and the ball. Executing a backward pivot on the left foot (Figs 55 and 56), and turning his back

to the defender (as in Fig 57), the dribbler will then pick up the ball or will dribble with his left hand (see Figs 58 and 59). A push off the right foot increases the pivoting speed. At all times, the dribbling player's body must be kept between the ball and the defender. The player also needs to keep his head up so that he can see and anticipate what is happening around him on the court. This dribble is also known as the spin dribble or the reverse dribble.

Change-of-Pace Dribble

As the name indicates, the change-of-pace dribble is used mainly to help a player alter his speed on the court, in order to trick the defender into relaxing his guard. The

Fig 55 Player dribbling with the right hand getting ready for a 360-degree turn.

Fig 56 The beginning of a backward pivot on the left foot.

Fig 57 The player turns her back to the defender.

dribbler may then take advantage of the situation. The execution is very simple: while dribbling continuously, the player suddenly changes his speed from fast to slow in order to deceive the defender into expecting a stop or a change of direction, while he quickly continues with his original move towards the basket.

Between-the-Legs Dribble

A safe and efficient way of changing hands and direction when dribbling, the between-the-legs dribble requires quick action from the dribbler. When dribbling with his right hand, the player will place his left foot forward while the right one stays at the rear (as in Fig 60). At this point, when the feet are wide, the player will bounce the ball between his legs (see Fig 61), sending it to the other side (left) of his body, where he will collect it with his left hand (Fig 62), which will continue the dribbling. Having the opposite foot to the front will give the dribbler much-needed protection against a defender (see Fig 63).

Uses

Dribbling is used in a number of ways:

* To penetrate a defence in order to gain a shooting or a passing opportunity.
* To protect the ball when defence pressure is on (to escape from a defender who is closely marking you).
* To move the ball up the court.
* To create a better passing angle.
* To protect the ball in the closing minutes of a game.

Coaching Points

* Always use the fingers and the wrist to dribble the ball (to push it towards the ground).
* Good posture is required, with knees bent, head up, non-dribbling arm and opposite foot creating a barrier.
* Dribble the ball forward and slightly to one side of you (either right

Fig 58 When the turn is almost complete, the player will start changing the dribbling hand.

Fig 59 The player dribbles with the left hand in the new direction after the turn is completed – her body is between the ball and the defender at all times.

Fig 60 Left foot in front with the right at rear indicates the player is ready for dribbling between the legs.

Fig 61 The player bounces the ball between her legs.

Fig 62 The player uses the left hand to collect the ball.

Fig 63 The player protects the ball after the turn by having the opposite foot in front.

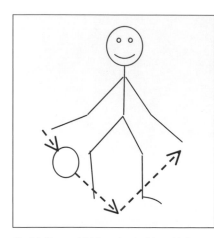

Fig 64 Player dribbling the ball in a V shape in front of his legs.

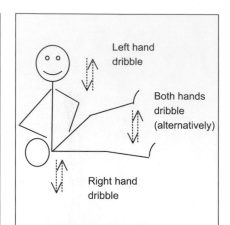

Fig 65 Dribbling while sitting down.

or left), and keep moving straight forward, away from a defender as much as possible.
• Use your peripheral vision, have your head up and keep the ball close and under control.
• Change hands depending on the type of dribble (behind the back, 360-degree and cross-over in particular).

Common Mistakes

• 'Slapping' or patting the ball.
• Ball bouncing too high (above waist level).
• Looking at the ball when dribbling.
• Bouncing the ball on the feet or too far away from the body.

Drills

Dribbling is one of the basic skills that are taught to beginners right from the first couple of training sessions. The coach needs to make sure that all players develop this skill correctly, and that means learning it properly from the start.

Dribbling on the Spot (Stationary)

All players stand around the centre circle (facing inside the circle), each with a ball. The coach asks them to dribble the ball in different ways:

• with the right hand, first at hip level, then at knee height, then below the knee (low dribble), then at shoulder height (really high dribble);
• with the left hand, following exactly the same pattern (normal dribble, low, very low, high);
• dribbling the ball alternately with both hands (bouncing it in a V shape in front of the legs) (see Fig 64);
• standing still, moving the ball around the feet by dribbling it so that from the front it goes to the right side, then at the back and again to the front through the left side.

The practice is progressed by increasing the speed of the dribble for any of the above drills. Additionally, the difficulty can be increased by asking the players to keep their heads up – the coach can show numbers using his fingers and the players need to respond.

Coaching points

• Try to control the ball using the wrist and fingers;
• Find a comfortable height at which to bounce the ball.

For the next stationary drill, players are sitting down with their feet wide (see Fig 65). They bounce the ball with the right hand outside the right leg, with right and left hands alternately in between their legs, and with the left hand outside the left leg. The coach challenges them to do this without catching the ball in two hands (continuous dribble), and can set targets such as ten dribbles (or more) in each of the three spots.

Next, players lie down on their back and dribble the ball with the right hand on the right-hand side of the body, and with the left hand on their left-hand side. Then they lie on their front and dribble the ball in the same way.

Standing up again, they can then attempt to dribble the ball between their legs. To make it easier at the beginning, they should bounce the ball reasonably close to them, in order to control the ball, and then send it through their legs. As they progress, they can try to dribble continuously through the legs by using one hand at a time, alternately, and sending the ball between your legs. The final move should look like a figure of '8'.

Dribbling on the Move

All players are lined up at one of the end lines of the court, each player with a ball (see Fig 66). At the coach's signal, they start walking towards the other end of court while dribbling the ball with right hand. On the way back they are asked to dribble with their left hand. The coach needs to stress the fact that this drill is not a race or a relay, but individual work to improve dribbling skills.

The same drill is then performed at jogging speed. Next, the players dribble with the right hand up the court and then return to the start position walking backwards, still dribbling the ball. (When moving backwards, players need to look behind them out of the corner of their eyes for any obstacles or other players who might trip you over.) This is repeated for the left-hand dribble. As they make progress, they can increase their speed, running forwards and then backwards while still dribbling the ball. The ball must be bounced at hip level so that the player maintains control.

Dribbling Relays

All players, whatever their level (beginners, advanced, seniors), enjoy an element of competition as part of the session. A

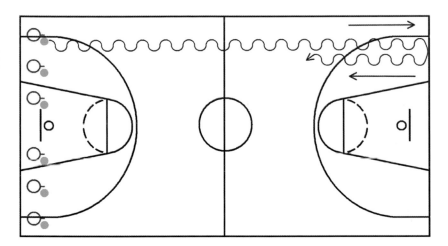

Fig 66 Players' positions for drill practising dribbling on the move.

Dribbling Between Cones

For this drill, you need at least four balls and eight big cones. The squad is split into two groups; one group lines up at one corner of the court (Point A on Fig 68 overleaf) and the other at the opposite corner (point B on Fig 68).

One player from each group at a time runs towards the opposite basket, dribbling the ball through the cones (going to the right-hand side of the first cone and not through the middle of the court). When he arrives at the other end of court, he will pass the ball to the first person (waiting in the opposite queue) who has no ball and will then join the end of that queue. When Player 1 at each end goes over the half-way line, Player 2 starts his turn.

Coaching points

- Change hands when dribbling past a cone.
- Keep the head up.
- When running and dribbling, avoid going in big semicircles. Stay as close as possible to the cone (almost like running in a straight line).

The drill may be progressed by increasing the speed of the running. Later, it may be combined with taking a lay-up after going round the last cone. The player gets his own rebound, passes to the first person waiting in the closest queue and joins the queue.

Zig-Zag Dribbling

This drill has the same formation and same principles as the previous one: two groups of players at opposite corners of the court. When Player 1 goes over the half-way line, Player 2 starts his turn. One player in each group will start dribbling the ball and jogging in a zig-zag shape, changing direction and his dribbling hand (see Fig 69 overleaf).

When changing directions, different types of dribbling can be used:

- normal dribble – from left hand to right in front of the body (or cross-over);
- between the legs;

dribbling relay is fun, competitive, easy to organize and fulfils an important role – it keeps improving dribbling skills. The players are grouped into teams with an equal number of players in each team (see Fig 67). If in either group is one player down, someone in that group will have to run twice.

At an agreed starting signal (a whistle, a clap of hands, or a shout of 'go'), the first player in each group dribbles the ball with his dominant hand all the way to the other end of the court, then dribbles back and offers (without throwing) the ball to the next teammate, who will do the same. The first player then joins the end of queue. The winning team is the one whose players have all completed the run.

The coach can impose certain restrictions, such as a right-hand dribble to the end line and a left-hand dribble on the way back. He may increase the distance that must be covered using dribbling, or he may include another technical element at the end of the court, such as a pass with the wall.

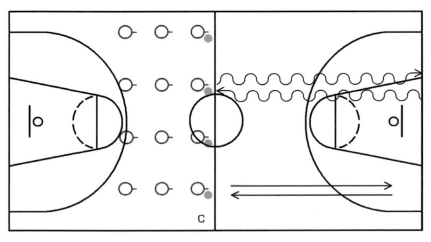

Fig 67 Dribbling relay.

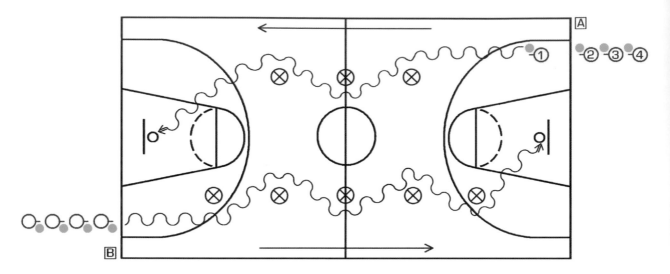

Fig 68 Dribbling between cones.

- behind the back;
- 360-degree (spin dribble).

After changing direction (and dribbling hand), there must be a change in speed (with a short, 3- to 4-m sprint). The player should also seek to protect the ball with the non-dribbling hand and keep the head up.

There are a number of ways of progressing the drills:

- combining dribbling with taking a lay-up when reaching the opposite basket;
- increasing the speed;
- introducing a defender who is not stealing the ball or obstructing the

dribbling, 1 vs. 1 along the court. The defender plays defence using a defensive stance and will go backwards zig-zagging all the time, keeping the same distance between him and the attacking player.

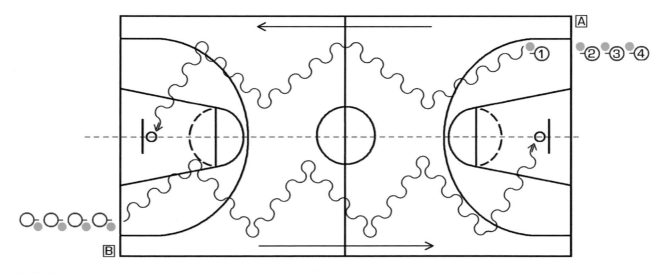

Fig 69 Zig-zag dribbling.

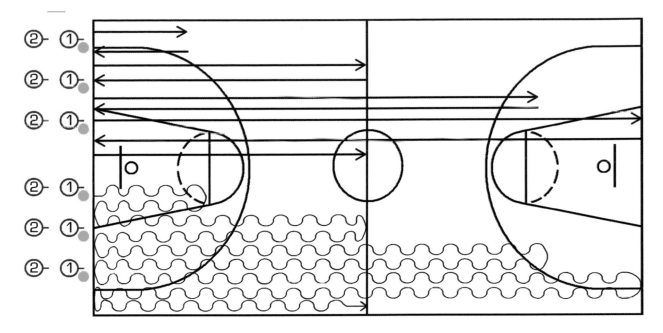

Fig 70 'Suicide' with dribbling.

'Suicide' with Dribbling

The players wait in pairs at one end of the court (outside of it), Number 1s with the ball, Number 2s without. At a signal, the Number 1s dribble and sprint in a straight line to touch the free-throw line (or the floor level with it), then run back to touch the start place (the end line of the court), then sprint to touch the half-way line, then back to the end line, then sprint to touch the other free-throw line and back to the end line, then sprint towards the opposite end line, back to the starting line and finish with a sprint over the half-way line (finish line) (see Fig 70).

This is a great drill for improving dribbling but also for conditioning and improving fitness levels. While the Number 1s have a rest, the Number 2s do the same drill. The drill can be performed with the right hand only then with the left hand only.

It can be progressed in a number of ways:

- right hand on the way to the free-throw line, the half-way line, the other free-throw line, the other end line, and left hand on the way back to the starting point;
- running facing forwards on the way to the free-throw line, half-way line, the other free-throw line, the other end line, and running backwards on the way back towards the starting point;
- two suicides in a row – one without the ball and the second one with the ball (pick up the ball waiting at the end of the court and dribble it).

Shooting

The main objective in the basketball game is to shoot and score more points than the opposition. As a consequence, accurate shooting is a high priority for any basketball player and working towards improving this skill must be incorporated in the training sessions. There are a number of important principles in shooting (the first three relating to the player's 'mental' approach, and the last five to his 'physical' attributes):

1 *Concentration*: while taking a shot, the player needs to concentrate on the target (the hoop) from the moment he takes/receives the ball until he releases it. It is about mental discipline and, through continuous practice, good shooters can develop their concentration to the extent that they cannot be distracted by any noise (such as that made by spectators) or pressure.

2 *Ability to relax*: closely related to concentration, the ability to relax will enable the shooter to perform efficiently under pressure. The pre-shot routine is performed calmly by the shooting player who needs to have good balance and to have the ball under control.

3 *Confidence*: when taking a shot, every player must be confident that the ball will drop through the basket. Making a correct decision as to when to shoot or what type of shot to take will increase confidence levels.

4 *Sighting (or locating the target)*: for every shot he takes, the player

Fig 71 Excellent follow-through demonstrated by the GB guard Jarrett Hart, who leaves his arm fully extended after taking a free throw.

Fig 72 GB forward Luol Deng shows the correct position of the feet (right foot in front of the left) when shooting a free throw with the right hand.

8   **Follow-through**: a follow-through moment in which the forces generated and impacting on the ball are allowed to diminish is an essential part of the shooting sequence. This is usually done by leaving the shooting arm extended after the shot (see Fig 71). Some players rise on the balls of their feet in addition to extending the arm.

There are several different types of shot but three of them are considered to form the basis of the basketball player's scoring repertoire: the set shot (free throw), the lay-up shot and the jump shot. As well as these three types, there are also close-range shots, the hook shot and the slam-dunk shot.

Set Shot (Free Throw)

Description
Correct positioning of the feet and the way the arms hold the ball are vital for shooting accuracy and precision. With the ball in his hands, the player will first position his feet – they should be shoulder-width apart, with the right foot slightly forward (half of a sole) for right-hand shooting players (see Fig 72). The feet/soles are parallel with each other and perpendicular to the board line; they provide a very good balance for the whole body, with the shooter's weight being equally distributed from side to side and back to front, to prevent any swaying motion. The line of the shoulders is parallel to the board and they should stay the same during the shooting action, without turning.

The ball is held in front of the chest just below shoulder level (see Fig 73). The position of the shooting hand is on the lower back side of the ball (behind the ball), the fingers spread comfortably wide and pointing upwards, with the palm facing the basket. The other hand supports the ball from the side, providing additional balance and control. It falls away the moment before the release. The ball should rest on the finger pads of the shooting hand, never on the palm.

needs to remain focused on the target (which could be the ring or, in case of a bank shot, the painted rectangle above the basket), from the moment the shot is begun to the completion of the follow-through move.

5   **Body balance**: when properly balanced, a shooter can coordinate the effort of his legs, trunk and arm muscles to produce a net force in the direction of the basket resulting in a nice, clean shooting action, completed by a follow-through move. Good balance comes from a good stance (feet usually shoulder-width apart). The player's movement during the shooting action should be up and down on the spot or towards the basket.

6   **Applying force on the ball**: several muscles or parts of the body apply force on the ball when shooting. The best results are achieved when all these separate forces are brought into a smooth, coordinated effort: a powerful flick of the wrist and fingers; a sudden extension of the arm, snapping the shoulder and elbow; and a sharp knee-locking thrust with the legs, while rising on the balls of the feet.

7   **Hand–eye coordination**: all forces imparted to the ball by the shooter should pass through the fingertips, which should be comfortably spread on the ball. This will allow the fingers to make fine trajectory adjustments at release and will provide a 'soft' natural backspin.

Fig 73 GB International Andrew Sullivan holds the ball in front of his chest ready for a free-throw shot.

You should be able to slide a finger from the other hand between the ball and the palm of the shooting hand; if you cannot get it through, you are holding it incorrectly.

The arms are relaxed, close to the body, as if you were gently holding two books under each arm. The elbows are tucked in, reasonably close to the body. The right elbow is directly under the ball, directed at the basket. The shooting action has two parts: Moment 1, when the ankles, knees and hips are bent (see Fig 74) and Moment 2, when the legs (ankles, knees, hips) and arms are straightened upwards and the ball is released (see Fig 75).

As the shooting arm reaches full stretch, a powerful snap of the wrist gives the ball backspin. The action of the set shot is finished with the follow-through, and the player ends with the shooting hand upwards, palm facing the floor, and fingers pointing towards the basket (see Fig 76).

TOP TIP

The shooter needs to maintain a continuous action (single-motion delivery) from the moment the shot starts until the ball is released. The BEEF acronym is used by coaches to focus the attention of the players on the key elements for shooting:

- B = balance;
- F = elbow under the ball;
- E = eyes on the target;
- F = follow-through.

Use

The set shot is used primarily for free throws (as its name suggests) but also for long-range shots.

Coaching Points
- Emphasize a continuous movement/action: bend your knees, extend your legs and your arm, and finish with a powerful flick of the wrist.

Fig 74 GB centre Pops Mensah-Bonsu gets ready for the first part of the free-throw shooting action by flexing his hips, knees and ankles.

Fig 75 The second part of the free-throw shooting action – GB international Andrew Sullivan extends his arms before releasing the ball.

Fig 76 Excellent follow-through action performed by GB centre Pops Mensah-Bonsu after the ball is released.

- Remember the follow-through move of the arm after the shot.
- Ball, wrist, elbow and front foot must be in a perpendicular line on the board.

Common Mistakes

- Not having the elbow of the shooting hand right under the ball.
- The shooting arm dropping down and/or to the side.
- Failing to finish the shot with a powerful wrist action.
- Holding the ball incorrectly (with the palms).
- 'Pushing' the ball instead of throwing it.
- Not being properly balanced.

Drills

Solo

Each player stands 2m from the basket and takes set shots, trying to follow all the instructions given in relation to the correct shooting action: position of feet, position of hands and fingers, knees and arms action, follow-through after the shot.

After a couple of minutes, players are instructed to move backwards (3–4m from the basket) and continue shooting.

In pairs

With one ball between two, one player will take a set shot (from 3–4m in front of the basket). His partner collects the rebound and passes the ball back to the shooter. After five consecutive throws, the players change roles.

The drill progresses with each player taking five (or ten, or fifteen, and so on) consecutive shots from five spots around the basket (3–4m away from different angles on the left and right) (see Fig 77). The partner rebounds and passes the ball back, and the roles are swapped after each set of shots.

'Tour de France' (or 'Shooting around the World')

Two or three (or more) players shoot, one at a time, from positions indicated to them by the coach (see Fig 78). The first player shoots from Position 1; if he makes

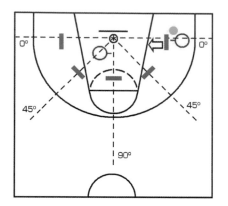

Fig 77 Five spots for set shots shooting in pairs drill and shooting angles.

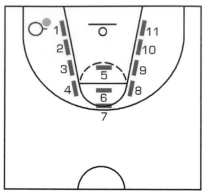

Fig 78 Shooting spots for 'Tour de France' ('Around the World') game.

the shot, he moves to Position 2 for his next shot, and so on. If he misses, Player 2 has his turn and follows the same pattern. When his turn comes round again, Player 1 starts from the spot where he missed his last shot. Those players not shooting get the rebound and pass the ball back to the shooter. The winner is the player who scores from all positions.

Shooting free throws in teams

This is a very good drill for coaching big groups. Players are split into several teams of three to four players in each team, positioned 3–4m from a basket (see Fig 79). On the signal, the first player in each group

takes a free throw, then goes and gets the rebound (whether he scores or not) and passes the ball to the next person, before joining the back of the queue. When a player scores, all his teammates shout out loud how many points their team has scored; the winning team is the first to get to 5 points (or 10 with more advanced players). The coach will then rotate the teams so that everyone is shooting at different baskets.

14–21

In pairs, one ball for each pair, Player 1 takes a free throw from the free-throw line (or from 3–4m away) and then runs

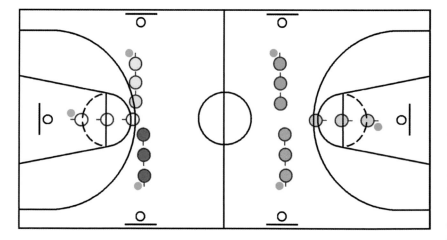

Fig 79 Positioning of the players for shooting free throws in teams.

TOP LEFT: Fig 80 GB guard Flinder Boyd (number 14 in white jersey) runs towards the opposite basket ready for a lay-up.

BELOW LEFT: Fig 81 GB guard Flinder Boyd jumps to take a lay-up.

BELOW RIGHT: Fig 82 GB forward Luol Deng reaches up to score a lay-up.

to get the ball for his second shot. If he scores the first attempt he gets 2 points; if he misses he gets no points. Whether he scores or misses, he goes to take the rebound, ideally before the ball touches the floor (although with beginners one bounce of the ball can be allowed). If he makes his second shot it is worth 1 point only (regardless of the outcome of the first shot). If he scores both shots, he will have 3 points and will continue to shoot by going back to the free-throw line and taking the next set of two shots. If the player misses one of the two shots, he passes the ball to his partner, who will go on to take his two shots. The first to score 21 is the winner.

Alternatively, when a player has reached 14 points, one of his two shots has to be with the left hand for right-handed players (right hand for left-handed players). Another restriction is not allowing the ball to bounce on the floor after the first shot, forcing the shooter to run quickly and rebound it before touching the floor.

Lay-Up Shot

Description/Technique
As a general rule, if approaching the basket from the right a player should take a right-hand lay-up; similarly, he should take a left-hand shot on the left. Ideally, when

shooting a lay-up, players should approach the basket from a 45-degree angle (see Fig 77 for shooting angles) and should use the backboard.

The lay-up is made up of four parts: the run or the approach (Fig 80); the jump up and towards the target (Fig 81); the reach up and score (Fig 82); and the landing. When a right-handed player receives a pass or finishes a dribble and picks up the ball in two hands (Fig 83 overleaf) with both feet on the floor, he will be allowed to take two steps – right foot (see Fig 84 overleaf), then left foot (Fig 85 overleaf). Jumping off the left foot (upwards and forwards, as in Fig 86 overleaf), he will swing the right knee upwards during the flight as if performing a high jump in athletics (see Fig 87). He shoots the ball with the right hand softly against the backboard so that it bounces off the backboard straight into the net. Right-handed players should aim for the top right-hand corner of the small square printed on the backboard (see Fig 88).

As in the set shot, there should be a complete follow-through – the shooter alights with hips down, knees bent and body weight low, ready to move immediately into position for a rebound.

For a left-hand lay-up the sequence is left foot (Fig 89), right foot (Fig 90), swing the left knee up (Fig 91), take the shot (Fig 92), and land.

Use
A lay-up shot is used by a player who dribbles past defenders and under the basket. It can also be an efficient finish for a player who receives a pass, close in, while cutting towards the opposite basket.

Coaching Points
- Approach the basket from a 45-degree angle.
- Use and send the ball softly on to the backboard.
- The running action is transformed into a jumping (take-off) action by driving the knee (on the same side as the shooting hand) upwards.
- Hold the ball with both hands for as long as possible and place the shooting hand behind the ball.
- Aim the ball at the top right-hand side corner of the square drawn on the board when shooting from the right-hand side.

Common Mistakes
- Shooting the ball too hard off the backboard.
- Losing control of the ball during the two steps or during the take-off.
- Holding the ball with one hand only, which leads to unsafe control.
- The player using hops and skips during the cut towards the basket and jumping forwards instead of upwards.

Fig 83 The player picks up the ball in two hands before taking two steps for the lay-up.

Fig 84 The player starts the lay-up by taking a step with the right foot.

Fig 85 The player takes a second step – with the left foot – during the lay-up.

Fig 86 The player takes off from the left foot, jumping upwards and forwards.

Fig 87 The player swings his right knee up.

Fig 88 The ball is sent into the top right-hand side corner of the square drawn on the board.

Fig 89 The player takes a step with the left foot as the first part of a left-hand lay-up.

Fig 90 The player takes a step with the right foot.

Fig 91 The player swings the left knee up.

Fig 92 The player reaches up and takes the left-hand lay-up shot.

Fig 93 Position of the feet when learning the lay-up.

Fig 94 Lay-up drill with dribble from the 3-points semicircle.

Drills

Teaching the lay-up

In order to teach the lay-up, the coach will ask the right-handed players to stand 3–4m away from the basket in a 45-degree angle (as in Fig 93), with the left foot in front (right foot in front for left-handed players, on the left-hand side). The player bounces the ball once, catches it and then moves by taking two steps – right, left. After the second step the player has to jump upwards (at the same time the right knee has to be lifted upwards, to get more height into the jump). While in the air, the ball is released with the right hand on to the basket – on the top right-hand side corner of the small square drawn on the board. The player will land on both feet, ready to move to the next action.

Players are encouraged to count '1-2' (or to say 'right-left') when they start the lay-up so that they get used to taking only two steps. For left-handed players, the process is left step, right step and up (swing left knee upwards), and shoot with left hand, sending the ball on the top left-hand side corner of the small square.

From the 3-points semicircle the player has to dribble towards the basket before taking two steps (right-left for right-hand players) and throwing the ball (see Fig 94).

At the beginning the drill may be performed at walking speed and then jogging. It may be progressed by increasing the distance, starting from the half-way line, walking first and then jogging. The speed can be increased as the players become more confident in taking the steps before the actual shot.

Lay-ups from three directions

In small groups (three to four players in each group), one at a time, players dribble and take lay-ups, get their own rebound, pass the ball back to the next person in the group, and join the back of the queue. The three groups are positioned in front of the basket so that players come from the left at a 45-degree angle (Group A in Fig 95 overleaf), from the front (Group B) and from the right at a 45-degree angle (Group C). After scoring ten lay-ups as

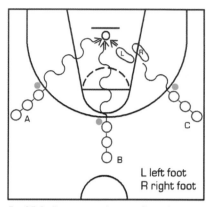

Fig 95 Drill practising lay-ups from three directions.

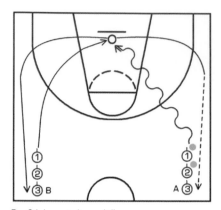

Fig 96 Lay-up lines drill.

a group (players count each time they score), the whole group will move to the right (Group A instead of B, B instead of C and C instead of A) for another set of ten, and so on, until all players have taken lay-ups from all three spots.

Lay-up lines
This drill is usually used during the pre-match warm-up. Players are lined up in two lines facing one basket, as in Fig 96. Group A (with two balls) will be the drib-bling and shooting players while Group B will be the rebounding players. Player 1 in Group A (with the ball) dribbles towards the basket and takes a lay-up. At the same time, Player 1 in Group B advances to the basket and goes and gets the rebound no matter the outcome of the lay-up from the Group A player. After shooting, Player 1 from Group A runs to the back of Group B in order to become a rebounder; after rebounding, Player 1 from Group B drib-bles the ball close to the side line towards Group A, passes to the first player without the ball (to Player 3) and joins the queue to become a shooter.

This is a very good drill, which allows players to rehearse dribbling, taking lay-ups, rebounding and passing. Players should be encouraged to jump and get the rebound (so that the ball does not hit the floor) instead of just waiting for the ball. After 4–5 minutes (or after scoring fifteen to twenty lay-ups as a team), move the

balls to the left (Group B) so that players practise left-hand lay-ups.

Note: most of the drills used for practising dribbling (pages 50–53) are also useful for practising lay-up shots.

Jump Shot

Description/Technique
One of the most effective offensive weapons, the jump shot is very similar to the set shot, except that it is taken after a vertical jump (from a quick movement following a quick stop). To begin the jump shot the player needs to establish a balanced position with his feet shoulder-width apart facing the basket. The take-off (the vertical jump) can be from either a stationary position (rather rarely) or a position on the move (more frequently) after dribbling, pivoting or receiving a pass. The ball is held in a similar manner, brought up to shooting position and released in an almost identical way to the set shot (see Fig 97).

The ball is released when the player reaches the highest point of his jump (and not after starting his descent) (see Fig 98). The follow-through should be completed with the shooting arm fully extended and with a powerful wrist and fingers snap, as in Fig 99. A proper landing after is another important element of the shot:

the jump should be vertical and the player should land on the same spot from where he took off. During the whole action of the shot, the shooter's eyes should be fixed on the basket (see Fig 100). This requires considerable concentration as the shooter's hands and forearms cross his line of vision. The player should finish the shot just as he started it, smoothly and well balanced, ready to move either to jump for a rebound or to pick up a defensive role. It is recommended that young players and/or beginners should not be taught this type of shot until they have mastered the technique of performing set shots and lay-ups to a reasonable standard.

Use
The jump shot is very frequently used in modern basketball. It can be used after the player has performed a number of other techniques/skills: after the dribble; after receiving a pass as an open player or after the cut; after pivoting; after using a fake (a shooting fake, or a pass fake); or after grabbing an offensive rebound.

Fig 97 For a jump shot the ball is held and brought to the shooting position in a manner similar to that for the set shot.

Fig 98 The player releases the ball at the highest point of his jump.

Fig 99 An extension of the shooting arm and a powerful wrist snap complete the follow-through after the jump shot.

Fig 100 GB centre Pops Mensah-Bonsu (white jersey) keeps his eyes on the target during a jump shot.

Coaching Points

- Try to have feet shoulder-width apart when preparing for the jump (right foot slightly forward if shooting with the right hand).
- The hand, forearm and elbow are in a straight line up the body.
- Follow through after the shot (arm extended, flick your wrist and fingers).
- Jump vertically upwards and land on the same spot.
- Release the ball when you reach maximum height during the jump.
- Use the non-shooting hand to protect, adjust and control the ball right until the shot is taken.
- Concentrate and keep your eyes on the basket.
- Be well balanced and have the ball under control by holding it with both hands.

Common Mistakes

- Not jumping vertically and failing to land on the same spot.
- Losing balance in the air.
- Releasing the ball too early (before reaching the maximum height on the jump) or too late (after the descent has started).
- Lack of follow-through action (arm not extended and/or no flick of the wrist).
- Too low a trajectory of the ball.
- Taking the shot too far away from the basket.

Drills

Exactly as for free throws or lay-ups, the secret for being a good jump shooter is to practise constantly. When learning the jump shot, start off close to the basket and follow all principles in the description. After mastering the shot from close range, the distance can be increased progressively using the spots indicated in Fig 101.

Jump shots in pairs

One ball between two players. One shoots five or ten jump shots in a row while his partner rebounds and passes the ball back. Use the same positions as in Fig 101 and change roles regularly.

Five players with three balls

Five players take jump shots from inside the 3-points semicircle (see Fig 102 over-leaf). The three players with a ball take a jump shot, then go to collect the ball no matter the outcome of their shot, and pass it to one of the two players without a ball. After the pass, the player runs towards the outside of the 3-points semicircle, touches the floor with his hands, and then goes to find a different position (inside

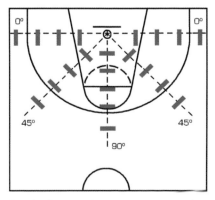

Fig 101 Positions for learning the jump shot.

the semicircle) to shoot from. The drill continues until one player scores ten times as an individual or the whole group of five scores ten (or fifteen or twenty, depending on their level).

Three queues jump shots

Player 1 (see Fig 103) takes a jump shot, goes and gets his own rebound, passes the ball to someone in the same queue, runs to the half-way line and then joins a different queue. Players 2 and 3 follow a similar pattern. The drill continues until one player scores ten times or a time limit is up. This is an ideal drill for warming-up.

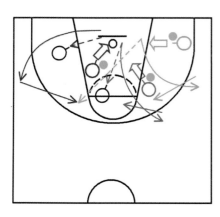

Fig 102 Jump shots drill with five players with three balls.

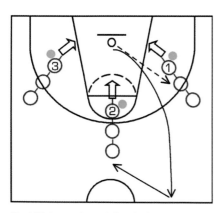

Fig 103 Jump shots drill with three queues.

Close-Range Shots

There are several types of shot that every player should be able to execute closer to the basket, including the tip-in shot (tipping in after offensive rebounding), the close-in shot after a quick stop (power move shot), and the reverse lay-up (or lay-back). According to some coaches, the lay-up shot is also classified as a close-range shot, but it is generally treated as a separate category of shot because it is such a fundamental skill in the game.

Tip-In Shot (Tipping In after Offensive Rebounding)

Description

The tip-in shot should not be viewed as a lucky slap at the ball but as a regular shot in the repertoire of any player of any height. Following any shot by a teammate, an offensive player should get himself ready in a rebounding position, facing the basket, well balanced, with knees flexed, and arms and elbows up and ready. Timing in relation to the ball and its flight is vital – the tip-in shooter needs to time his jump and take-off to make contact and catch the ball just as he is reaching the top of his jump. With his fingers spread, the player aims to get control of the ball while he is in the air and, using a similar action to that used for a set shot or jump shot, he straightens his arms and hands and tips the ball with a soft trajectory into the basket with a flick of the wrist and fingers.

Common Mistakes
- Jumping too soon or too late.
- Tipping the ball in too hard so that it bounces out of the ring/basket.
- Being positioned incorrectly and failing to time the jump with the flight of the ball.

Drills
- In pairs, facing each other, practise tipping in, passing the ball to each other after jumping and catching the ball while in the air with two hands (and releasing it before landing).
- Individually, practise tip-ins at the wall and then move to the board.

Try, for example, sets of ten or see how many you can make in 20 or 30 seconds. Alternatively, after ten tips on the board, shoot the ball so that you can score.
- In pairs, practise tip-ins by passing to each other using the board and over the ring.
- For a whole team practice, position the players in single file on the right or left of the board, one ball with the front player (see Fig 104). After throwing the ball on the board/ passing it to the next player in the queue, Player 1 will run to the back of the queue. Player 2 will jump, catch the ball in the air and then throw the ball on the board for Player 3, who will do the same for the next one. The drill continues for a set time (30 seconds, 1 minute) or for a set number of passes (thirty, fifty).

Close-In Shot after a Quick Stop (Power Move Shot)

Description

The execution of this type of shot is exactly the same as for the jump shot (see page 60). However, the main aim here is to shoot the ball before the defender can recover from your quick stop. After the power move and the stop, the offensive player can shoot straight away after a strong, powerful upward jump, or after a shooting fake, in order to

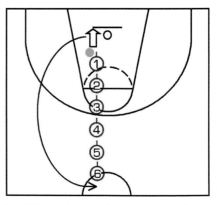

Fig 104 Whole team tip-ins at one basket.

get a defender off balance. For the shot to be efficient the attacking player should be very well balanced and should shoot softly using the backboard, if he is in an area less than a 45-degree angle to the basket (see Fig 77 for shooting angles). Ideally, each time a power shot is taken, the player should either score or draw the foul.

Common Mistakes

- Being off balance before and during the shot.
- Bad timing with defender's actions – not being quick enough and/or not using a fake, which will lead to a blocked shot.

Drills

- 1 vs. 1 on half-court: the attacking player starts playing 1 vs. 1. When he gets closer to the basket (less than 3–4m away), he attempts the power move shot (see Fig 105). Initially, he tries with the jump stop and shoots straight away but then introduces a shooting fake. One player performs five actions, then the players swap round. Count how many times each player scores.
- 2 vs. 2 on half-court, exactly as above. One team has five actions then the other team has five. Keep the score.

Reverse Lay-Up (Lay-Back)

Description

Sometimes, a player cutting or driving under the basket finds himself with the ball right under the basket, too late for a safe and proper lay-up shot. In this case, the player has two shooting options: a short hook (or semi-hook, which is very similar to the hook shot, see below) or a reverse lay-up (or lay-back) shot. The reverse lay-up is initiated from the side opposite to the side from which the basket is approached. For example, if a player is coming from the right-hand side of the basket/ring, he will take two steps while he is under the basket and will finish the shot from the left-hand side, very close to the basket and to the board.

This shot is usually made with the strong hand but an ambidextrous shooter might consider the advantage of using his weak hand for what will be an almost conventional lay-up. The palm of the shooting hand will face the basket, with the fingers up and well spread and the thumb pointing towards the end line. The shooting hand rotates inwards towards the little finger. The ball is released by a soft flick of the wrist and fingers, which will give the ball a natural reverse spin.

Common Mistakes

- Taking the two lay-up steps too far from the ring and too close to the

baseline so that the ball will hit the back of the board or the soft padding support underneath it.
- Because of good defending, the player may find himself in a position in which he wants to shoot but will either get the shot blocked or will land with the ball in his hands trying to avoid the blocked shot.

Drills

As for any type of shot, the more you practise the better you will be. The lay-up lines drill (see page 60) is useful, but the player will aim to go under the basket when taking the two steps and shoot the ball from under the basket on the opposite side to where he has come from (see Fig 106).

The Hook Shot

Description

Despite the fact that it is not used very frequently, the hook shot is still a valuable and effective weapon, used by centers and forwards in particular when they are close to the basket. This type of shot is a modification of the lay-up, with the shooter jumping off one leg, usually after two small, quick steps: right, left, jump and shoot (for right-hand shot). The right-handed attacking player, with his back towards the basket, receives the ball and pivots to his left (see Fig 107 overleaf), or dribbles and takes two small steps (right, left). He will then take off his left foot and lift his right knee (exactly as in the lay-up), completing a continuous, sweeping overhead arc towards the basket. As he jumps, the ball (which has been held in two hands in front of the chest, as in Fig 108 overleaf) is taken up in the right hand (at the same time as the right knee swing, as in Fig 109 overleaf), with the arm fully extended and the palm holding the ball facing upwards (as in Fig 110 overleaf).

The shot is finished with a wrist flick through and fingertip control so that the ball spins and the shot is soft when it hits the ring; a correctly executed follow-through will see the shooter facing the basket on landing, with the arm fully

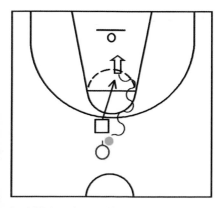

Fig 105 1 vs. 1 on half-court (with a power move shot attempt).

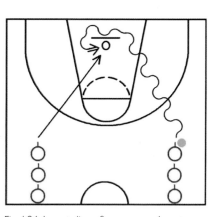

Fig 106 Lay-up lines for a reverse lay-up shot.

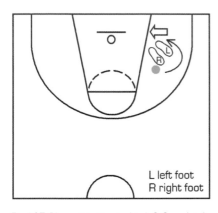

L left foot
R right foot

Fig 107 Player pivoting to his left for a hook shot.

Fig 108 The ball is held safely in two hands in front of the chest ready for a hook shot.

Fig 109 The player leaves the ball in one hand while he swings up his right knee.

extended and close to the ear, palm facing the floor, and in a good position for a rebound (Fig 111).

Common Mistakes

- Finishing the shooting action with the arm sideways instead of being next to the ear.
- Failing to hold the ball with two hands for safe control, which can lead to the ball being lost.

Drills

For individual practice, the player repeatedly takes hook shots, positioned with his left shoulder towards the basket (for a right-hander); he steps with his left foot and takes off this leg while he lifts up the right knee. The ball is passed from two hands to one hand only. The right hand goes right up and with a wrist flick the ball is sent to the basket.

The same drill may be practised by two players, one acting as shooter and one as rebounder.

Hook shots can also be practised in threes, with two balls for each group of three players. The player without the ball will be the one shooting hook shots. He will turn up from the left side to the right side of the key following a path as illustrated in Fig 112. With his arms up (showing a target for his teammate to pass to), Player 1 will receive the ball from

Fig 110 The ball is taken up in the right hand – arm extended and palm facing upwards.

Fig 111 The player flicks his wrist to finish the hook shot. Note the follow-through action: the shooter has the arm close to his ear (palm facing the floor) and is facing the basket on landing.

Player 3 and then shoot using a hook shot. Player 1 rebounds the ball, passes it back to 3 and then cuts towards the other side to receive a pass from Player 2 and to take a hook shot with the left hand (see Fig 113). After ten shots, the players change roles.

Slam-Dunk Shot

Description

One of the most spectacular ways to score points in the basketball game is to slam-dunk (see Fig 114). The player needs to be able to jump well enough to have

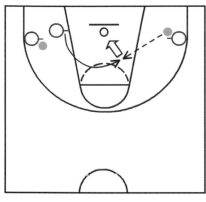

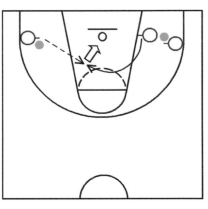

Fig 112 Hook shots in threes – the player goes from left to right to receive the ball for a hook shot.

Fig 113 Hook shots in threes – the player goes from right to left to receive the ball for a hook shot.

RULES

Player in the act of shooting

A *shot* for a field goal or a free throw is when the ball is held in a player's hand(s) and is then thrown into the air towards the opponents' basket.

A *tap* is when the ball is directed with the hand(s) towards the opponents' basket.

A *dunk* is when the ball is forced downwards into the opponents' basket with one or both hands.

A tap and a dunk are also considered as shots for a field goal.

his hand(s) over the ring height (3.05m). He comes to a stop under the basket, pushes off with both feet and, while in the air, puts the ball down into the basket with both hands, as in Fig 115. Another way to perform the dunk is to take off on one foot and, using one hand only, to put the ball through the net from the top downwards, as in Fig 116. However, a two-hand dunk is preferable because the chances of the ball slipping out of the hand are greatly reduced.

Basketball players can dunk forwards or backwards, after rotating 360 degrees through the air, after receiving the ball through the legs, and so on. This variety provides great entertainment for the spectators and enjoyment for the players.

Common Mistakes
* Poor timing of the jump.
* Taking off too far away from the basket.
* Holding the ball in one hand only, with the risk of dropping it or losing it.

Fig 114 GB centre Pops Mensah-Bonsu slam-dunks while two Israel defenders try to stop him.

Fig 115 GB forward Joel Freeland slam-dunks using two hands.

Fig 116 GB forward Joel Freeland demonstrates the one-hand slam-dunk.

Drills

Without a ball, players perform several consecutive jumps trying to reach the backboard, the net and then the ring (either using normal lay-up steps and jumping high on the second step or stopping and taking off on both feet).

With a smaller-sized basketball (5 or 6), players try to jump high and push the ball from the top of the net downwards, into the basket. Once this has been mastered, the players attempt the same with a normal-sized ball.

Footwork and Other Important Offensive Skills

Basketball is a game that requires excellent balance and control of the body while moving at various speeds on the court. Because of this, footwork and all the other offensive skills (running, stopping, pivoting, changing direction and cutting, jumping and rebounding, getting open/losing a defender) are of paramount importance for any player. Coaches should highlight the fact that a sound knowledge of these fundamentals and the ability to perform them both quickly and within the limits of the rules are essential for successful play (at both individual level and team level).

While the skills of jumping and getting open are performed without the ball, all the others may be executed both with and without the ball. When learning and practising these skills they can be rehearsed as stand-alone drills or (and this is highly recommended) in combinations with passing, dribbling and shooting.

Running

Description and Use

A natural running action – head up high, active movement of the arms, on the balls of the feet – should be used by any player who wants to receive the ball (when catching it) and also when running without the ball (in a fastbreak situation, for example). Running forwards (facing the direction in which you are running) and running backwards (facing the opposite direction) are the most frequent types of running employed when playing basketball. Running sideways is also quite common, especially when trying to get open to receive a pass.

Running is particularly important in relation to catching the ball or passing on the run because all players need to perform these actions within the limitations set out in the rules of the game – no more than two steps are allowed after catching the ball with two hands.

Common Mistakes

- Running flat-footed.
- Looking at the floor while running, rather than keeping the head up.
- Lack of arm movement while running.

Coaching Points

- There should be continuous movement of the arms alongside the body, with the palms moving between hip and chin level.
- The player should always be on the balls of the feet to enable quick reactions and changes of direction.
- The head should be kept up, with the eyes looking at the opposite ring level.

Drills

It is assumed that all players know how to run when they come to play basketball but sometimes the coach may need to spend some time teaching them the proper way of running (especially at beginner level and with big or tall players). Running drills can be performed in isolation but usually they are rehearsed in combination with the other fundamental skills of passing, dribbling or shooting.

Running drills that incorporate various other types of action will enhance the athleticism of players. These might include running with the knees up, running with the heels up (touching the bottom), skipping, running with long strides (as in the triple jump in athletics), running and alternately lifting the knee up and kicking forward with the foot, running with the legs extended forwards, and running with the legs extended backwards.

Stopping

Description and Use

With or without the ball, the stopping action has to be performed quickly and with perfect balance. A player in possession of the ball must take into account the limits specified by the rules when stopping, using either the stride stop (1-2 count stop or stopping in two times) or the jump stop.

Stride stop (1-2 count stop or stopping in two times)

After catching the ball while both feet are in the air, the player will land on one foot (Fig 117), followed immediately by the other foot, following a natural running action. The first foot to come in contact with the floor will become the 'pivot foot'. Ideally, the pivot foot should be the left foot for a right-handed player and the right foot for a left-handed player. The stride stop is also known as '1-2 count stop', and it is useful for the player to count '1-2' when his feet touch the ground in order to stop. The second foot to touch the floor must be at a reasonable distance from the first to ensure good balance (see Fig 118).

Jump stop

The main advantage of this stopping action is the fact that either foot can be chosen as the pivot foot. At the end of the dribble, or when somebody is about to receive the ball, the player will jump, catch the ball while both feet are in the air (Fig 119), and land on two feet simultaneously (with both feet parallel and shoulder-width apart), as in Fig 120. On landing, the knees are bent, and the ankles and hips flexed in order to absorb the shock.

Common Mistakes

- Travelling when stopping with the ball (taking extra steps).
- Having the feet too close together or too far apart, creating a loss of balance.
- Head looking down.

Fig 117 The player lands on one foot – the first part of the stride stop.

Fig 118 The player's second foot will land on the floor – there is an optimum distance between the feet leading to a balanced position.

Fig 119 The player catches the ball while both feet are in the air.

Fig 120 The player lands on both feet simultaneously, bending his knees, and keeping ankles and hips flexed.

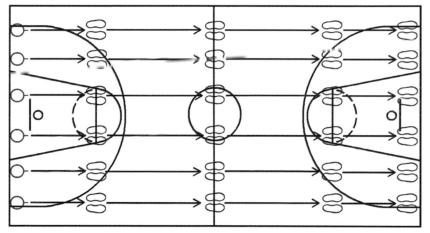

Fig 121 Drill practising stopping areas for the stride stop and jump stop.

Coaching Points

- A low body position must be maintained.
- The player should land with the feet shoulder-width apart, knees bent, hips relaxed, with his body weight evenly spread.
- The head must be kept up.
- The ball should be close to the body, held with both hands.

Drills

The skills of the stride stop and the jump stop are more easily taught without the ball when the player is first learning them. Once they have been mastered by the players, the coach can move them on to performing the following drill with the ball.

Starting at one end line of the court, without the ball, all players work at the same time, trying to stop in one time (jump stop) in the areas highlighted in Fig

Fig 122 The player starts the pivoting action using his left foot as the pivot foot.

Fig 123 The player pivots away on his left foot to protect the ball.

Fig 124 The right foot (stepping foot) will move to a new position during pivoting.

Fig 125 Keeping the knees bent gives a well-balanced position during pivoting.

RULES

A *pivot* is the legal movement in which a player who is holding a live ball on the playing court steps once or more than once in any direction with the same foot, while the other foot, called the pivot foot, is kept at its point of contact with the floor.

Establishing a pivot foot for a player who catches a live ball on the playing court:

- While standing with both feet on the floor, the moment one foot is lifted, the other foot becomes the pivot foot.
- While moving, if one foot is touching the floor, that foot becomes the pivot foot.
- If both feet are off the floor and the player lands on both feet simultaneously, the moment one foot is lifted, the other foot becomes the pivot foot.
- If both feet are off the floor and the player lands on one foot, then that foot becomes the pivot foot. If a player jumps off that foot and comes to a stop, landing on both feet simultaneously, then neither foot is a pivot foot.

121 (the first free-throw line, the half-way line, the second free-throw line and the other end of the court). The drill is then repeated, with the players being required to stop in two times (1–2 count). As they progress, they perform the same drill, but with a ball. Similarly, the speed of the drill is increased as they improve their skills.

Pivoting

Description and Use

The pivot or turn is a legal manoeuvre that allows the player in possession of the ball to change and improve his position in order to shoot, pass, dribble or protect the ball. It can also be used before receiving the ball. The *pivot foot* is the first foot to

touch the ground after receiving the ball, or after a jumping and rebounding action in case of a stride stop. When landing after a jump stop (or when catching the ball standing still), any foot can be chosen as the pivot foot. Using the pivot foot as a swivel point (with the ball of the foot remaining in permanent contact with the floor), the player is free to move in any direction and to rotate his body any way he wants; the pivot foot should not move from its point of contact with the floor (see Figs 122, 123 and 124). The player must be well balanced, with knees bent and feet shoulder-width apart (although sometimes it may be necessary to take a longer step in order to regain balance). The force of rotation is supplied by the outside foot – the *stepping foot* – which the player with the ball can

use to move in a circle shape around his pivot foot (see Fig 125).

Common Mistakes
- Lifting the pivot foot off the floor before releasing (for a pass or a shot) or dribbling the ball.

TOP TIP

When receiving the ball, try to pivot immediately so that you can face the opposite basket. While pivoting, always hold the ball with both hands in front of your chest. Right-handed players should try to have the left foot as the pivot foot, while left-handed players should choose the right foot as the pivot foot.

Fig 126 Player going towards his right and getting ready to change direction to his left.

Fig 127 For a change of direction, the player has his knees flexed, a low body position and the feet (soles) pointing in the new direction.

Fig 128 A push-off on the outside foot (right foot) towards the new direction.

- Taking extra steps on stopping and pivoting because of the body weight being too far forward, resulting in a travelling violation.
- Holding the ball in one hand only during pivoting.
- Pivoting and using the stepping foot as the pivot foot.

Coaching Points
- The pivot foot should be in touch with the floor using the ball of the foot.
- A fairly low, well-balanced position, with knees flexed should be maintained.
- The ball should always be held with both hands for better and safer protection.

Drills
The pivoting action can be learned as a stand-alone skill but more frequently (and this is preferable) it is integrated with other fundamental moves such as stopping, receiving and releasing the ball (dribble, shot or pass).

The players assume the same formation as for stopping (see Fig 121, page 67), lined up at one end of court. They start jogging towards the opposite end. On hearing the signal, they stop using a stride stop and pivot, making a full circle around the pivot foot. On the second signal, they start jogging again until they hear a third and

then a fourth signal, and so on. The coach signals four stops and should encourage the players to use their left and right foot alternately as the pivot foot (right-left as well as left-right on the stride stop).

Next, players perform the same drill, this time using a jump stop. Again, players are encouraged to alternate their pivot foot.

Later, the drills may be performed with a ball (with each player dribbling the ball while jogging towards the other end line of court in a straight line). In addition a defender can be introduced to put pressure on the player who pivots.

Another drill involves 4 vs. 4 or 5 vs. 5 on the half-court, in a passing game. Players are not allowed to dribble or to shoot. They may only pass the ball, stop and pivot while under pressure, with man-to-man defence being used.

Changing Direction and Cutting

Description and Use
Due to the nature of the game of basketball (ten players using fast moves within a limited space), there are a number of situations in which players need to change direction, in order to get open to receive a pass or to avoid running into a defender.

When changing direction, the player should have the feet shoulder-width apart, with knees flexed, and the body lowered.

The feet are positioned so that they point in the new direction, as in Figs 126 and 127. The player now pushes hard off the outside foot in the opposite direction to the one in which he intends to go (see Fig 128). For example, if a player is going to his right and wants to change direction to go to the left, he needs to push off the outside (or right) foot (see Fig 129).

In order to be effective (for example, to get rid of a defender), the player needs to be able to sprint powerfully in the new direction. A clear change in the pace of his movement is required.

The skill of changing direction may be performed in combination with another fundamental move that all players should

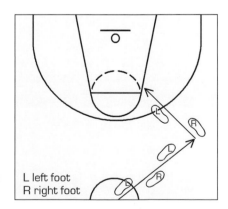

Fig 129 Player pushing off his right foot for a change of direction towards his left.

Fig 130 An attacker passes to a teammate.

Fig 131 The attacker goes away to fake a move to the right side of court away from the ball.

Fig 132 The attacker stops and starts changing direction for a cut to the left (by pushing off on the outside foot).

Fig 133 The attacker cuts towards the basket – he is between the ball and the direct defender.

Fig 134 The cutter has his arms up to signal to his teammate.

Fig 135 The cutter receives the ball and is on his way to take a shot.

master: *cutting to the basket*. The cut can be used as a tactical weapon when a teammate has the ball and needs to change direction, change pace, pivot, or use fakes, quick stops and starts (either performed as individual actions or in combination). The main aim of the cut is to get free from the close guard of a defender. The move of the cutter (the player who cuts towards the basket) needs to be timed according to the position of the ball. One of the most suitable moments to cut is straight after passing because this is when the defender tries to intercept the pass (moving his body towards the

Fig 136 Player performing a convincing feint towards the ball.

Fig 137 A quick change of direction performed by pushing off the outside foot.

Fig 138 The defender is left between the ball and the attacking player performing the back-door cut.

Fig 139 The cutter is getting open towards the basket to receive a pass.

receiver and thus creating space) or when he tends to relax.

There are two types of cut: the front-door cut and the back-door cut. A *front-door cut* is initiated by an attacking player without the ball who will move/fake away from the ball (Figs 130 and 131) and will then perform a quick change of direction towards the basket (Fig 132), so that he will be between his teammate with the ball and his defender (Fig 133). It is advisable for the cutter to have one arm up (or both, as in Fig 134), to signal to his teammate with the ball that he is on the way to the basket in a good position to shoot and hopefully score (Fig 135).

A *back-door cut* can be used when a player without possession is being overplayed by his guard, between him and the ball. The cut starts with a convinc-

ing feint towards the ball (as in Fig 136), followed by a change of direction, pushing off hard on the outside foot (opposite to the direction of the cut) (Fig 137). The defender will be left between the ball and the attacking player who is cutting, as in Fig 138; the attacker is getting open towards the basket (Fig 139) and will take a lay-up (Fig 140).

Common Mistakes

*   Feet too close together, leading to a loss of balance.
*   Feet crossed over.
*   Failing to push off the outside foot.
*   Keeping going in a straight line instead of making a clear change of direction, creating a 'V' shape.
*   No difference in pace after the change of direction.

Fig 140 The player performing the back-door move will take a shot.

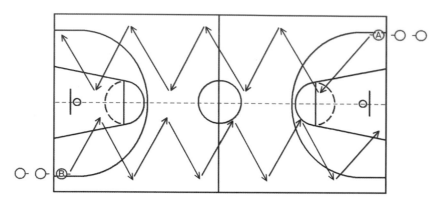

Fig 141 Zig-zag run.

Coaching Points

- Push off the outside foot to change direction.
- Keep the body position fairly low, and remain well balanced.
- Sprint powerfully (covering 3–4m at least) once you are going in the new direction.

Drills

Tag in pairs

All players are grouped in pairs spread out on the court, having numbered themselves as 1 and 2. Player 1 starts by trying to catch Player 2; once he has been tagged, Player 2 then chases Player 1, trying to tag him, and so on. If the playing area is restricted (half-court, for example), players will have to constantly change direction in order not to be caught and to avoid all the other players.

Zig-zag run

Two groups of players line up in a single file behind either Player A or Player B, as in Fig 141. In turn, players run forward in a zig-zag shape, changing direction by pushing off the outside foot. As Players A and B pass over the half-way line, the next player in the queue starts his turn.

Zig-zag dribble

This is a progression of the previous drill, but now players have a ball each. Following the same zig-zag pattern, players dribble the ball in front of their legs (crossover), behind the back, between the legs, and in a 360-degree pivoting action. The coach should emphasize the need to change the dribbling hand each time when the player goes in a new direction.

Zig-zag attacker vs. defender

The formation is the same as in the previous drill, but this time players are grouped in pairs – attacking player vs. defender. Initially, the defender plays 'passive defence' – simply moving and being in the correct defensive position, without trying to steal the ball. On the way back, the players change roles. As the drill progresses, the defender may become active and attempt to steal the ball.

Fig 142 GB players Luol Deng (number 9 white jersey) and Pops Mensah-Bonsu (number 7 white jersey) demonstrate very good jumping ability when trying to get the rebound.

Fig 143 GB forward Nick George gets the rebound with his arms extended and fingers spread on the ball.

Fig 144 GB centre Pops Mensah-Bonsu rebounds the ball with both hands.

Fig 145 Player catching the ball with two hands.

Fig 146 Player landing on both feet after a rebounding action.

Jumping and Offensive Rebounding

Description and Use

Considering the fact that basketball is played by people who are taller than average, it is obvious the ability to jump is essential (see Fig 142). A good jump will help an offensive player without the ball to get a rebound, or enable a player in possession of the ball to take a good jump shot (see page 61), with minimum risk of being blocked. For a successful rebounding action, the jumper must maintain his balance and needs to time the jump accurately. To ensure good balance, he should establish a wide base (feet more than shoulder-width apart), with knees slightly flexed, and should be on the balls of his feet. The arms are held quite high, with fingers spread wide, ready to catch the ball (see Fig 143). In terms of timing, the rebounder needs to synchronize the height and the direction of his jump with other factors related to the ball, such as its trajectory, whether it hits the board or the ring, any spin on the ball, and so on. The rebounder will elevate himself towards the ball and, at the highest point of his jump, depending on how far away from the ring he is, will attempt either to tip the ball into the ring or to catch it safely with two hands (as in Fig 144). Another frequently used option is to pass the ball to a better-placed teammate while still in the air.

After catching the ball (see Fig 145), the rebounder will try to land on both feet (taking care not to travel) (Fig 146), and immediately either look for another jump for a shooting opportunity or pass the ball out of the 3-seconds area to a team-mate. Taller players often prefer to land and keep their arms extended upwards (holding the ball) so that the ball is not easily stolen by smaller players, or in order to make a quick shot.

Common Mistakes
- Being flat-footed when attempting to jump for an offensive rebound.
- Poor timing of the jump in relation to the position of the ball.
- The rebounder not being properly balanced.
- Lack of height on the jump.

RULES

Goal tending and interference with the ball

Goal tending occurs during a *shot for a field goal* when a player touches the ball while it is completely above the level of the ring and:

- It is on its downward flight to the basket, or
- After it has hit the backboard.

Goal tending occurs during a *shot for a free throw* when the player touches the ball while it is in flight to the basket and before it touches the ring.

The goal tending restrictions apply until:

- The ball no longer has the possibility of entering the basket during the shot.
- The ball has touched the ring.

Interference occurs during a shot for a field goal when:

- A player touches the basket or the backboard while the ball is in contact with the ring.
- A player reaches through the basket from below and touches the ball. This is valid also on a pass and also after the ball has touched the ring.
- A defensive player touches the ball or the basket while the ball is within the basket and it prevents the ball from passing through the basket.
- A defensive player causes the backboard to vibrate or grasps the basket in such a way that, in the judgement of the official, the ball has been prevented from entering the basket.
- An offensive player causes the backboard to vibrate or grasps the basket in such a way that, in the judgement of the official, the ball has been caused to enter the basket.
- A player grasps the basket to play the ball. This is valid also after the ball has touched the ring.

Penalty

If the violation is committed by an *offensive player*, no points can be awarded. The ball shall be awarded to the opponents for a throw-in at the free-throw line extended, unless otherwise stated in the rules.

If the violation is committed by the *defensive player*, the offensive team is awarded:

- One (1) point when the ball was released for a free throw.
- Two (2) points when the ball was released from the two-point field goal area.
- Three (3) points when the ball was released from the three-point field goal area.

The awarding of the points is as if the ball had entered the basket.

If the violation is committed by a defensive player during a last or only free throw, one (1) point shall be awarded to the offensive team, followed by the technical foul penalty charged against the defensive player.

Coaching Points

- Make sure you are well balanced, on the balls of the feet, with feet wide and arms ready to catch the ball before the jumping action.
- Extend your arms upwards to retrieve the ball after a vigorous jump.
- Keep an eye on the ball and on its flight.
- Try to bring the ball strongly to the chest with both hands.

Drills

Consecutive jumps facing the basket
Jumping ability can be improved by practice. In this drill, without the ball, players jump and attempt to touch the ring several times in a row (ten or fifteen times, or for a specified time, such as 30 seconds or 1 minute). If the ring is too high, the net or the backboard could be the target.

Skipping rope exercises
On one foot or both feet, within a time limit (1, 2 minutes) or by counting the number of jumps (100, 150, and so on).

Consecutive jumps on the same foot
Players are lined up behind the end line, and have to jump on their left foot only all the way to the other end of court. On the way back, they jump on the right leg.

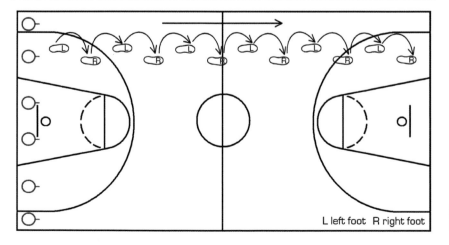

L left foot   R right foot

Fig 147 Consecutive jumps, alternating the take-off foot.

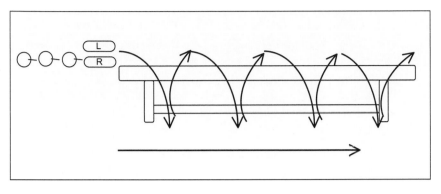

Fig 148 Jumps over a bench.

Jumping on the spot with knees high

Players jump on the spot with the knees high, either for a specified time (30, 45 seconds) or for sets of ten (or more) consecutive jumps.

Consecutive jumps, alternating the take-off foot

Players are lined up at one end of court and asked to perform jumps, alternating the take-off foot (taking big strides, as in the triple jump) (see Fig 147). Try to find out who has the most powerful jump by counting how many strides each player will take to finish one length of the court – the lowest number wins!

Jumps over a bench

One player at a time performs consecutive jumps over the bench from one side to the other, as in Fig 148. As a safety precaution the next player will start jumping only when the player in front has finished his go. Ensure the bench is stable before starting the drill.

Getting Open
(Losing A Defender)

Description and Use

Every player on the court has specific tasks to perform, depending on his

position and on the stage and status of the game (attack, defence, sideline possessions or free-throw shooting). The attacking player who is not in possession of the ball still needs to contribute to the team effort by getting open to receive the ball in an advantageous position where he constitutes a threat, because he may shoot, dribble or pass. Having said that, meaningless movements should be avoided; unplanned moves are not only useless, but may even interfere with play. It is vital that the player coordinates his own moves with the actions of the player who has possession. Communication between the potential receiver and the ball carrier is very important, and some coaches strongly advise their players to send a clear signal to the player with the ball.

All the fundamental skills (plus the use of fakes – see page 76) can be employed in order to get open and lose the defender. A player can get open in two ways: either coming towards the ball and then suddenly moving/running away and getting open (see Figs 136–140); or going away first (as in Fig 149) and then changing pace quickly (Figs 150 below and 151 overleaf) and coming towards the ball to receive a pass (see Fig 152 overleaf).

Good timing between the player who is getting open and the ball carrier is essential,

Fig 149 The player goes away in a move to confuse the defender.

Fig 150 The player stops in order to change direction.

Fig 151 The player moves into a new direction by changing pace quickly (pushing on the outside foot).

Fig 152 The player comes towards the ball with the arms in front of the chest, showing he is ready to receive the ball, and eventually receives the pass.

so that the pass is received before the defender has had time to recover. A player who can free himself at the right time (which is when the passer is ready) will be a serious attacking threat to any opposition.

Common Mistakes

- Bad timing when getting open, so that the teammate with the ball is not ready.
- If the player getting open does not perform a convincing change of direction or fake, the defender will still be able to guard closely.

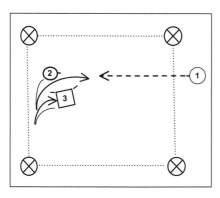

Fig 153 Getting open (drill in three players).

- Failing to submit a signal to the ball carrier.
- The receiver standing still and not catching the ball with two hands.

Coaching Points

- Successive fundamental moves can be performed when getting open.
- The change in speed and rhythm needs to be obvious.
- When receiving, try to catch the ball with two hands.
- Be alert to what is happening around you.
- Send all passes at chest level.

Drills

Getting open in pairs

Players position themselves in groups of three in a restricted area (4 × 4m or 5 × 5m). Player 1 is inbounding, Player 2 is in offence and he needs to get open to receive the ball while the defender (Player 3) aims to intercept the ball (see Fig 153). After five inbounding actions, jobs are changed: Player 1 becomes an offensive player, Player 2 will be the new defender and Player 3 will inbound the ball. The players score each time a successful pass is sent.

2 vs. 2 and 3 vs. 3 – continuously getting open

This drill is a passing game, with no shooting and no dribbling, on a half-court. To make it more competitive, each team has to pass the ball ten (or fifteen, or twenty) consecutive times. If they manage to do this, the other team receives a punishment. If played 4 vs. 4 or 5 vs. 5, the playing area is extended to the full court.

Fakes

Description and Use

A fake (or feint) is a movement used by an offensive player (with or without the ball) with the intention to confuse or mislead a defender. In other words, it is about making your opponent commit himself by convincing him that you are going to do one thing and then doing something completely different. A complete player will be able to perform several types of fake, including the following:

- the passing fake (when a player pretends he is passing to get the defender out of his position) (see Figs 154–157);

Fig 154 The attacker fakes the pass to a teammate.

Fig 155 The defender gets out of position and creates some space towards the basket.

Fig 156 The attacker changes his position quickly, ready for a dribble to the basket.

Fig 157 The attacker dribbles past the defender on his way to the basket.

Fig 158 The attacking player has knees, ankles and hips flexed, as he does when he is ready to shoot.

Fig 159 Attacker initiates the shooting fake by 'showing the ball' to the defender – the defender jumps as if trying to block the shot.

Fig 160 *While the defender is still in the air, the attacker is ready to move and to dribble towards the basket.*

Fig 161 *The attacker dribbles past the defender.*

Fig 162 *The attacker is on his way to the basket.*

Common Mistakes

- Excessive use of fakes.
- The player using a fake failing to respond to an error by the defender.
- Rushed movements.
- Loss of balance because of excessive faking, or failing to bend the knees and therefore having a relatively high position.

Coaching Points

- Be well balanced when initiating a fake.
- After a fake, the move into the new direction needs to be powerful and quick enough to leave the defender behind.
- Hold the ball with both hands.

Drills

Spread out on the court and working individually, players stop (stride stop or jump stop) on hearing different signals and, using the correct footwork, perform two or three fakes of their choice.

In pairs, 1 vs. 1 (attacker vs. defender), the attacking player puts into practice some of the fakes – at least two to three each time the coach sends the signal to stop.

- the shooting fake (used to make the defender jump unnecessarily) (Figs 158–162);
- the dribbling fake (showing the intention of a dribble and then doing something else);
- the foot fake (in strict connection with footwork and rules related to footwork);

- the arm and hand fake;
- the head and shoulders fake; and
- the fake with the eyes.

Top-class players use various combinations of all these types of fake in an attempt to mislead the defender and draw him off-balance.

CHAPTER 6

ATTACKING COMBINATIONS BETWEEN TWO AND THREE PLAYERS

In order to create a successful and efficient basketball team, a coach must coordinate the efforts and movements of five players into an agreed pattern of play in which, ideally, all contribute to the overall goal. This integration of a number of individuals into a unit is based on a proper execution of the fundamentals of the game. Frequently, the offensive play structure is based on combinations between two or three players, which will eventually (and hopefully) lead, at the end of the 24 seconds, to a basket scored or at least to a good scoring opportunity. The most frequent combinations between two or three players are 'give and go' (pass and cut, or pass and move), setting screens and the use of screens, playing 2 vs. 1 and 3 vs. 2 situations, and playing 1 vs. 1 situations.

'Give and Go' (Pass and Cut)

Description and Use

The 'give and go' (or pass and cut, or pass and move) is a fundamental attacking combination between two players. This basic offensive play involves a pass and a move into space (preferably towards the basket) for a quick return pass (see Fig 163). Player 1 will pass to his teammate on the right (Player 2) and will fake a move towards the left side of the court so that the defender A will move, trying to follow him. After the fake, a quick change of direction and a powerful cut towards the basket will enable Player 1 to get into a good scoring position, where he will receive the ball back from Player 2.

Any two players on the team can initiate and use this combination: guard and guard, guard and forward, guard and centre, forward and centre.

During the cut, it is advisable for the player to signal for the ball with the hand closest to the basket, or both hands up above shoulder level, so that the teammate is aware of the cut, knows that he can pass safely and has a target to aim for. Accurate passing is essential, as is a convincing fake and a strong move towards the basket. The cut can be a 'front-door' or a 'back-door' cut (see page 71).

Common Mistakes

- The attackers who are part of the combination being too close to each other.
- Inaccurate passes (the first pass and the return pass).
- Using fakes that are not convincing enough.
- The attacking player not reacting quickly enough to a defender mistake.
- The attacker who is cutting failing to signal the cut with his arm(s).

Coaching Points

- The player who is cutting needs to signal to his teammate, using the arm closest to the basket, or both arms.
- The player who is cutting needs to sprint vigorously away after a fake.
- The attackers should allow plenty of space between them (at least 4 to 5m).
- After the pass, try to cut towards the opposite team basket.

Drills

'Give and Go' in Pairs
In pairs, one ball for each pair. Player 1 will pass to Player 2, then will go away for a fake in front of a cone. After changing direction, he will cut towards the basket (an increase in speed will now be obvious), signalling to his teammate for a return pass (see Fig 164 overleaf). On receiving the ball he will take two steps (a lay-up while running) and shoot. This is the ideal scenario. If he is too far away from the basket, he will dribble once and then take a lay-up.

'Give and Go' as a 2 vs. 2 Game
This is the same drill as before but with defenders. The defenders will initially be passive – they will only move following the

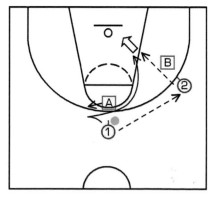

Fig 163 'Give and go' combination between two players.

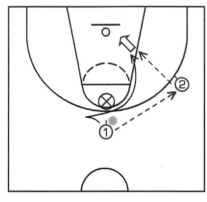

Fig 164 'Give and go' drill in pairs.

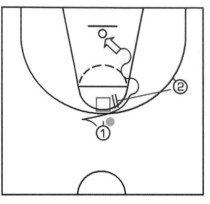

Fig 165 Attacker 2 setting a screen for his teammate, Player 1, to get open.

RULES

Screening: Legal and Illegal

Screening is an attempt to delay or prevent an opponent without the ball from reaching a desired position on the playing court.

Legal screening is when the player who is screening an opponent:

- *Is stationary* (inside his cylinder) when contact occurs.
- Has both feet on the floor when contact occurs.

Illegal screening is when the player who is screening an opponent:

- Was *moving* when contact occurred.
- Did not give sufficient distance in setting a screen outside the field of vision of a *stationary* opponent when contact occurred.
- Did not respect the elements of time and distance of an opponent *in motion* when contact occurred.

Charging

Charging is illegal personal contact, with or without the ball, by pushing or moving into an opponent's torso.

Blocking

Blocking is illegal personal contact which impedes the progress of an opponent with or without the ball.

A player who is attempting to screen is committing a blocking foul if contact occurs when he is moving and his opponent is stationary or retreating from him.

attacker but will not attempt to intercept or steal the ball – but in the progression, the drill becomes a normal game of 2 vs. 2. The defenders are active and are allowed to play proper defence (steal the ball, intercept, and so on).

'Give and Go' as a 3 vs. 3 Game

3 vs. 3 game at one basket with a special scoring system: if a team scores after a 'give and go' combination they will receive 4 points. Everything else is 1 point or 2 points.

Screens

Description and Use

A 'screen' (or block or pick) is an attacking move performed by two players as part of their offensive pattern of play. The main aim of this combination is to allow a teammate (with or without the ball) to get free temporarily from his defender. In order to set a screen (or a pick screen), the player without the ball – Player 2 on Fig 165 – will act as a screen, trying to block the path of the defender guarding attacking Player 1. When he sees that the 'screener' (the player who sets the screen; see Fig 166) is in position (about half a metre away, with feet shoulder-width apart, in a strong and well-balanced position, arms folded across the chest, knees slightly bent, and his shoulder line perpendicular to the defender's shoulder line, see Fig 167), the attacker with the ball will fake away and then change direction (Fig 168), dribbling and driving

Fig 166 The teammate (the screener) comes to set a screen.

Fig 167 The screener is in position (arms folded, well balanced). The defender's shoulder line is perpendicular to the screener's chest.

Fig 168 The attacker benefiting from a screen will go in a new direction.

Fig 169 The attacker benefiting from the screen will dribble towards the basket.

very close to his teammate. The dribbling player's foot will be as close as possible to the screener's foot and their shoulders will be almost touching (Fig 169). This means that there is no space for the defender to slide between the attacker and his screening teammate. The screener must remain motionless once the screen has been set and should not lean towards the defender to anticipate physical contact.

The same principles apply whether you are screening for a teammate who has the ball or one who is cutting to get open for a pass. When setting a screen, the attack-ing player may stand to the side of, in front of or behind the opponent, and this leads to three types of screen:

1 the *pick screen*, which is set at the side of the defender;
2 the *front screen*, which is used to create an opportunity for a shot (the screener will be positioned in front of a defender); and
3 the *rear screen*, in which the attack-ing player will run the defender into a stationary teammate who is acting as a post.

Screen and Roll

As well as simply setting a block to obstruct the path of a defender, the screener can also make himself available to receive a pass – this is particularly important in the situations when the defenders have 'switched men'. When this is happening, the screener will *screen and roll* (or pick and roll; or block and roll). This move involves the screener pivot-ing ('rolling') in such a way as to move facing the basket and facing the teammate using the screen, while trying to keep the

Fig 170 A screen is set for the attacker with the ball.

Fig 171 The attacker with the ball benefits from the screen and dribbles towards the basket.

Fig 172 The screener rolls facing the teammate, who dribbles.

Fig 173 The screener keeps the defender on his back during the roll while the defenders change men.

Fig 174 The screener steps forwards and makes himself available for a pass.

defender on his back throughout the roll (see Figs 170, 171 and 172). After making sure the defender is behind him (see Fig 173), the screener can step forward towards the basket, signalling for the ball (see Fig 174) and get in a very good position to score an easy basket.

Common Mistakes

- The screener moving in his attempt to 'catch' the defender and block his way, instead of standing still. This will lead to an illegal moving screen.
- The screener leaning into the defensive player as he goes to set the screen (instead of adopting an upright position).
- The person with the ball dribbling too far away from the screener on the way to the basket, allowing the defender to move through the screen.

Coaching Points

- The screener must be stationary.
- The player (with or without the ball) who receives the screen needs to

cut and/or dribble really close to the screener, so that their shoulders are almost touching.
- The attacker receiving the screen will need to use a fake once the screen is in place.
- The screener must have a good position, half a metre away from the defender, with his shoulder line perpendicular to the defender's shoulder line.
- The player who is going to use the screen must wait for the screener to occupy and establish his position before he starts his moves.
- When rolling, the screener will roll towards the shoulder that is closest to the shoulder of the teammate benefiting from the screen.

Drills

Drill 1

Players sort themselves into groups of three with one ball at one basket; two of them are offensive players, while the third is a defender. Offensive Player 1 has the ball and will send a verbal signal to his teammate (Attacker 2) to come and set a screen (as in Fig 165). When the

screen is set, Attacker 1 will fake away and then dribble towards the basket using the screen. After five actions for Player 1, the players rotate and change roles: Attacker 1 becomes the defender, the defender becomes Attacker 2 and Attacker 2 will replace Attacker 1.

In the beginning, the defender will be passive and will not try to steal the ball or avoid the screen.

As the practice progresses, the defender will become active and play defence as if in a game situation

Drill 2

The second drill is the same as Drill 1, but this time Player 2 has the ball and will pass to Player 1, who will then wait for a screen from Player 2 (see Fig 175).

Drill 3

2 vs. 2 at one basket. Attacker 2 (with the ball) will pass to Attacker 1 and then 2 will go to set a screen for 1 (see Fig 176). When the screener is in place, 1 will fake away and then drive towards the basket using the screen.

Option 1: both defenders are passive – they just follow the attackers they are marking without trying to steal or to switch man.

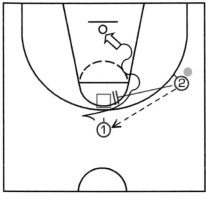

Fig 175 Attacker 2 will pass to teammate 1 and then will go and set a screen.

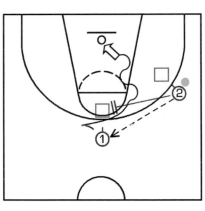

Fig 176 Two attackers vs. two defenders at one basket – the attackers are using the screen to get one of them open.

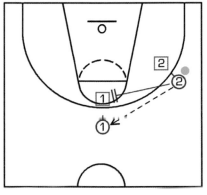

Fig 177 Attacker 2 passes and then goes to screen for teammate 1.

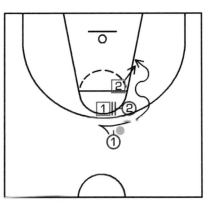

Fig 178 Defender 2 will switch the man he is guarding when attacker 1 dribbles towards the basket.

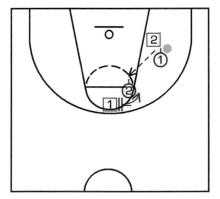

Fig 179 Attacker 2 rolls towards the basket, and attacker 1 (who is now guarded by defender 2) will pass to him.

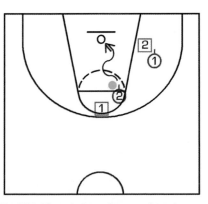

Fig 180 After receiving the pass from 1, attacker 2 dribbles once and takes a lay-up shot.

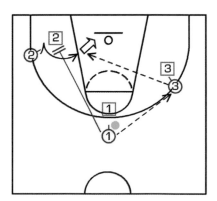

Fig 181 3 vs. 3 play with pass and screen away.

Option 2: defenders are active – 2 vs. 2 game at one basket. The players perform five possessions each and then change roles (with attackers becoming defenders).

Option 3: 2 vs. 2 pick and roll (screen and roll). Attacker 2 sets the screen and, after Attacker 1 cuts past him, rolls, facing the teammate benefiting from the screen. The defender shouts 'switch' and changes man, leaving the screener having the defender behind him. Player 1 now returns the pass to Attacker 2 who steps forward for an easy lay-up (see Figs 177, 178, 179 and 180).

Drill 4

3 vs. 3 at one basket. The focus here is the pass and screen away. Attacker 1 will pass to the right to Attacker 3 (see Fig 181), and then will go and screen away for Attacker 2. When the screen is in place, 2 will fake away and then cut towards the basket. On his way, 2 will receive the pass from 3 and will finish with an easy lay-up.

This drill may progress from the defenders being passive to the defenders being active. As a third option, the players can perform a pass, screen away and roll. Player 3 has 2 options: to pass to 2, who cuts after receiving the screen, or to pass to 1, who will roll after setting the screen (see Fig 182 overleaf).

Fig 182 Two options for attacker 3: either to pass to attacker 2, who benefits from the screen, or to pass to 1, who will roll towards the basket after setting a screen.

Fastbreak Situations

One of the easiest ways to score points in the fast-moving game of basketball is to use the fastbreak. In a fastbreak situation the easy points come about through a proper use of numerical superiority – every team and every player should take full advantage whenever this moment of superiority occurs and teams/players should actively create these opportunities as part of their offensive patterns. By moving the ball extremely quickly towards the opposition's basket and by creating a 1 vs. 1, 2 vs. 1, 3 vs. 2 (and even 4 vs. 2 or 5 vs. 2) playing situation – two or three offensive players running fast or sprinting on offence to obtain a numerical advantage against one or two defenders – a fastbreak is created. A fastbreak may also be initiated and played by one attacker against one defender in a 1 vs. 1 situation.

If played properly, the fastbreak is one of the most effective ways to score points and is also very entertaining for the spectators.

2 vs. 1

Description and Use
In a fastbreak situation in which two attackers play against one defender, the offensive players must spread out and fill the outside lanes, as in Fig 183. Usually, the court is split along its length into three lanes or 'channels': a middle lane (between imaginary lines drawn from each side of the backboard), a right-hand side lane (on the right, when facing the opposition's basket) and a left-hand side lane (see Fig 184).

The attackers keep passing the ball to each other until they enter the scoring area – just outside the 3-points semicircle. At this point, without slowing down, one of them takes control of the ball by dribbling it towards the basket (see Fig 185). This player now has two options:

1 if the defender stays still and does not come to stop him, the attacker will continue his run and finish with a lay-up shot;
2 if the defender does come towards him, the attacking player needs to respond appropriately. A quick pass to an open teammate is the best solution – in this way, 2 vs. 1 is transformed into 1 vs. 0, creating a very easy scoring opportunity (undefended lay-up).

Common Mistakes
- The attackers being too close to each other, making it easy for the defender to guard both of them.
- The attacker with the ball dribbling towards the area (or the lane) where his teammate is.
- The attacker with the ball deciding what to play (for example, to pass) before reading the defence. Reading the situation and making the right decision are crucial.
- The ball handler jumping to pass – he will either rush into an unprepared shot or will pass incorrectly.
- The dribbler failing to pass quickly enough when the defender commits to stop the ball.
- Poor passing (behind the moving teammate, at foot level, and so on).

Coaching Points
- Be a scoring threat – keep dribbling/driving to the basket until the defender comes to stop you.
- Accurate chest passes are recommended.
- Keep enough space between you and your teammate.
- When dribbling, use the outside hand to keep the ball away from the defender (for example, if the dribbler is on the right-hand side lane he will dribble with the right hand).
- Do not jump to take a pass when the defender is coming to you.

Fig 183 Two attackers vs. one defender.

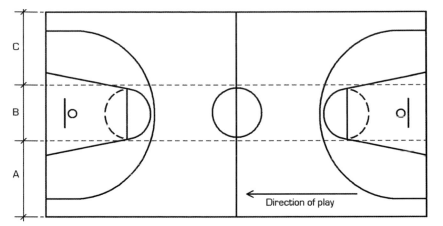

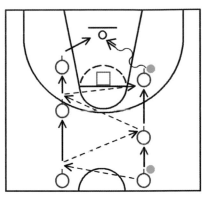

Fig 184 The court split into three lanes/channels: A = left-hand side lane (for a direction of play from right to left); B = middle lane; C = right-hand side lane.

Fig 185 2 vs. 1 fastbreak.

Drills

2 vs. 1 on half-court

Players are grouped in pairs on both halves of the court with one defender at each end (see Fig 186). They need to play 2 vs. 1 at one basket. The shooter (or the player losing the ball) will become a defender, and the defender will replace the attacking player.

Three-man weave with 2 vs. 1 full court on the way back

Players are in groups of three, each group with a ball. All three players run one length of the court, performing a three-man weave (passes between three with changing positions, as in Fig 41). The player who takes the shot becomes a defender; the other two players get the rebound or, if the basket is good, inbound the ball from behind the end line, playing 2 vs. 1 (see Fig 187). If at the end of the three-man weave (the first length of the court), the shooting player misses the shot, then the other two players get the rebound and play straight away.

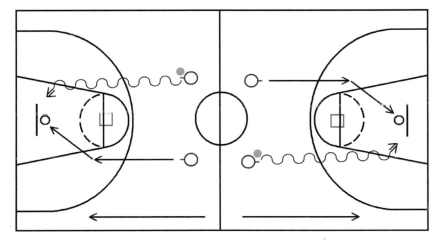

Fig 186 2 vs. 1 half-court drill.

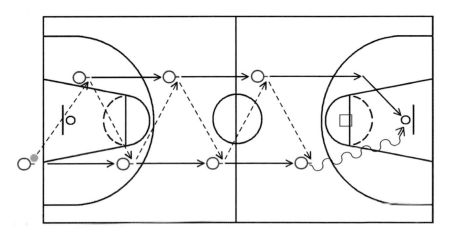

Fig 187 2 vs. 1 after three-man weave on the full court.

2 vs. 1 full-court continuous play

Two players (1 and 2) with a ball start the drill from the central circle; all other players are positioned on the court as in Fig 188. Attackers 1 and 2 play 2 vs. 1 against Defender 1. If they score, Defender 1 inbounds the ball by passing to Player 3 who is waiting for an outlet pass at the free-throw line extended at a 45-degree angle. If Attackers 1 and 2 miss the shot (or if Defender 1 intercepts the ball) then Defender 1 will become an offensive player and will pass to 3 in order for both of them to go to the other end of court to play 2 vs. 1 against Defender 2.

The drill continues following a similar pattern – Defender 2 (who is positioned at the free-throw line) becomes an offensive player (to play 2 vs. 1 with Player 4 waiting on the side line opposite the free-throw line) and goes (using passing or dribbling) towards the opposite end of court for a 2 vs. 1 play against the defender waiting there. Out of the two offensive players, the one who takes the shot (or the one losing the ball) will become a defender while the other will go to the sideline to join the queue.

Progression: after losing the ball (as a consequence of a shot, or after a poor pass or travelling, and so on), the offensive players will play defence up to the half-way line before becoming a defender or a passer.

3 vs. 2

Description and Use

The 3 vs. 2 fastbreak situation is similar in some respects to the 2 vs. 1 scenario, and some of the principles apply equally to 3 vs. 2 moments. The three offensive players need to 'fill in' the lanes (see Fig 184), so that there is a player in the middle and two wings. After a rebound and an outlet pass, the ball needs to be passed to the player in the middle. This is when the 'be ahead of the ball' principle comes into play. The two wings need to run fast to be ahead of the ball line. (Players 1 and 2 are ahead of the ball line in Fig 189.)

When approaching the scoring area (the 3-points semicircle), the middle

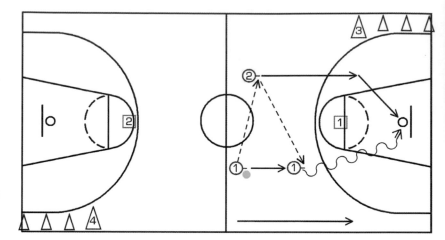

Fig 188 2 vs. 1 full-court continuous play drill.

player (with the ball) will dribble and go towards the free-throw line for a jump shot (see Fig 190). If the defence opens up and gives him some space, the middle player should take advantage and go for a lay-up. If the defenders play good defence, he will have to pass right or left (see Fig 191). By passing early, the 3 vs. 2 situation is transformed into 2 vs.1 (after receiving the pass from 1, Attackers 2 and 3 are playing against Defender 2) and all the principles relating to playing 2 vs. 1 should be applied.

Common Mistakes

- Poor passing.
- Wing players not being ahead of the ball.
- Players being too close to each other (not sufficiently spaced out).
- The player with the ball (usually the middle player) dribbling towards a teammate instead of penetrating to the basket, presenting the defenders with an easy task.
- Offensive players not jumping or getting the rebound after a shot.
- Offensive players spending too much time in the key – this leads to a 3-seconds violation.
- The player with the ball running straight into the defender – this will result in an offensive foul.

Coaching Points

- When close to the scoring area, pass the ball early to create a 2 vs. 1 situation (from 3 vs. 2).
- Go to get the rebound following a shot.
- Read the defence and force them to commit to one side.
- The ball should be passed on to the middle lane as soon as possible and the wing players should be ahead of the ball.

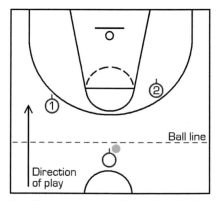

Fig 189 Attackers 1 and 2 are ahead of the ball line.

Fig 190 Three attackers vs. two defenders scenario.

Drills

3 vs. 2 at one basket

Three attackers play against two defenders at one basket only (on the half-court). The focus for offensive players is to go for a lay-up (easy points) instead of an unprepared jump shot.

Later, the drill may be extended to the full court, with attackers having only one dribble per player when they receive the ball.

Eleven players continuous fastbreak

This is a continuous 3 vs. 2 drill for eleven players (or at least nine) on the full court (see Fig 192 overleaf). Attackers 1, 2 and 3 play 3 vs. 2 against Defenders 1 and 2. The principles described above relating to 3 vs. 2 play also apply here. If the group of three players scores, then the defender

who gets the ball (Defender 1 or 2, who is closest to the ball) inbounds from out of bounds by passing to Player 4 or 5; these two will be waiting at a 45-degree angle from the basket. If the attackers miss, the defender who gets the rebound sends an outlet pass to either 4 or 5 and then all of them (Defender 1, together with Players 4 and 5) go and play 3 vs. 2 against Defenders 6 and 7, who are waiting at the other end of the court in front of the basket. The offensive player who scored or lost possession will become a defender while the other two will replace Players 8 and 9 (who went 3 vs. 2 towards the opposite end with the defender who got the ball) on the sidelines for an outlet pass.

The drill is progressed by allowing the attackers only one dribble each time they receive the ball. Next, there may be no dribbling at all, only passing and moving.

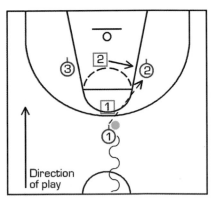

Fig 191 Three attackers against two defenders (3 vs. 2) – playmaker (1) passes to the right to attacker 2.

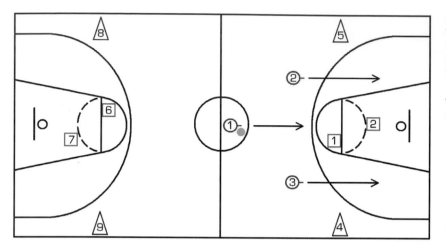

Fig 192 3 vs. 2 with eleven players (3 vs. 2 continuous fastbreak drill).

3 vs. 2 followed by 2 vs. 1

Three attackers start from behind the end line and inbound the ball, trying to go towards the opposite basket and play three against the two defenders who are waiting on the court. After a basket is scored, the two defenders become offensive players and play 2 vs. 1 against the player who has just scored (or lost the ball). This player needs to sprint back in defence in an attempt to stop the fastbreak.

1 vs. 1

Description and Use

1 vs. 1 (attacker vs. defender) situations are the starting point for almost all attacking collective combinations that a team uses in order to score points. It is also the basic attacking option to initiate the fastbreak (the primary break). There is a strong interdependence between the individual value of a player and that of the whole team. Consequently, the quality of each player and his contribution will have an impact on the overall team performance.

There are two types of situation:

1   1 vs. 1 *without the ball*, in which the attacking player tries to get open in a

position that will allow him to receive a pass and score easily (see also page 75); or

2   1 vs. 1 *with the ball*, when the attacker tries to overtake/beat the defender in order to go and take a lay-up or a jump shot from a convenient position (see Fig 193). Alternatively, he may be able to create space for a free teammate to cut and to receive the ball, which will lead to easy points being scored.

1 vs. 1 with the Ball

If the attacker receives the ball after a pass from a teammate or acquires it as a consequence of a defensive or offensive rebound, interception or steal, and he did not dribble, this is a 'triple threat' position. The offensive player with the ball has three main options: to shoot, to dribble, or to pass (see Fig 194). There are two other alternatives – to fake (fakes may be used in combination with any of the triple threat options) or even to hold the ball (but for no more than 5 seconds if he is closely guarded – see Rules box).

In all 1 vs. 1 situations the offensive player needs to 'read' the defender; if he feels he can beat the defender on the dribble, then he should take it all the way to the basket and attempt a lay-up. If the defender plays good defence against the

dribble, then the attacking player should try a jump shot from close to the basket. In both situations, the moves should be executed properly because they form the basic options for a fastbreak.

There are a number of common mistakes made by defenders that an offensive player should look to exploit:

- poor positioning – the defender not being in the right place (on the imaginary line between the ball holder and his own basket); the defender being too far away from the player he is guarding;
- poor balance – the defender not adopting a proper defensive stance. He may have the legs straight or feet crossed when moving; he may be jumping up to check an anticipated shot; he may be moving towards the attacker and reacting slowly to moving backwards; he may even be moving backwards and allowing the offensive player to take an uncontested shot; or he may be caught off balance moving laterally when the offensive player uses a fake for changing direction.

Common Mistakes

The attacking player needs to avoid a number of common errors:

- failing to read the situation properly and not reacting quickly to defensive placement errors;
- poor control of the ball when initiating a 1 vs. 1 situation;

RULES

Closely guarded player

A player who is holding a live ball on the playing court is closely guarded when an opponent is in an active guarding position at a distance of no more than one (1) metre.

Rule – a closely guarded player must pass, shoot or dribble the ball within five (5) seconds.

TOP TIP

It is recommended that the player holding the ball in the 'triple threat' position (when he has the option to shoot, dribble or pass) should have feet shoulder-width apart, with the body weight evenly distributed on each foot, and a slightly low position, with knees flexed, head up and the ball held in two hands in front of the chest (for better protection). From this position, the attacker should pivot to face the opposite team's basket and to read the movements on the court. If a teammate is in a better position, a pass should be sent straight away. If the ball holder has a chance for an open shot (if the defender is in a poor position, for example) this should be taken, especially if he is very close to the basket. Lastly, if there is a clear path towards the basket, the player should start dribbling the ball.

- poor choice of offensive options – shooting instead of dribbling, for example;
- keeping the head down;
- rushing his movements, which will lead to incorrect footwork when starting dribbling;
- excessive dribbling (and bouncing the ball merely out of habit); and
- excessive use of fakes, as well as using fakes that are not sufficiently convincing.

Coaching Points
- Always keep the head up to see the position of defenders and team-mates, and to read the play.
- Start from a triple threat position, well balanced, and ready to react quickly.
- Hold and protect the ball with two hands.

Fig 193 GB forward Rosalee Mason (number 4 in white jersey) in a 1 vs 1 situation against a Lithuanian defender.

Fig 194 GB forward Megan Moody (number 14 in white jersey) simply received the ball (without dribbling) – she is in a 'triple threat' position.

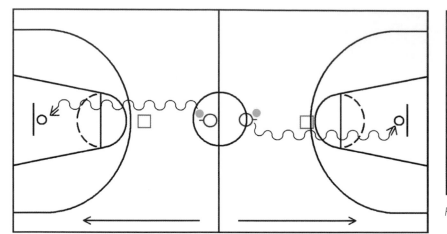

Fig 195 1 vs. 1 play on half-court.

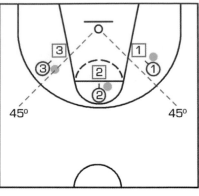

Fig 196 1 vs. 1 play from three positions.

- Pivot and face the basket as soon as you receive the ball.
- Be a threat when dribbling and go towards the basket.
- Use simple and efficient fakes when playing 1 vs. 1.

Drills

1 vs. 1 on half-court

In pairs, one ball for each pair. One player is the attacker (with the ball) while the other is the defender. They play 1 vs. 1 (attacker against defender) at one basket until one of them scores (see Fig 195). If the defender steals the ball, he becomes the offensive player and continues the drill at the same basket. Offensive rebounds are allowed and players keep playing until a basket is scored.

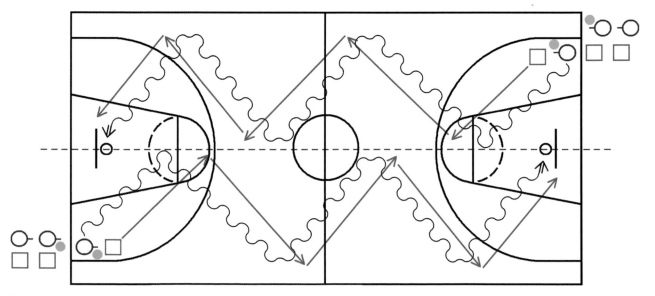

Fig 197 1 vs. 1 play (zig-zagging) on the full court.

The drill may be progressed in a number of ways:

- five possessions for each player, with a focus on taking a lay-up shot;
- five possessions for each player with a focus on taking a jump shot from very close to the basket (2–3m, maximum 4m);
- five possessions as before but with each player having one shot maximum per possession, so the first possession is over after one shot;
- 1 vs. 1 play with the first player to score 11 points winning the game. This is a simplified version of street-ball – instead of 3 vs. 3, players play 1 vs. 1. The player who scores keeps possession and restarts the play (after checking the ball with the defender) from the top of the key.

1 vs. 1 from three positions

In pairs, each pair with a ball. Players (attackers vs. defenders) occupy three positions on the court just inside the 3-points semicircle, as shown in Fig 196: one pair at a 45-degree angle on the right-hand side of the court, the second pair in front of basket on the free-throw line and the third pair on the left of the court at a 45-degree angle.

There are a couple of options with this drill:

1   One pair at a time will play 1 vs. 1 at one basket until the offensive player scores or until the defender gets the ball (by stealing it, knocking it out of the offensive player's control or through a defensive rebound). Once the first pair has finished and cleared the area, the second pair starts and does the same. The same applies for the third pair. Each player has five possessions and then they change roles. After all six players finish five possessions each, the pairs change their position on the court: the first pair replaces the second, the second replaces the third, and the third goes instead of the first. The drill is then repeated.

2   1 vs. 1 with shooting. In turns (one pair at a time), each attacking player takes a jump shot. The drill starts with a passive defender, who does not attempt to block the shot. After five shots each, the defenders become active. After the shot, the defenders box out and both players go to get the rebound. If the attacker gets the offensive rebound after his own shot, he will have one more shot (six instead of five). The drill follows a pattern similar to that of the previous drill so that all players shoot from three different spots on the court.

1 vs. 1 full court

In pairs, each pair with a ball. The court is split into two lanes, along its length. The player with the ball starts dribbling and changing direction in a zig-zag manner, as shown in Fig 197. When he reaches the imaginary line that splits the court (the red line between the two baskets on Fig 197), he changes the hand dribbling the ball and then, when he reaches the side line (without touching it), he switches back again. The defender (using the basic defensive stance and proper footwork) tries to play defence, maintaining the optimum distance (one arm and a half away from an attacking player who is dribbling). When the first pair goes over the half-way line, the next pair can go. After they complete a length, players change roles on the way back (after joining the queue at the other end).

CHAPTER 7

TEAM ATTACKING PLAY

Man-to-Man Offence

As soon as a team gets in possession of the ball, all five players should coordinate their effort and work together to create a favourable situation that will allow them to score in one of three ways:

1 an undefended lay-up;
2 an open shot from close distance; or
3 a jump shot.

Generally, the coach will devise an organized system of attack, which will be coordinated on-court by the playmaker and will be followed by the players. Attacking team play against a man-to-man defence is usually built upon individual attacking skills and techniques (individual players using dribbling, shooting, passing, fakes, running, stopping/footwork/pivoting, changing direction, getting open, jumping, playing 1 vs. 1 situations) and also upon offensive combinations between two or three players (give and go; setting a screen and screen and roll; playing 2 vs. 1, 3 vs. 2, 4 vs. 2 and 5 vs. 2 situations; using set plays; see pages 79–91). All players must be familiar with the basic playing positions, the transition game, the fastbreak, positional play (including play calls or motion play and playing systems), and the principles of attack.

Basic Playing Positions

Each offensive system requires players to play in a particular position depending on their dribbling ability, height, size and general ability. Every player must possess a variety of fundamental skills that will help them both offensively and defensively – everyone should be able to pass and receive the ball accurately, to move quickly

from a defensive situation into an attacking one and the other way round, to rebound the ball at both ends of court, to play good defence and to contribute unselfishly to the team's attacking effort. However, in offensive moments, all five player positions demand specific skills and attributes. The five offensive spots are most often referred to as point guard, shooting guard, small forward, power forward and pivot (center) (for details, see page 14).

Transition Game

'Transition game' is a generic term used to describe the moment of change from defence to offence (and also from offence to defence) as a consequence of the ball changing possession. This change of possession can happen after a basket is scored, after a player gets a rebound or after an interception, a steal or a side-line possession (after a turnover). The quicker the transition, the better the chances are for creating a numerical superiority or positional advantage before the opposition can have their players back on their own territory and get the defence organized. Clearly, a short transition game (that is, the time it takes a team to get the ball into the front court ready to start the offensive patterns after getting possession) – of just 3 to 4 seconds– will be more efficient because it will give the offensive team 20 to 21 seconds to shoot the ball. This can be achieved by using two to three passes to teammates who are running towards the front court. To some extent, transition is the building block and the initial phase prior to and leading to a fastbreak situation.

This change from defence to offence occurs in a few situations:

- *After a basket is scored* – your team now has possession and will inbound the ball behind the end line of the court. The quicker your team inbounds the ball and brings it from the back court to the front court the better the chances for a longer offence. For a quick inbound, the player closest to the basket (usually the center) should pick up the ball, step outside the court and look for a pass to one of the guards. Remember: never send a long pass (towards the half-way line or over it) if you are right under the basket. To avoid this, take two to three steps sideways, outside of the board projection on the floor, so that the ball does not hit the backboard.

- *After a defensive rebound* – once again, for a quick and short transition play, the player getting the defensive rebound should land, pivot and protect the ball, and look for a pass to the playmaker as soon as possible in order to initiate the fastbreak (the offence).

- *After a turnover from the other team (side-line possession)* – getting the ball from the opposition as a consequence of their mistakes is a good opportunity to initiate your own offensive actions. On a side-line possession from the front court, teams should have set plays for inbounding the ball – screens, cuts, getting open and fakes are all techniques that may be used for a safe inbound, which will lead to a potential scoring situation.

- *After an interception or steal* – good defence (that leads to an interception or a stealing of the ball) can create a psychological advantage in the game, which needs to be used for scoring points from easy situations. When obtaining the ball in this manner, all players should concentrate to transform the possession into valuable points – this usually occurs after a quick transition and playing 2 vs.1, 3 vs. 2 or 1 vs. 1 situations.

Fastbreak

The fastbreak has two forms: the primary break and the secondary break. For more on these two forms, see, respectively, page 100 and page 101.

Positional Play

When players on offence come up against a strong defence that slows down the attacking rhythm and eliminates the fastbreak opportunities (allowing no 2 vs. 1 or 3 vs. 2 play, for example), the attacking players will have to stick to positional play. This is an offensive playing system based on set motions of the players. When the playmaker calls a play (usually via a verbal, visual or physical signal by showing a number using his fingers – see Fig 198 overleaf), the attackers follow a pre-learned pattern of play. This involves the movement of the ball and a series of screens, cuts and passes that will lead to the team scoring from a favourable position. Because of the movement of the players, the positional play is also referred to as 'motion offence'. Generally, the positional play is based on playing 1 vs. 1, 2 vs. 2 or 3 vs. 3 situations but there are also play calls (motions) that involve all five attacking players.

Considering the players available to him (in terms of height, dribbling and shooting / passing ability), a coach will then decide on an offensive playing system which is appropriate and suitable to the quality of players available and based on using and maximizing players' strengths. There are a number of common types of attacking system from which a coach can choose.

Attacking System with One Pivot

The attacking system with one pivot (or four players outside and one inside) makes good use of the tallest and biggest player in the team. The pivot could be used as a moving player, playing on both the right-and left-hand side of the offence. The usual distribution of the remaining players (see Fig 199 overleaf) is one guard (1), two forwards (2 and 3) and one corner player (4) to play alongside the pivot (5). Another option could be two guards (1 and 2) and two corner players (3 and 4), plus the movable pivot (5) (see Fig 200 overleaf for clarification).

Attacking System with Two Pivots

This is one of the most commonly used systems (three players outside and two inside), which creates a very well-balanced floor, with players well spread and with clear offensive roles. As is obvious from Fig 201 overleaf, the playmaker 1 will have good support from the forwards 2 and 3, while the big guys – pivots 4 and 5 – will be in the low-post position. They will be close enough to the basket but also ready to take part in the team attacking combinations between themselves, with the guard or with the forwards. Good shooting ability (both from a jump-shot or a set-shot situation) is essential for guards

Fig 198 GB point guard Lisa Hutchinson (number 12 in white jersey) provides a visual signal to her teammates, telling them the number of the set play.

and forwards, together with very good ball control. Being rather small but very agile, these players will frequently change positions and will benefit from screens set by the tall guys. It is one of the best offensive systems, which offers good threats both inside and outside.

Attacking System with Three Pivots

This system uses two pivots in tandem and the third one on the other side. There are teams that use three big guys at the same time on court. If this is the case, these teams can choose the offensive system with three pivots – two of them (3 and 4) in tandem on one side (one high, next to the free-throw line, and one low, close to the basket), while the third one (5) will go to the low post on the opposite side. The remaining two players (1 and 2) could be two very mobile guards – as in Fig 202 – or could be one guard and one corner player (on the same side as the pivot, who is alone).

Attacking System with Four Pivots – Double Tandem

If a team can afford the luxury of having four tall players at any time on the court,

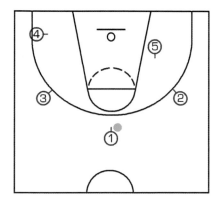

Fig 199 Attacking system with one pivot (and one guard, two forwards, one corner player and one pivot).

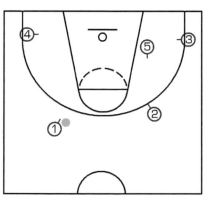

Fig 200 Attacking system with one pivot (and two guards and two corner players).

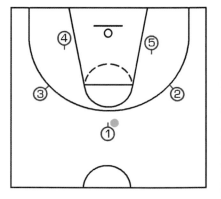

Fig 201 Attacking system with two pivots (one guard, two forwards and two pivots).

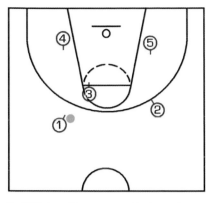

Fig 202 Attacking system with three pivots (two guards, two pivots in tandem and a third pivot).

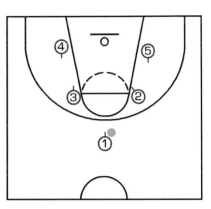

Fig 203 Attacking system with four pivots (two pivots in double tandem plus a guard).

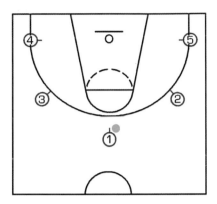

Fig 204 Attacking system with no pivots (five players outside in a horseshoe shape).

this system (one player outside and four inside) should be used. The pivots will be situated in pairs, just outside the 3-seconds space, in tandem – one of them could be playing on the low post (4 and 5 respectively), close to the basket, while the second one (2 and 3) could be high, next to the free-throw line, as shown in Fig 203. The playmaker/guard (1) will have clear defensive responsibilities (court balance, protection and prevention of fastbreaks) as soon as the team loses the ball. If he is involved in the play close to the basket, then this responsibility will be covered by the pivots playing high post.

Attacking System with No Pivot

This system uses five players outside. When playing basketball there are situations when either a team does not have any tall enough players to play inside (on pivot position) or the team has tall players but they are fouled out. In both cases, the playing system with no pivot could be the solution. The five small players – who are displayed on court as in Fig 204 – all need to compensate for the lack of height with speed and ball-handling ability that are higher than average. Their ability to penetrate using dribbling, or 'give and go' moves, should make them a team that can create problems. Another area in which they need to excel in order to compen-

sate the lack of height is in the use of aggressive defensive tactics.

Court Balance and Protection

No matter what offensive system is used by a team against a man-to-man defence, all players must make sure that there is at least one player slightly backwards to ensure protection just in case possession is lost, and in order to stop a potential fastbreak. While on offence, all players need to be spaced out so that court (or floor) balance is achieved. This means that all players are evenly distributed across the floor, instead of all or most of them being gathered around one spot only.

Defensive responsibilities start even during the running of an offensive play call. If the team is using one guard only, there needs to always be somebody in the team who is covering the defensive responsibilities of the guard, especially when he is in action close to the basket. If there are two guards, then they are covering for each other, protecting the basket by trying to stop the fastbreak and/or to slow down the offence until the remaining players come back in defence. As a general rule, players should understand and be aware of their teammates' movements in every situation, be it offensive or defensive.

Common Mistakes when Using Man-to-Man Offence Set Plays

- Players failing to follow the pre-scribed pattern of play.
- Players not having patience to run the play right down to the last couple of seconds of their attack.
- Poor passing during the set motion.
- Players failing to get open at the right time or moment (so timing and synchronizing actions are poor).
- Players not understanding the movements required of each of the five offensive positions.
- Players failing to fulfil the responsibilities of each position.

Teaching Set Plays/ Offensive Motions

When teaching a new set play for an attacking system, the coach should pick five players and have them on the court without any defenders. Once they are in their positions, the players begin by walking through the movements (in slow motion), guided by the coach. The set play is allocated a number or a name that will be easily recognized by the players. The set play includes certain combinations between two or three players that are performed in a specific order (which needs to be respected by the players), so that they can create a situation in which to score easy points.

Once the play motion is mastered to a reasonable level and players know what they have to do, with or without the ball, defenders may be introduced. Initially they will be passive (they will follow their man and position themselves but will not try to steal, intercept the ball or block the shot). Gradually, the next step is for defenders to become active, playing as if they are in a real game situation. All the players in the squad need to be given a chance to practise during session time, both in offensive set-ups and also in defence.

Once the team has learned the set play during training, the coach will arrange some friendly games with weaker opposition (preferably), so that the new patterns may be applied in a game situation. It is recommended that two to three set plays be learned (plus one to two for side-line possession) during the off season so that players become familiar with and are ready to use the new play calls when the new season starts.

Principles of Attack

Most offensive systems used for positional play (when the fastbreak opportunities for quick play such as 2 vs. 1 and 3 vs. 2 are not viable because of good defence) are based upon the 1 vs. 1 relationship and on combinations between two or three players. Having said that, the secret for a successful offensive set motion lies in how well the players execute the agreed plan, and not only in what system a team or coach chooses to use.

The attacking players need to learn a few basic principles that will lead to the creation of a good shooting opportunity for each possession:

- accurate and, equally important, quick passing to a teammate who is in a good penetrating offensive position;

- the movement of the ball and of the players with or without the ball should lead to an uncontested shooting opportunity;
- floor balance – players well spread out on the court to cover all the areas;
- adopting a 'triple threat' position each time a player receives the ball and pivoting to face the opposite basket;
- good selection of the right offensive system, based on the qualities of the players (tall players to be positioned near the basket, for example);
- fundamental skills and techniques properly learned and applied in game situations;
- try as much as possible to take a lay-up or a jump shot from close range;
- never force or hurry a shot. Players need to develop an understanding of when to shoot and when not to;
- the offensive system needs to be flexible and to adapt depending on the type of defence the opposition is playing;
- players should not congest the keyhole area, placing too many hands around the ball in a small space; and
- every team should have at least two to three players who are attempting to get the offensive rebounds. Also, every team should aim for a quick transition game.

Zone Offence

Players at beginner level are recommended to start learning to play man-to-man defence. All other teams must have an offensive playing system that can be used against a zone defence. Having secured the possession, every team playing in offence needs to find the solution to send the ball to the best-placed player at the right time. That is why it is important to have set plays (motions) that could be used against a man-to-man defence but also in case of a zone defence.

When choosing which attacking pattern should be performed, a coach needs to

consider his own players' abilities and height, as well as the type of zone defence that is being employed by the opposition (2-1-2, 2-3 – see page 128 for a description of different types of zone). Two of the main characteristics of playing a zone offence are the frequent use of outside shooting (which has to be good, with high percentages) and a quick movement (passing) of the ball into spaces that are not covered by the defensive players. In fact, most of the fundamental techniques and skills described earlier are applicable and can be equally successful against a zone. Obviously, some of the fundamentals will be used more than others and an overview of the most frequently used techniques when playing a zone is given here.

Fundamental Skills When Attacking a Zone

Passing
Accurate and quick passes with two hands from chest height or over the head are vital when playing against a zone defence mainly because the ball can move more quickly than the players. Good movement of the ball will contribute to spreading the zone and consequently create spaces that need to be exploited. When passing, attackers should ideally look to pass to the closest person. If the zone is moving from right to the left, for example, the pass

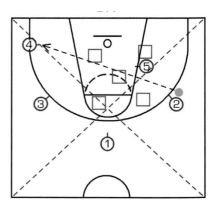

Fig 205 Passes over a zone are not recommended.

should go the other way round – against the flow of the zone. It is also important to remember not to pass over the zone (see Fig 205 for a visual representation). Sometimes a 'skip pass' can be used, when the passer misses out (skips) a man on the perimeter to get the ball more quickly to the receiver.

Dribbling

Generally, it is recommended to keep dribbling the ball to a minimum. There are, however, a few situations that need a different approach:

- dribble the ball between two defenders only when they are far away from each other;
- dribble the ball along the baseline with the clear intention of going to the basket;
- dribble the ball with the intention of keeping it in your team's possession (for example, bring the ball from inside the 3-points semicircle towards the half-way line in order to restart a new 24-second attack).

Cutting

Cutting is one of the most efficient moves against a zone defence. If properly used, it has the potential to create a shooting opportunity on the move, or can bring about a situation of numerical superiority that will eventually lead to great scoring opportunities. As a general principle, only one cutter at a time should go in one direction – it is quite difficult for a ball handler to pass to two players who are cutting at the same time and in the same direction.

Defensive Balance

As with man-to-man offence, every attacking system against zone defence should have incorporated safety factors. These factors take the form of one or two players (usually the guards) who have a major role in preventing an easy basket from the opposition's fastbreak in case of a lost possession. They will be playing just outside the 3-points semicircle and will be covering each other when one of them is driving towards the basket.

Screens

Screens can be used in an effective manner against a zone defence. The main use of a screen is to facilitate a shot over that screen from a teammate. When a screen is set, the continuation of the situation needs to be accurately timed with the ball path so that an easy scoring chance is created.

Offensive Rebounding

Due to the fact that the defenders are not always able to box out all the attackers that are situated in the zone they are supposed to defend, offensive rebounding opportunities are available. At least two to three attackers should attempt to go and get the offensive rebound.

Shooting

Attacking players should aim to take only those shots that are not hurried or deflected, closely marked or off-balance. Choosing unwisely can lead to poor shooting percentages, which in turn can have an impact on team morale and on the outcome of the game. Good outside shooters are required when playing against a zone and coaches should develop shooters who can consistently shoot from 4–6m range.

Danger Areas

The space between the defenders can be vulnerable especially when this space is increased. The attacking team should look for the 'gaps' and try to get advantage from them – they may be found in the corners of the court and in the area close to where the pivot plays (see Figs 206, 207, 208, 209 and 210 overleaf for gaps in different types of zones).

Overloading

Overloading a zone defence increases a team's chances for a good shooting and/or scoring opportunity. Overloading involves attacking players moving on a particular place on the court within the zone of responsibility of one defender, so that there will be more attackers against one defender. This defender will struggle to guard both attackers adequately at the same time. See page 98 for examples of overloading.

Advantages and Disadvantages of Playing Zone Offence

- Zone defences create vulnerable spaces that need to be speculated. For example, in case of 1-3-1 zone, the corners on both sides have very limited coverage and they are usually exploited by the attackers.
- It is a very useful system when your team has very good outside shooters.
- It is very efficient if your team uses the fastbreak as a principal offensive solution.
- It is not very efficient if the attacking team does not have outside shooters.
- It is vulnerable to quick offences if the possession is lost after a poor pass.

Zone Offence Principles

- It is generally acknowledged that the best offence against a zone defence is to fastbreak before the defenders can get into their set positions. The fastbreak as an option (which must always be a major component in any attack against a zone defence) should be used as soon as the team gets possession of the ball.
- Try to identify early what type of zone the defenders are using and take this into account when choosing the attacking formation.
- Two of the most important factors to remember when attacking a zone are: players need to be patient; and players should take a good shot every time their team has possession.
- Attackers need to be well spaced out on the court. This will lead to spreading the zone (this can also be achieved by passing the ball), creating gaps and vulnerable spaces. A gap occurs where the areas of responsibility of two defenders in the zone meet.
- Accurate passes should be used to move the zone or individual defenders out of position.

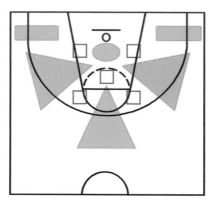

Fig 206 Weaknesses of 2-1-2 zone defence that need to be exploited.

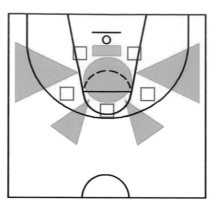

Fig 207 Weaknesses of 3-2 zone defence that need to be exploited.

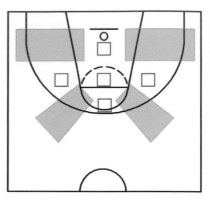

Fig 208 Weaknesses of 1-3-1 zone defence that need to be exploited.

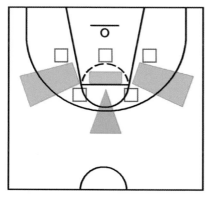

Fig 209 Weaknesses of 2-3 zone defence that need to be exploited.

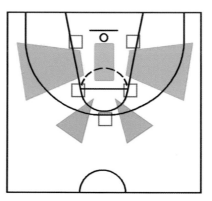

Fig 210 Weaknesses of 1-2-2 zone defence that need to be exploited.

- Successful outside shooting is an important weapon and, in order to be successful when playing this type of offence, any team needs at least one or two players who can shoot and score from behind the 3-points semicircle.
- Maintain a good rebounding position and go for a rebound every time a shot is taken.
- When receiving the ball, players should pivot and look at the basket first of all, threatening the defence (getting into the 'triple threat' position).

- The overload principle should be used as much as possible, placing two attackers in one defender's zone of responsibility.
- Dribbling may be used to create 2 vs. 1 opportunities or to improve passing angles.
- Teamwork is the key to success.

Types of Zone Offence

The attacking formation adopted against a zone defence will largely depend on the type of zone formation adopted by the

zone. The most common zone defences are 2-1-2, 2-3, 3-2, 1-2-2, 1-3-1 (for details, see page 128). All the principles given above should be applied no matter what attacking formation the team decides to use. The most efficient types of zone offence display are the following:

1-3-1 Attacking Formation
This is very useful against a 2-1-2 zone defence (see Fig 211 for the players' formation in both offence and defence).

A 1-3-1 attacking formation is also very efficient against a 2-3 zone line-up (see Fig 212). This formation is ideal for creating an overload on the same side with the pivot (player 5 on Fig 212), who will set a screen for player 2, who will come through under the basket to receive the ball from 1 via 3 and to be ready to take the shot.

2-1-2 Attacking Formation
This attacking formation is mainly used in a number of situations:

- against a 3-2 zone defence, as in Fig 213. A pass inside the key to player 3, combined with a cut towards the basket from players 4 and 5, will create a favourable 3 vs. 2 situation;
- against a 1-2-2 zone defence – attackers are displayed on court as in Fig 214;

- as before; a pass from the top to player 3 inside the key creates another 3 vs. 2 situation;
- the pass goes to player 4. Now player 3 has two options: to cut/go towards the basket and receive the ball, or to go and set a screen for player 5;
- against a 1-3-1 zone display – by passing the ball from 1 to 2 and then, after a dribble towards the sideline, player 2 will pass to 5. In this way a 2 vs. 1 situation is created (attacker 5 with the ball and attacker 4 on the left of key against the defender closest to the basket in the 1-3-1 zone set-up). (See Fig 215.)

1-4 Attacking Formation

The 1-4 attacking formation may be used with success against a 1-3-1 zone defence (see Fig 216 for players' display). An early pass is sent from 1 to 3. When 3 controls the ball, 5 cuts towards the basket and receives the ball. From here, 5 either plays 1 vs. 1 or can pass to 4, who cuts straight to the board in a 2 vs. 1 situation.

1-2-2 Attacking Formation

This is a very useful formation against a 2-1-2 zone defence. In Fig 217, player 3 will go to overload towards the left-hand side, benefiting from screens set up by 5 and then by 4. The ball gets to 3 after playmaker 1 passes to player 2 on the left wing.

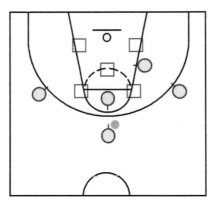

Fig 211 1-3-1 attacking formation against a 2-1-2 zone.

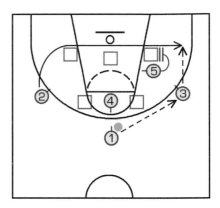

Fig 212 1-3-1 attacking formation against 2-3 zone (with an overload on the pivot's side).

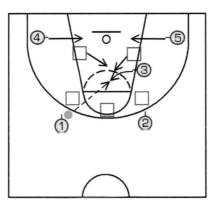

Fig 213 2-1-2 attacking formation against a 3-2 zone defence.

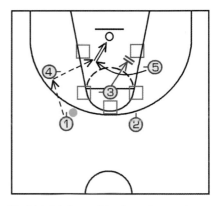

Fig 214 2-1-2 attacking formation against a 1-2-2 zone defence.

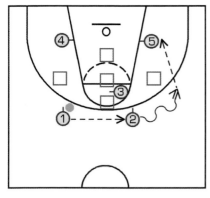

Fig 215 2-1-2 attacking formation against a 1-3-1 zone defence.

Fig 216 1-4 attacking formation against 1-3-1 zone defence.

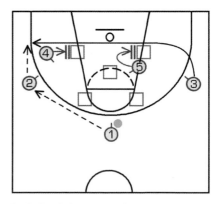

Fig 217 1-2-2 attacking formation against 2-1-2 zone defence.

Fig 218 4 vs. 4 drill (1-2-1 attacking formation against 2-2 zone set-up).

Fig 219 Positioning of the players for triangle passing drill.

Drills for Attacking a Zone

4 vs. 4

Four defenders play zone in a 2-2 formation against four attackers who use a 1-2-1 line-up as in Fig 218. All defenders are allowed to intercept or steal the ball and to block shots. Attackers are trying to create space by penetrating between defenders using 1-2 dribbles. Alternatively, if they do not have the ball, they should cut towards the basket or move into a space that is not covered by the defenders. The player close to the basket (player 4 on Fig 218) is free to run along the baseline to change his position from right to left and even to cut inside into the middle of the zone.

The drill runs for five possessions for the attackers and then the roles are changed. Keeping the score will identify the winning team.

Triangle Passing

This is one of the drills that could be used as preparation in order to learn how to attack the zone. In groups of three – as in Fig 219 – attackers are required to send quick and accurate passes in front of their teammate so that a quick shot may be taken. When receiving the ball, players threaten the basket, pretending to take a shot, and afterwards they keep passing.

As the drill progresses, after a couple of minutes passive defenders could be introduced and, later, active defenders. Without defenders, after counting five passes within each triangle, players 1 and 2 swap places. The changes could be as low-post and high-post movements.

Fastbreak Drills

Fastbreak drills (see page 103) can be rehearsed during the training session so that players get used to the idea that they need to apply it in a game situation against a zone defence.

Attacking a Combined Defence

Despite the fact that is not a very common type of defence, every attacking team should be aware of and prepared to play against a combined defence. A combined defence (or combination defence) is, essentially, a combination between man-to-man and zone defence. The two most common types of combined defence are 4 plus 1 – also called 'box and one' (four players playing in a 2-2 zone formation while the fifth player is playing man-to-man) (see Fig 220); or 3 plus 2 – also called 'triangle and two' (three players playing zone in a triangle formation while the other two are playing man-to-man) (see Fig 221). For more detail on combination defences, see page 132.

In both cases, attacking teams need to free any players that are closely man-to-man guarded. One of the most efficient ways of doing this is to set screens for the player(s) to use. Alternatively, the attackers need to react quickly and pass immediately when the closely guarded player is getting open using his own solutions, such as sudden changes of direction, cuts, fakes and so on.

Generally, all the fundamental techniques (individual and/or combinations between two or three players) used for offensive purposes are also applicable in the situation of attacking a combined defence. As is clear from Figs 220 and 221, 1-3-1 or 1-2-2 attacking formations may be successfully used against this type

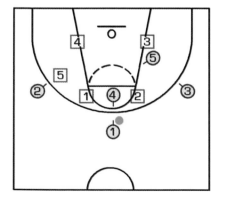

Fig 220 1-3-1 offence against 4 plus 1 (box and one) combined defence.

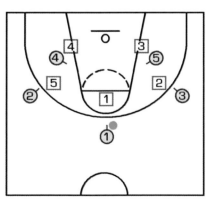

Fig 221 1-2-2 offence against 3 plus 2 (triangle and two) combined defence.

of defence. A well-prepared and patient offensive team may be able to work against the unfamiliar defence and still come away with a good shooting (and scoring) opportunity.

Fastbreak

Use

No matter what type of defence a team is playing (man-to-man, zone or combined defence), the fastbreak is one of the most effective ways to start an attacking situation, and an easy way consistently to score easy baskets. Basketball is a game of fast action and the fastbreak attack is the best medium for providing action and quick scores. Those easy baskets are produced by proper and efficient use of numerical superiority when switching from defence to offence. Teams cannot afford either to lose possession or not to score when using the fastbreak.

The fastbreak has a number of advantages:

- players will get into favourable positions to score lay-ups or easy baskets mainly because the defenders are not getting back in defence in time;
- most of the fastbreak drills are excellent conditioning for the team, so two objectives are achieved at the same time – practising the fastbreak and conditioning;
- it can be used against any type of defence (especially against a zone) and many of the skills learned to bring the ball up the court are transferable, depending on whether the opposite team is playing full-court or half-court pressure defence;
- it gives a team the chance to control the tempo of the game; and
- it makes every player a potential scorer.

It is worth noting that there are some disadvantages to the fastbreak:

- it is difficult to use when a team lacks players that are sufficiently skilled in handling the ball. This would lead to

an increased number of turnovers; and
- it takes (generally) valuable practice time.

Primary Break and Secondary Break

Running an effective fastbreak puts extreme pressure on the opponents, affecting their playing rhythm and forcing their coach to adjust the defence. Generally, the fastbreak is split into a primary break and a secondary break. If executed properly, the *primary fastbreak* should create offensive situations that will lead to a 1 vs. 1 play, 2 vs. 1 or 3 vs. 2 situations (and even 4 vs. 2 or 5 vs. 2). It leads to a numerical superiority within a short space of time (no more than 4 to 6 seconds after getting the possession), via the use of quick movement of the players (usually sprinting on offence), safe passing and, possibly, dribbling towards the basket.

A classic fastbreak will see a guard with the ball in the middle lane dribbling up the court, forwards and pivots filling the lanes, a trailer for extra support and one player in position (behind everyone else) to maintain safety (for defensive balance). For details of the 1 vs. 1, 2 vs. 1 and 3 vs.

2 situations, see pages 84–91. Despite the fact that they are rather rare, the 4 vs. 2 and 5 vs. 2 situations can also happen in a game during the primary break – the principles relating to 2 vs. 1 or 3 vs. 2 apply in these cases too. Constant repetition during training sessions will ensure that players become fluent in playing and in choosing the options available to them during the initial stages of the fastbreak.

If a primary-break situation is not sorted out quickly and efficiently by the attackers, or if the 1-2 defenders are playing good defence by succeeding in stopping the quick break, the *secondary break* begins. Most commonly, the secondary break starts when one of the players (Player 2 in Fig 222) who initiated the fastbreak dribbles the ball towards the baseline (usually forced by the good defence). This player will look for a pass inside because Player 4 (who arrives as a trailer) should enter the scoring area from the opposite side of the floor from where 1 and 2 are. Using a diagonal cut (also known as a 'first wave' cut), 4 will make himself available for a pass inside and for a potential lay-up on the move.

If this move is not successful (4's way to the basket is blocked by good defence and 2 cannot pass to him), a number of situations can develop:

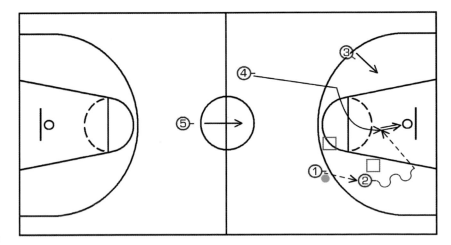

Fig 222 Secondary break: pass to a diagonal cut from opposite side (after a dribble towards the end line).

1 if he has not received the pass, player 4 keeps going and leaves the inside area open for player 3 to cut inside (this cut is also called the 'second wave') and to receive the ball for a potential lay-up (see Fig 223);

2 if both 4's and 3's moves (cuts) have been denied, 2 should reverse the ball to 1 who can then look on the left for a screen from 3 for 4 (or the other way round), which will free a teammate towards the basket (see Fig 224);

3 Player 1 will pass to 5 who arrives just outside the 3-points semicircle and goes to set a screen for 2, who will then cut inside the key and receive the ball from 5 (see Fig 225).

The secondary break will last for another 6 to 8 seconds after the primary break, so it is really important for attacking players to react quickly and to read the situation. Doing this will allow them to use cuts, quick passes or to dribble the ball so that a shooting opportunity will occur before the remaining defenders arrive back in defence. If all five defenders are back, this is the moment when the fastbreak (primary and secondary) will transform into positional play (set play).

Fastbreak Phases

In the world of basketball coaching it is generally agreed that there are three phases to a fastbreak:

1 getting into possession of the ball and making the first pass/dribble out;
2 moving the ball up the court; and
3 passing the ball to a position for a shot.

Getting into Possession of the Ball and Making the First Pass/Dribble Out

During the game, possession can be obtained as a consequence of a number of following situations:

- a rebound after a 1-point, 2-points or 3-points shot;
- an interception;
- a steal;
- out-of-bounds possession from anywhere outside the court: behind the team's own end line following a basket received; from the side lines and behind the other end line after a violation by the opponents or as a consequence of a jump ball and alternating arrow possession rule.

Once possession has been gained, the attacking team will immediately try to move the ball to the front court. This team has several options; their choice depends on the situation in which the possession occurred:

- if the team gets the defensive rebound, the player with the ball needs to send a pass away from the congested area in front of basket – most of the time, this pass is an outlet pass at a 45-degree angle towards the side line (the free-throw line extended);
- powerful dribbling is an option when the rebounder has no player to whom he can pass. Two to three dribbles should be enough to move away from the crowded 3-seconds space;
- the easiest way to fastbreak the opposition is to have one player sprinting down the court and to have the rebounder passing straight to this man (usually a javelin pass or an over-the-head pass);
- in the case of side-line possession, attackers should aim to get open towards the opposite basket as soon as the inbounder receives the ball from the referee to put the ball back in play.

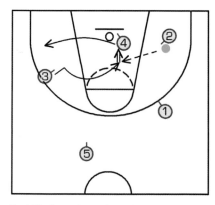

Fig 223 'Second wave' cut during a secondary break.

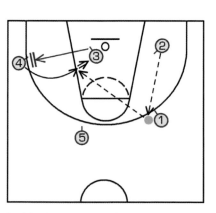

Fig 224 Another option for the secondary break: pass from the top to the opposite side after a screen is set.

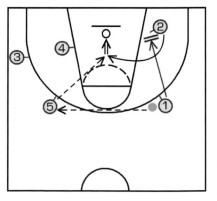

Fig 225 Lateral pass from the playmaker and then screen away as one of the last options for a secondary break.

Moving the Ball Up the Court

Once the ball is on its way to the opposition's court and the break is launched, at least two or three attackers should run fast, forward, so that they can get ahead of the ball line to support the ball carrier and to create that much-needed numerical superiority.

Sometimes it is possible for the person receiving the outlet pass or even for the rebounder to dribble the ball all the way down to the opposition's basket and to take an uncontested lay-up (especially if the defenders are slow in getting back to their positions). Being able to pass safely on the move is a major requirement for a successful fastbreak. Players should think about filling the lanes as the ball is moved (dribbled or passed) towards the opposite basket. After going over the half-way line, the ball should be in the middle lane – from here, the player has the option to pass to the left or to the right to teammates who are cutting straight to the basket.

Passing the Ball to a Position for a Shot

While in possession and dribbling the ball in the middle lane, the ball handler should aim to go all the way to the opposition's basket for an easy lay-up. If the defenders are on his path, the player should go to the free-throw line, where there are two major options for him. He can perform either a jump shot or a pass (right or left) to a teammate who is cutting straight to the basket (see Fig 191, page 87), in order to take a lay-up, or a jump shot from a good position (close to the basket).

Common Mistakes during Fastbreak

• The team using the fastbreak moving the ball down the court too fast, with the risk of losing control.
• Players jumping to pass (and committing a travelling violation).
• Teammates passing to a player who is closely guarded.
• Players failing to decide what to do with the ball when close to the

basket (whether to stop for a jump shot or go all the way for a lay-up).
• Teammates passing the ball behind a player as he runs forward (instead of passing in front of the player so that he can run into the ball).
• Excessive dribbling when bringing the ball down the court.
• Players running slowly instead of sprinting.

Coaching Points

• Keep the head up all the time when in possession to spot the best-placed teammate (open man) and to read the situation correctly.
• Always pass ahead to a running player.
• Always fill the lanes and have one player for defensive purposes, usually the last trailer.
• Space out when filling the lanes – at least 3–4m apart.
• Use a chest pass as much as possible when on a fastbreak.
• Keep the ball in the middle lane in order to move it up the court.
• Use the 'player ahead' principle – after a pass, the player should move ahead towards the opposite basket looking for a return pass.

Drills for the Fastbreak

Together with the drills relating to the primary break (2 vs. 1, 3 vs. 2, 1 vs. 1), the following drills are very useful in teaching the basic principles of the fastbreak, as well as being very good for conditioning players.

Passes between Three Without Changing Places

See page 43 for a description of the drill and see Fig 40 for a diagrammatic representation.

The drill is progressed by each group of three running the drill for three lengths, continuously. Afterwards, one defender is introduced so they play 3 vs. 1.

Three-Man Weave

This drill involves passes between three players with the added difficulty of changing places. See Fig 41 for a description.

Fastbreak Drill in Pairs (Long Pass Break)

In pairs, each pair with a ball. The player with the ball – Player 1 in Fig 226 overleaf – takes a free throw while his partner (Player 2) waits at a 45-degree angle (free-throw line extended) close to the side line (without touching it). After the free throw, Player 1 has two options:

1 if the basket is good, 1 will get the ball out of bounds and will inbound the ball to teammate 2;
2 if the basket is not good, 1 will quickly go to get the rebound, will pivot to face 2 and will pass to him. After the pass, 1 will run as shown in Fig 226 overleaf towards the other basket and will receive a pass from 2 in the central area of the court (over the half-way line) for a fastbreak. After catching the ball in two hands, 1 will dribble and take a lay-up. After the shot, 1 will continue his run, this time towards the basket he initially took the free throw at. His run will be in the shape of a letter 'C', almost touching the side line before turning his head back to see the pass that is coming from 2. (After his first pass, Player 2 follows the pass and the man with the intention of getting the rebound.) If the basket is good, 2 will quickly inbound with a long pass – ideally over the half-way line – for 1 who runs on the fastbreak. (In the case of a miss, 2 will pick up the ball and pass to 1 on fastbreak.) The same pattern follows: 1 dribbles for a lay-up after catching the ball while 2 follows his own pass in order to get the rebound (preferably before the ball touches the ground).

After this, players change roles and join different queues. Player 2 takes a free throw, while 1 waits ready for an outlet pass.

After five free throws each, the receiving group (players in the queue waiting for the

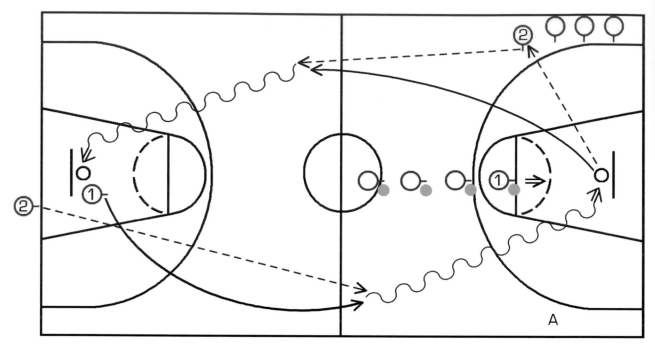

Fig 226 Fastbreak drill in twos (long pass break).

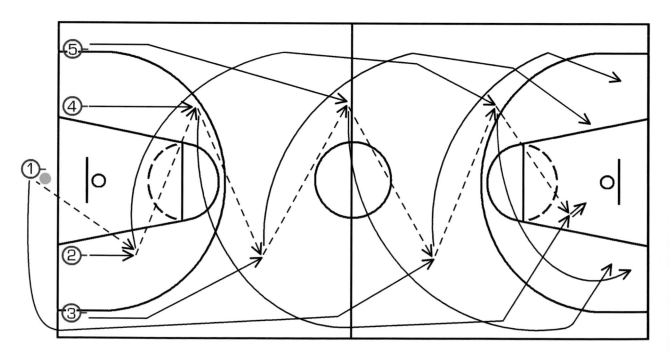

Fig 227 Five-man weave.

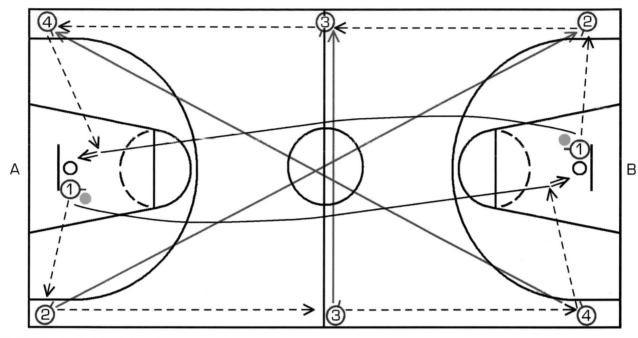

Fig 228 Fastbreak drill with four players.

outlet pass) will go on the other side of court – Point A in Fig 226 – and the drill will run for a left-hand dribble and lay-up.

3 vs. 2 All the Time
This eleven-player continuous fastbreak drill is shown in Fig 192.

Five-Man Weave
This is a variation of the three-man weave drill that requires careful attention, thought and accurate passing. Groups of five players are lined up along the baseline, as in Fig 227. The player in the middle lane (Player 1) has the ball and passes to the closest teammate (probably 2), then cuts behind two players (2 and 3) to the side of the pass. After receiv-

ing the ball, Player 2 will pass to Player 4 and then cut behind Players 4 and 5. This pattern continues to the opposite basket for a lay-up.

Fastbreak Drill with Four Players
Players are in groups of four, each group with a ball, positioned as in Fig 228. Player 1 starts the drill with a pass to Player 2 at the corner of the court (outlet pass) and then runs towards the opposite basket. Player 2 passes to 3 at the half-way line and then runs across the court to the opposite corner – as in Fig 228. Player 3 passes the ball to 4 and then runs to the other side line of the basketball court at the half-way line. Player 4 passes to 1, who is now cutting to the basket and then runs

across the court to the opposite corner. When he receives the ball from 4, Player 1 takes a lay-up (no dribble), then he gets his own rebound and continues the drill with a pass to Player 2, who is now waiting on the corner to the right of the basket. The drill continues with 1 running and receiving the ball for a lay-up after 2 passes to 3, 3 passes to 4 and then 4 passes to 1. Player 1 runs ten lengths (ten lay-ups) and then he replaces Player 2; 2 replaces 3, 3 replaces 4 and 4 becomes 1 (the player running and taking lay-ups). Eventually, everyone will run ten lengths.

Later, players can change the direction of the drill, going clockwise (with the first outlet pass to the left), so that they are forced to take lay-ups with their left hand.

PART III

DEFENCE – SKILLS, TECHNIQUES AND TACTICS

CHAPTER 8

INDIVIDUAL PLAYER DEFENCE

Basketball is a game in which all five players on the court need to contribute to both offensive and defensive moments. Naturally, many players prefer to attack (to dribble or to shoot the ball) instead of working hard on drills that will improve their defensive ability and skills. Much attention is given to scoring points, particularly by the media covering the game at the higher levels, and this can cause problems between coaches and players. Coaches need to convince their team members of the importance of defence. Many coaches subscribe to the theory that 'good defences win matches' and in recent years there has been a growth in the number of teams playing really effectively in defence. The ability of each individual player to play well in defence is vital to any team's success.

Irrespective of the type of defence played by a team, an individual player should take into consideration some basic *defensive principles*, which should be applied during the game:

- aim to gain possession of the ball without giving up the score; discourage and prevent the opponents from taking easy shots from your own danger area;
- put pressure on the ball by marking/guarding closely the ball and any potential receivers, anticipate passes or players cutting (using dribbling or not);
- communication in defence is fundamental and is key to successful cooperation of team members in order to stop the attacking team from scoring and in order to obtain possession;
- match opponents according to ability, size/height and floor formation;
- a quick transition game – changing from attack to defence – has clear

benefits for the defending team in terms of preventing the opponents from gaining numerical or positional advantage and starting a fastbreak;

- the position of the defender in relation to the attacker he is guarding is essential – all the time the defender should position himself on the imaginary line between the attacking player he is marking and his own basket (see Fig 229).

Basic Defensive Technique

Defensive Stance
The defence begins when possession of the ball is lost and this is the moment when all defenders should adopt the proper defensive stance (unless they are sprinting back in defence, closely guarding an opponent). The defensive stance is the

Fig 229 GB centre Pops Mensah-Bonsu (number 7 in white jersey) demonstrates good positioning in defence, having positioned himself on the imaginary line between the attacker and his own basket.

Fig 230 GB forward Joel Freeland (number 11 in white jersey) adopts the correct stance while playing defence.

common athletic ready position, similar to those seen in other sports such as tennis (for example, when receiving the service), football (the goalkeeper getting ready for a free kick) or volleyball (the players' position when receiving a serve). In basketball this position enables the defender to respond quickly to any challenge from the opposition (attacking team) and to adjust his position in relation to the ball, direct player, other attackers, his own team-mates, and his own basket.

When applying a basic defensive technique (adopting a proper defensive stance) the defender should be well balanced, with knees bent, feet spread approximately shoulder-width apart (up on the balls of the feet). The head is up and the arms are raised and extended in order to prevent a

pass, block a shot or steal the ball from an opponent's dribble. See Fig 230.

From this fundamental defensive position the defender can move to maintain the same distance in relation to the direct opponent. He uses what is called *defensive footwork* – a sliding action of the feet from side to side, with the feet not meeting or crossing, while keeping low centre of gravity. The defender needs to use his arms to distract the attacker in his efforts to shoot, pass or dribble the ball (see Fig 231). With the arms out the defender seems bigger and passes can be intercepted more easily. Coaches often encourage players learning how to play defence to 'make themselves big'.

In turning to the side, the player pivots on the opposite foot – for example, if a

Fig 231 GB forward Joel Freeland (number 11 in white jersey) tries to distract the attacker's efforts to shoot the ball by having his arms fully extended upwards.

Fig 232 The defender is moving towards the left at the same time as the attacker.

Fig 233 The attacker is changing direction – this is when the defender starts pivoting on the left foot.

Fig 234 The defender moves in the new direction (towards the right).

defender is moving towards the left and suddenly needs to change direction and turn to the right (to stay with the direct attacking player), he pivots on the ball of the left foot and resumes sliding to the right (see Figs 232, 233 and 234).

Defensive Situations

When teaching players how to play defence, the coach needs to emphasize that there are two important scenarios: defending an attacking player without the ball and defending one with the ball. When defending an attacker without the ball, the defender needs to adjust his stance so that he can see – using his peripheral view – the ball and the opponent he is guarding at the same time. Using arms to point at the ball and at the direct player can be very useful, especially with beginner players (see Fig 235).

Every time the ball moves, the defender needs to move. It is advisable for a defender in this situation to step back one or two steps to anticipate and to cover any fakes and/or cuts. Also, the defender needs to be alert to avoid a screen.

The second scenario – defending an attacker with the ball – presents three potential situations that need to be treated differently by the defender: an attacker with the ball who did not dribble; an attacker who dribbles; and an attacker who has just finished dribbling.

Defending an Attacker with the Ball Who did not Dribble

In this case the defender should be one extended arm and a half away from the attacker, on the imaginary line between his own basket and the player, adopting the basic defensive stance (see Fig 236). The defender needs to concentrate hard and beware of fakes and drives, at the same time remembering all the triple threat options that are available to the attacker (pass, shoot or dribble).

Defending an Attacker Who Dribbles

Using defensive footwork or even running, the defender tries to maintain the same distance without allowing the attacker to overtake him (or to go under the basket area) (see Fig 237). Ideally, the defender should direct the attacker so that he is using his weakest hand when dribbling.

Defending an Attacker Who has just Finished Dribbling

Once he has finished dribbling, the attacker has only two options left: to pass or to shoot. This is the moment when the defender can put extra pressure on the attacker by getting really close to him (less than half an extended arm's length), and with both arms out wide open, in the hope of forcing the attacker to send a wrong pass, take a hasty shot or commit a 5-seconds violation (see Fig 238).

Common Mistakes

- Defender's legs not flexed and the defender failing to adopt a low position.
- Defender crossing the legs when moving.
- Loss of balance.
- Excessive use of arms, which come in contact with the attacker, leading to a foul.
- The defender jumping upwards when using defensive footwork (when moving backwards or sideways), instead of using sliding movements.

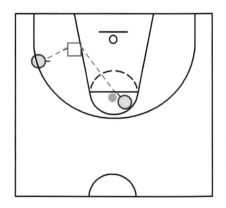

Fig 235 The defender uses his arms to point towards the player he is guarding and to the ball.

TOP LEFT: Fig 236 GB guard Jarrett Hart (number 4 in white jersey) defends a player who did not dribble.

TOP RIGHT: Fig 237 GB guard Jarrett Hart (number 4 in white jersey) defends a player who dribbles.

Fig 238 GB forward Megan Moody (number 14 in white jersey) puts pressure on the attacker who has just finished dribbling.

Coaching Points

• Keep the head up, knees bent, arms out.
• Feet should be shoulder-width apart (on their toes).
• Do not jump when moving in defence – use sliding movements.

Drills

Basic Defensive Stance Drill

The whole group of players is lined up at one end of the court in two rows, as in Fig 239. At the coach's signal, the players start jogging forwards. On a whistle, they perform a jump-stop landing and adopt the basic defensive stance. The coach corrects any players who are not adopting a correct defensive position. Players repeat the same thing at the first free-throw line, the central line, the second free-throw line and the end line – Points A, B, C and D on Fig 239.

Defensive Stance – Circle Formation

In a circle formation, players run on the spot with knees and heels high. On the whistle they stop and adopt the basic defensive stance. After any corrections, players repeat the drill responding to the coach's signals.

Defensive Slides

Players are split into two groups and individually, one at a time, perform defensive slides in a zig-zag manner, following a pattern as in Fig 141. The court is split into two parts along its length. Players need to change direction (by pivoting on the

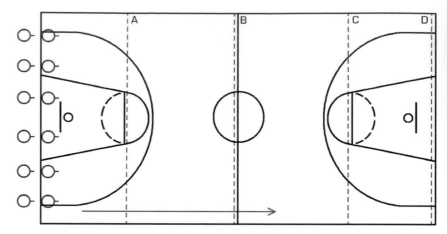

Fig 239 Basic defensive stance drill.

balls of their feet) when touching the side line with their foot or when reaching the imaginary line between the two baskets.

1 vs. 1 with No Ball

The attacker jogs following a zig-zag pattern, without trying to beat the defender (to overtake him), while the defender, using defensive slides, tries to maintain the same distance and the same position – all the time between the man and his own basket. On the way back, the players change roles.

1 vs. 1 Attacker vs. Defender with Ball

This is the same as the previous drill, except that the attacker has a ball and dribbles, but without trying to beat the defender. He simply dribbles in a zig-zag manner towards the opposite basket so that the defender can learn the technique properly – exactly as in Fig 197.

1 vs. 1 Play (as in a Match Situation)

As previous drill, but this time both players are active. The attacker tries to go past the defender in order to go and score while the defender tries to stop the attacker and steal the ball using defensive slides.

The 'Z' Drill (Sprint and Defensive Slides)

Players line up at Point A on the court, as shown on Fig 240. One at a time, they go from Point A to Point B (towards their right) using defensive slides; from B to C they run as fast as they can (sprint), then from C to D they use defensive slides; from D to E they sprint again and from E to F they perform defensive slides again. The drill finishes when the player reaches Point F – coaches should ask players to finish right on point F and not half-way through between E and F. When Player 1 is close to Point B, Player 2 starts his turn.

Interception

Description

Quite often, possession is obtained as a consequence of an interception. This is a defensive skill that requires anticipation, good footwork, quick reactions when the opportunity arises (see Fig 241) and quick decision-making (see Fig 242). Good defenders are usually good at intercepting the ball because they use their anticipation skills to see when the attackers have failed to send a safe pass.

Sometimes, a defender will fail in an attempt to intercept a pass and find himself in a poor defensive position. His teammates should then switch men quickly by guarding the attacker with the ball. At the same time, the player who is out of position should recover as quickly as possible and run back in defence to help his teammates.

TOP TIP

When playing defence always position yourself on the imaginary line between your man (the attacker you are guarding) and your own basket. And remember – do not jump when using defensive slides. If the attacker moves, you need to move too, especially if he is going towards your basket or sideways.

Common Mistakes

- Slow movement going towards the attacker and intercepting the ball.
- Defenders finding they have lost a good defensive position after attempting to intercept the ball.
- Teammates failing to cover if the interception does not work and if the defender is in a poor defensive position.
- After committing himself for an interception, the player not being able to regain balance immediately and running into the attacker – this will lead to a personal foul.

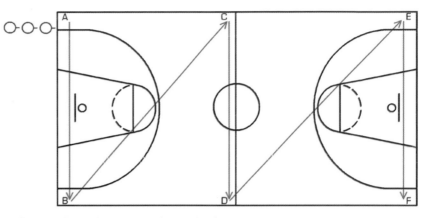

Fig 240 The 'Z' drill (sprint and defensive slides).

Coaching Points

- Always make sure that you can see both your man and the ball when playing defence – this will help you to make a good decision when attempting to intercept the ball.
- Use your anticipation to predetermine an offensive pattern (including a pass that will be sent to your man).
- Be alert all the time when on defence.

- Be on your toes for a quick movement.

Drills

Interception Drill in Threes

In groups of three two attackers against one defender, as shown in Fig 243 overleaf. Attacker 1 passes to his teammate 2 who is guarded by Defender 1 and who

will try to intercept the ball. If the ball is intercepted or gets to Attacker 2, the drill is restarted. After five possessions, the players change round so that everyone has a chance to rehearse intercepting the ball.

2 vs. 2 (or 3 vs. 3) with No Dribble

On the half court, groups of players (2 vs. 2 or 3 vs. 3) play a passing game without dribbling and without shooting – all other rules apply (travelling, 5-seconds rule, and

Fig 241 The defender sees the opportunity for an interception.

Fig 242 The defender makes a quick decision and steps forwards to intercept the ball.

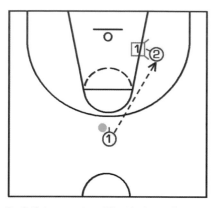

Fig 243 Interception drill with three players.

so on). This is a passing game in which defenders try to intercept the ball and to play good defence by guarding their men closely.

Stealing the Ball

Description and Use
Exactly as the name implies, stealing the ball is an action performed by a defender in order to take the ball from an attacker against the attacker's will – using legal

means. A defender can steal the ball from an attacker who is holding the ball in his hands – as in Figs 244, 245 and 246 – or he can steal the ball while the attacker is dribbling (see Figs 247, 248 and 249).

In order to steal the ball from someone's hands/possession, a defender needs to place two hands on the ball that is being held by the attacker and snatch it with a quick movement. This is a very effective move against the pivots, for example, because they sometimes have the bad habit of bringing the ball low after rebounding (instead of protecting it by keeping it above shoulder height). Similarly, coaches do not recommend that the big players dribble the ball, especially in the 3-seconds space and when they do not need to. This is a favourable moment for stealing the ball, mainly because some of the post players move slowly. When the dribbler pushes the ball forward, the defender, from a low defensive position, can suddenly squeeze between the ball handler and the ball.

Other players who might offer an easy steal are those showing off their ball-handling skills (dribbling in particular), who may leave the ball unprotected for a fraction of a second. Similarly, players who are dribbling high, or those who dribble in front of their body without protecting the

ball, expose themselves to defenders who are good at stealing. To steal the ball in this situation, the defender places his hand where the ball will bounce off after hitting the floor; from here, he can deflect it away or get in possession by dribbling.

Defending an attacking player with the ball is a pretty challenging task but with hard work and perseverance it can be mastered. It is a skill that is easily applicable in a game situation, for the benefit of the whole team.

Common Mistakes

- When trying to steal the ball from an opponent's hands, the defender

Fig 244 The defender gets ready to place her hands on the ball held by the attacker.

Fig 245 The defender has both hands on the ball and starts snatching it away.

Fig 246 The defender has stolen the ball and is ready to move away.

Fig 247 The attacker dribbles while a defender comes from behind to steal the ball.

Fig 248 The defender steals the ball by dribbling it.

Fig 249 The defender (who is now the attacking player) dribbles away.

grabs one of the attacker's arms – leading to a personal foul.

- When stealing from the dribble, the defender 'reaches in' – he gets too close to the attacker and cannot avoid contact with him. This also leads to a personal foul.
- Defender timing his move poorly with the attacker's moves.

Coaching Points

- Maintain a good defensive position (basic defensive stance) in front of the ball handler.
- React quickly when the ball handler brings the ball in front of him – that is an opportunity to steal the ball.
- Use your judgement and anticipation, and be determined when you want to steal the ball. If you decide to steal, go for it, and do not change your mind in the middle of the action.

Blocking Shots

Description and Use

One of the most popular defensive techniques, which is much enjoyed by both players and spectators, is blocking an opponent's shot (see Fig 250 overleaf). In order to do this, the defender who intends to block a shot needs to watch the ball and

the attacker's moves very carefully. If the defender sees the attacker at the beginning of a jump, as if he is going upwards for a jump shot (see Fig 251 overleaf), he can step forwards and try to slap the ball on its way up with his palm, leaving the arm extended (see Fig 252 overleaf). He does need to be careful though; if the technique is executed incorrectly, he can commit a foul (if he slaps the opponent's arm, for example); if he jumps after the attacker fakes a shot, he can be beaten on the dribble (the ball handler will dribble past the defender on the way to the basket).

Good timing is the secret for a clean block shot – the defender needs to synchronize his moves with the moment when the attacker releases the ball towards the basket. Sometimes the defender fails to block the shot. However, his effort might not be in vain because the simple fact of getting his hand close to the ball may be sufficiently distracting to make the opponent alter the shot.

Common Mistakes

- The defender having one arm on the attacker (on the shoulder, the back, and so on) while the other arm is blocking the shot.
- Defenders bringing their arm downwards when blocking a shot, getting in contact with parts of the attacker's body (head, shoulder, shooting

hand), leading to personal fouls and free throws.

- The defender jumping directly at the shooter.
- The defender going for the shooter's shot fake, jumping and then landing on the shooter – leading to a foul.

Coaching Points

- Try to block the shot as high as possible (jump high vertically and fully extend your arm).
- Aim to block the shot as soon as the attacker starts the shooting action (as the ball is leaving the attacker's hands).
- When in defence be on your toes so that you can react (jump) quickly.

Drills

1 vs. 1

In pairs in front of a basket, one attacker with the ball against a defender. The

---

TOP TIP

'The idea is not to block every shot. The idea is to make your opponent believe that you might block every shot.' Bill Russell

Fig 250 GB centre Pops Mensah-Bonsu gets his shot blocked by an Israeli defender.

Fig 251 The defender sees the opportunity to block a shot (the attacker is at the beginning of the shot) and jumps upwards.

Fig 252 The defender slaps the ball with her palm, blocking the shot.

attacker takes a shot and deliberately allows the defender to block his shot so that he (the defender) gets a feel for the blocking action. After five or ten actions each, the attacker becomes a defender, and the drill is repeated.

1 vs. 1 Shooting in Pairs

The defender aims to block every shot that the attacker is taking. To make the drill more challenging, the attacker is allowed to use one dribble if he prefers and also to use shooting fakes. After five possessions players change roles. The player with the higher number of blocked shots wins.

Fig 253 GB forward Kimberly Butler (number 11 in white jersey) blocks out her direct opponent.

Blocking Out Defensively (Boxing Out)

Description and Use

Blocking out (or boxing out) is an individual defensive skill that enables the defender to obtain an advantageous position in relation to his opponent, by placing his body between the attacker and his own backboard each time a shot is taken (see Fig 253). The main aim of this move is to facilitate easy access towards the ball, which will lead to a defensive rebound. In order to perform the box-out movement, the defender will first need to identify the position of the direct player he is guarding at the moment when a shot is taken (Fig 254), and see if that player is cutting towards the basket or not. In either case, the defender will pivot 180 degrees into the path of the opponent (as in Fig 255), so that the defender is facing his own basket and has the attacker behind his

Fig 254 The defender has seen the attacker taking a shot.

Fig 255 The defender pivots into the path of the opponent.

Fig 256 The defender is facing his own basket and has the attacker behind his back – having the knees bent and feet wide when boxing out gives him a solid stance.

> **TOP TIP**
>
> Blocking-out action is the first stage in rebounding and for this reason the two defensive skills are learned and practised together. The defender will box out first, maintain the blocking position for 2 to 3 seconds maximum and then jump powerfully to get the rebound.

back. With knees bent and feet wide, the defensive player who is boxing out will have a strong, solid stance (see Fig 256). From this position (blocking out the opponent) the defender will go strongly to the basket to rebound if a shot is taken.

Common Mistakes

- Excessive use of hands by the defender while boxing out – this will lead to a personal foul.
- Defenders do not concentrate and do not step in (or pivot) to box out the opponent.

Coaching Points

- Adopting a good, powerful stance (feet more than shoulder-width apart, knees slightly bent) is necessary to block and stop the attacking player with the body.
- Use peripheral vision to see the position of the other players (teammates and opponents) on the court.
- Box out first and then go to get the rebound.

Drills

Free-Throw Shots, Box Out and Rebounding

In groups of six players – three attackers and three defenders – one attacker shoots a free throw while the other players occupy positions around the key, exactly as in a game situation. After the ball is released by attacker 1, defender 1 will box out attacker 3, defender 3 will box out attacker 2 while defender 2 will go and box out the free-throw shooter (see Figs 257 and 258). All the defenders will go to get the rebound after the blocking-out situation.

Each attacker will shoot five free throws and then change roles with defenders. An element of competition (who can get the most rebounds) will make this drill more interesting to the players.

Jump Shots, Boxing Out and Rebounding in Pairs

In pairs (one attacker, one defender), one ball per pair as in Fig 259. Attacker 1 will take a jump shot; defender 1 will box out and then both will go to get the rebound. Once the area under the basket is clear (the ball is rebounded by Player 1), attacker 2 and defender 2 will do the same, as will attacker 3 and defender 3 afterwards. The attackers get five shots each, then change roles with the defenders. The aim is to see who gets the most rebounds.

After five shots each, players swap positions on the court in the following way: Player 1 replaces Player 2, Player 2 goes to shoot where Player 3 was and Player 3 replaces Player 1.

1 vs. 1, 2 vs. 2 and 3 vs. 3 with Boxing Out

1 vs. 1, 2 vs. 2 or 3 vs. 3 play on the half-court, as if in a normal game with a boxing-out action to be carried out each time a shot is taken. The drill may be also performed as a 5 vs. 5 game at one basket, with defenders attempting to box out each time a shot is taken.

Rebounding

Description and Use

There are many shots missed during a basketball game, so it is really important for the defending team to make every effort to regain possession of the ball. One way to achieve this is by defensive rebounding. Many of the fundamental principles relating

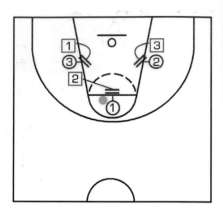

Fig 257 Positioning of the players for a free throw.

to jumping and offensive rebounding; (see page 73) are applicable when attempting to get rebounds while on defence. The player should adopt a well-balanced position with feet shoulder-width apart (on the balls of the feet), knees slightly bent and ready for the extension move, and hands and arms ready at shoulder height, with fingers spread wide and pointing upwards. They need to have good timing in order to reach the ball at the top of the jump, keeping an eye on the ball's flight.

After securing the ball in the air – preferably with both hands (see Fig 260 on page 120) – the defender should land with his feet wide, in a good, well-balanced position. Protection of the ball (bringing it with both hands to chest height) should be a major concern for the rebounder, especially because the opponents will also try to get the rebound. He should be looking for a quick outlet pass to any of his teammates (preferably the guard/playmaker) as a priority. If this is not possible, a dribble out from the crowded area under the basket may also be a good solution, which could lead to a fastbreak and a quick easy scoring opportunity.

There are situations during the game when one of the most efficient ways to secure the rebound is to box out (block out) first and then to go for the rebound. The defender needs to be aware where his own man (the attacker he is guarding)

Fig 258 The defenders have boxed out each of the attackers after the free throw

is on the court (or, as is the case with zone defence, the attacker or attackers in the area that he is covering), as this will lead to a successful box-out action first. Experienced players will develop a 'feel' for this action – they will not necessarily watch where the direct man is, but will naturally have an appreciation for his position and will box him out, while at the same time keeping an eye on the ball. One of the most desirable situations is to have all five defenders boxing out – in this way none of the attackers will be able to enter the danger area under the basket to rebound the ball.

Common Mistakes

- Most beginners will watch the ball or the player taking a shot and will not move or react to this.

- Waiting for the ball instead of jumping.
- Some players rebound the ball with their arms bent (instead of fully extended).
- Bad timing – jumping too early or too late.
- Incorrect appreciation of the ball's flight.

Coaching Points

- Do not jump until the ball has left the ring or backboard.
- Keep an eye on the ball while it is in the air.
- Try to see where your teammates are before and after the rebounding action for a quick outlet pass.
- Fully extend your arms when you get the rebound and have the fingers spread wide.

- When landing, land on both feet and keep the feet shoulder-width apart for good balance.

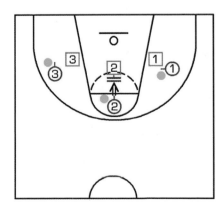

Fig 259 Drill practising jump shots, boxing out and rebounding in pairs.

Fig 260 GB forward Andrew Sullivan uses both hands to rebound the ball.

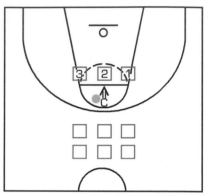

Fig 261 Shooting and rebounding drill in threes.

- Time your jump in relation to the flight of the ball.
- Put two hands on the ball and protect it as soon as you land.

Drills

All the drills related to jumping, offensive rebounding and blocking out (see pages 73 and 119) are useful for learning and rehearsing the defensive rebound.

The *shooting and rebounding drill* is another option. Players are divided into groups of three and are positioned in the 3-seconds space facing the coach, who is at the top of the key with a ball in his hands (see Fig 261). The coach shoots the ball and after the ball has left his hands the players turn around by pivoting and go to get the rebound. One point is awarded each time a player gets the rebound. For each group the coach shoots three times; after each shot the players change places between themselves before the coach shoots again (1 replaces 2, 2 replaces 3 and 3 replaces 1, and so on, after each shot).

CHAPTER 9

DEFENSIVE COMBINATIONS BETWEEN TWO AND THREE PLAYERS

Help Defence

Description and Use

The first consideration for each defender is to stop his man from scoring but he must also stay alert to help cover any attacker who might become more dangerous than his own man. Shifts (using defensive slides) are made only when necessary and the shift back to the original man should be made as soon as it is safe to make it. A man-to-man defence can be strengthened significantly when some defenders provide extra help in the middle of the court. Fig 262 shows an initial offensive set-up, with two pivots, two forwards and a playmaker (with the ball) and a man-to-man defence. When the ball gets to attacker 5 in the corner (after 1 passes to 2 and then 2 to 5), as in Fig 263, defenders 1, 3 and 4 are more effective if they move into the middle of the 3-seconds space (in front of the

basket). Now the court can be divided into the *strong side*, or 'ball side' (the half where the ball is), and the *weak side* (the half where the ball is not located).

As a consequence of defenders 1, 3 and 4 moving into the strong side, there are five defensive players in this area and only three attackers (1, 2 and 5), so the chances for the defenders to 'capture' the ball are increased. And even in the case of a long pass from attacker 5 to 3 or 4, there is a reasonable chance that the ball will be underthrown and intercepted, or overthrown and go out of bounds. Assuming the pass reaches attacker 3 (or 4), the defence has plenty of time to recover.

Having defenders 1, 3 and 4 playing help-side defence, the defensive team is able entirely to block the area under the basket and is in a dominating rebounding position as well. Help-side defenders can use this guide to position themselves on the court: the help-side defender,

the player he is guarding and the player with the ball form a shallow triangle, with the help-side defender in the paint. For example, in Fig 264 attacker 1 has the ball and defender 2 is guarding attacker 2 by moving into the point, forming in this way a shallow triangle with attackers 1 and 2.

In the example (see Fig 264), defender 2 has another responsibility on top of moving on to the strong side and 'filling in' the area. If Player 1 dribbles past his defender (defender 1), then defender 2 – who is playing help-side defence in a proper shallow-triangle position – will step forwards to stop attacker 1 dribbling all the way to the basket (see Fig 265 overleaf).

Defender 1 can also make himself useful by shouting 'help' so that defender 2 reacts quickly and – equally importantly – can retreat quickly to take over defender 2's place. This will enable him to anticipate and prevent a potential pass from attacker 1 to attacker 2 (see Fig 266 overleaf).

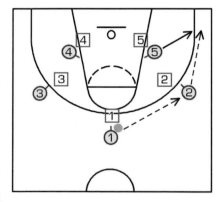

Fig 262 Man-to-man defence against an offensive set-up with two pivots, two forwards and a playmaker.

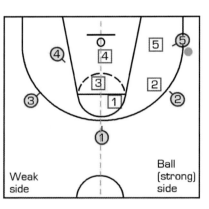

Fig 263 Defenders 1, 3 and 4 play help defence on the strong side.

Fig 264 Defender 2 is playing defence in the shallow-triangle position.

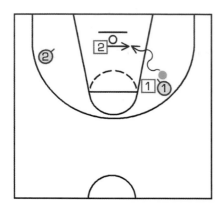

Fig 265 Defender 2 is playing help defence (helping teammate 1).

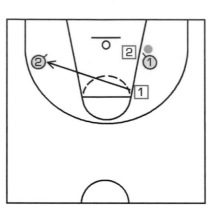

Fig 266 Defender 1 helps teammate 2 who has played help defence.

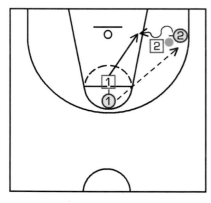

Fig 267 2 vs. 2 – help defence rehearsal drill.

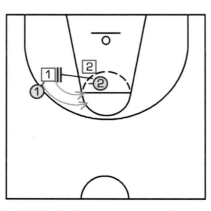

Fig 268 Defending against a screen by going 'over the top'.

- Have your arms wide and held up when helping out.

Drills

2 vs. 2 – Help Defence Rehearsal

2 vs. 2 drill on the half-court in front of a basket. After attacker 1 passes the ball to 2, defender 2 will deliberately let attacker 2 dribble around him along the baseline – this is when defender 1 will move across and leave his initial position to prevent attacker 2 from scoring an uncontested lay-up (see Fig 267). After five possessions for the attackers, the players change roles – attackers become defenders and follow the same pattern.

3 vs. 3, 4 vs. 4 and 5 vs. 5

Following a similar pattern to the first drill, help defence can be rehearsed using 3 vs. 3, 4 vs, 4 and/or 5 vs. 5 formations. Initially, one of the defenders will allow his direct attacker to dribble past him, but after five possessions (or after 5 to 10 minutes) all defenders can play actively as if in a game situation (without allowing anyone to dribble inside).

Defence against Screens (Switching Man in Defence)

Description and Use

Every defensive man must be alert to the possibility of a screen being used against him whenever the man he is guarding is in a position where a screen might make him an immediate scoring threat. Any time an offensive player sets a screen, the defence must talk to one another – the man guarding the screener must always clearly warn a teammate of a potential screen. Defending a screen will depend upon the verbal warnings given by the teammate marking the player setting the screen – they might use terms such as 'screen left', 'watch the pick', 'slide, slide', 'switch', and so on.

A lack of communication results in confusion and missed assignments, which may result in uncontested shots for the offence.

Common Mistakes

- Players on the weak side failing to move (or moving slowly) into the strong side to offer their support to defenders in this area.
- When beaten by an attacking player, defenders failing to shout 'help' to alert the closest defenders about the newly created situation.
- Once they have moved into a help-side position, defenders failing to move back on time to guard their man if the ball is returned to these attackers.

- Lack of communication between defenders.

Coaching Points

- Always talk in defence and ask for help if necessary.
- When moving into a help-side defence position, the defender must be able to see both his offensive player and the ball without turning his head from side to side (using his peripheral view).

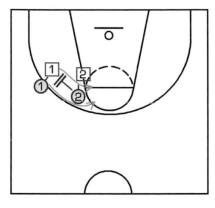

Fig 269 Defending against a screen by sliding.

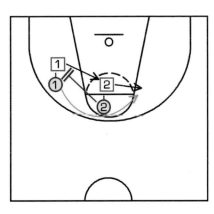

Fig 270 Defending against a screen by switching men.

3 vs. 3 at One Basket

3 vs. 3 play on the half-court with the main focus being on switching men when the screen is set. The players can use the same option as in the previous drill.

5 vs. 5 at One Basket

5 vs. 5 play on the half-court with the main focus being on switching men when the screen is set. The players can use the same option as in the previous drill and subsequently may extend the game to the full court.

Playing Defence in Inferiority Situations (1 Against 2 and 2 Against 3)

Description and Use

There are situations during a game when players going back on defence after losing possession will find themselves outnumbered by the attackers in the scoring area. The main defensive strategy when outnumbered is to slow down the ball, to prevent it getting closer to the basket. This will prevent an easy lay-up shot and possibly any good percentage shot until other defenders arrive to provide an equal number on defence. By using realistic fakes to stop the dribbler, or by bluffing at the offence, the defenders may be able to stall the offence, to delay the fastbreak attack or to cause the offence to 'hurry' and to force the least advantageous shooting opportunity until help gets there. In this way some of the effectiveness of the fastbreak is destroyed and the defenders will have done a good job. The most common fastbreak situations are 3 vs. 2 and 2 vs. 1.

2 vs. 1

The prevention of an easy basket is the top priority of the lone defensive man who is outnumbered. When defending against two attackers, the defender must run backwards to a position at the top of

The defender marking the player using the screen has three options available:

1 *Going 'over the top'*: defender 1 avoids the screen and stays with his opponent (see Fig 268);
2 *Sliding*: in sliding, the defender being screened moves between the screener and his teammate who is marking the screener. The teammate will have to step back to create space for the sliding player and can help by physically guiding him through (see Fig 269);
3 *Switching men*: the switch is used as a very last resort when the defender's progress is impeded. The defender marking the screener takes the player who is moving free and the defender who has lost his opponent quickly establishes a defensive position against the player who has set the screen (see Fig 270).

After an exchange of men, each defender is responsible for the man to whom he has been exchanged. However, if in switching there is a decided mismatch in the comparative height of the offensive and defensive men, a switch back must be made as quickly as possible. If this is not possible (the opportunity does not arise) the switches should remain until the play

is over or the defenders' team gets possession of the ball.

Common Mistakes

- Defenders failing to talk to each other when a screen is set.
- Both defenders going and following the player benefiting from a screen, leaving the player who set the screen free.

Coaching Points

- Always talk/communicate when playing defence against screens.
- Use peripheral view to see a screener approaching and to avoid being screened.
- Instruct players to exchange men if the command 'switch' is transmitted.

Drills

2 vs. 2 at One Basket

2 vs. 2 play on the half-court with the main focus being on switching men when the screen is set. As an option, the players can use sliding or going over the top when a screen is set (instead of switching men).

Fig 271 Defenders 1 and 2 play 'tandem defence' against three attackers.

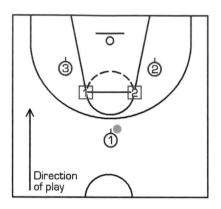

Fig 272 Defenders 1 and 2 play 'side-by-side defence' against three attackers.

the key (in front of the free-throw line), keeping the ball and both men in view. If the front man has the ball, the defender, while retreating, must delay him as far out as possible. When the cutter is ahead of the ball handler, the defender must open his stance towards the cutter, since he is the more dangerous man, keep the foul-line area covered and attempt to stop the dribbler. He must do all this without allowing the dribbler to make an easy pass to the cutter or execute a stop-and-go or change-of-pace dribble. In an ideal scenario, the defender is forcing the ball handler to stop dribbling and pick up the ball (and then moves slightly towards the other attacker to anticipate a potential pass), or forcing the attacker to take a quick shot from any distance further away than the foul line.

3 vs. 2

When caught in a 3 vs. 2 situation, the defenders can choose either of the two methods of defending: tandem defence or side-by-side play.

Tandem defence (or 'front and back' defensive alignment) will see the front defender occupying a position at the top of the key (in front of the free-throw line) and the back man just in front of the basket (in the middle of the 3-seconds space).

The front man must stop the dribbler as far out as possible and force a pass. When the pass goes to one side, the back man reacts and goes to the attacker on the side of the pass (the attacker who will receive the pass). The front man opens up towards the direction of the pass but slides quickly towards the cutter on the opposite side and at the same time is alert for a return pass to the middle man (see Fig 271).

The second option for the two defenders outnumbered by three attackers is to play *side-by-side* defence. In this, the defenders are parallel to each other, positioned near the ends of the free-throw line (as in Fig 272). The distance between them should not be sufficient to allow the offensive man to dribble between them for a lay-up shot.

It is preferable to use this method when the middle man is not a good ball handler or when the opponents are not a good fastbreak team. The defender on the side of the dribbling hand must try to stop the dribbler, using defensive fakes while retreating. If the dribbler stops, each man should fall off towards the cutter on his side, waving their hands and discouraging a pass-in, and make the middle man take the shot. If a pass is sent to a cutter, the defender on that side must move with the pass to get position between the cutter and the basket, to prevent the easy shot.

Whichever method they choose, the defenders must prevent the really easy or set-up shot. If they can force an extra pass or two, they should by then have help and no longer be outnumbered. Similar defensive principles apply for 3 vs. 1, 4 vs. 2, 4 vs. 3 and 5 vs. 2 situations.

Common Mistakes

2 vs. 1

- The defender not attempting to stop the player dribbling towards the basket.
- The defenders being passive in defence instead of being proactive to determine mistakes or to force attackers into early passes or unprepared shots.
- The defenders committing a foul and the attacker also scoring ('basket good and one free throw' situation).

3 vs. 2

- The back man not going to defend the first pass.
- The front man staying still after the first pass was sent instead of going towards the cutter on the opposite side to anticipate a potential pass.
- Both defenders positioning themselves too far away from their own basket, or too close.

Coaching Points

- Advise the player who loses the ball to drop back quickly for a defensive position (to be the first player back on defence).
- Challenge any good shot without giving away the rebound position.
- Always have in view both the dribbler and the cutter(s).
- Use defensive fakes and feinting motions to force the dribbler to commit himself early.
- Have the arms out to make passing difficult.
- Communicate with teammates.
- React quickly when losing possession and sprint back in defence.

Drills

2 vs. 1 on the Half-Court

One player is the defender on the free-throw line, while all the other players are in pairs waiting at the half-way line, as in Fig 186. Each pair has a ball. One pair at a time will play against the defender (2 vs. 1), taking into account the principles described above. The attacker who scores (or the one who loses the ball if no basket is scored) will replace the defender, while the defender will become an attacker and join the back of the queue.

The drill may be progressed as follows:

- the attackers are allowed only one dribble each time they receive the ball;
- the attackers are not allowed to dribble – only pass and move;
- the attackers are allowed to take only one shot, rather than playing until they score (or lose the ball).

2 vs. 1 All the Time

This is the drill relating to playing 2 vs. 1 and 3 vs. 2 situations (see Fig 188).

It may be progressed as follows:

- the attackers are allowed only one dribble each time they receive the ball;
- the attackers are not allowed to dribble – only pass and move.

3 vs. 2 on the Half-Court

This is the same as the first drill, but this time the players are practising 3 vs. 2 – groups of three attackers against two defenders who are waiting at one basket (see Fig 273). After playing 3 vs. 2, the attacker who takes the shot (or the one who loses the ball) becomes a defender, while the defender who gets the rebound or intercepts the ball becomes an attacker together with the remaining two attackers, and joins the queue.

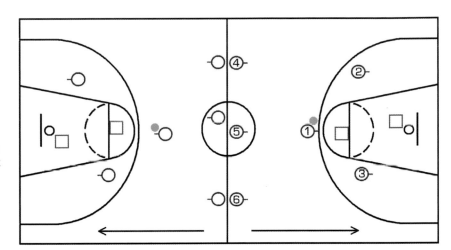

Fig 273 3 vs. 2 drill on half-court.

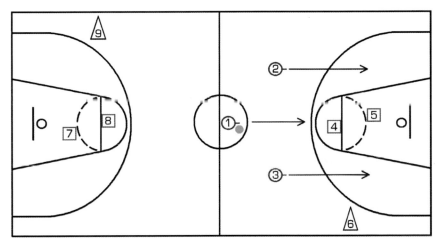

Fig 274 3 vs. 2 continuous fastbreak drill with nine players only.

The drill may be progressed as follows:

- the attackers are allowed only one dribble each time they receive the ball;
- the attackers are not allowed to dribble – only pass and move.

3 vs. 2 Continuous Fastbreak Drill

This is a continuous 3 vs. 2 drill on the full court, with eleven players (see Fig 192, and page 88). Although the ideal number is eleven players, this drill can also be practised with nine. In this case, both defenders will go with the attacker waiting on the side line after the three attackers have scored or lost the ball (see Fig 274).

CHAPTER 10

TEAM DEFENCE

The beauty of the game of basketball is the fact that all players are required to fulfil attacking roles but also (and this is equally important) defensive roles. To be a complete player, the individual needs to be able to play well in both moments of the game. All individual defensive skills and techniques, together with successful combinations between two or three players, need to be integrated together in a team effort.

Discipline, concentration, hard work and determination are the foundation pillars of a good efficient defence. Offence and defence are constant during the game. Defence does not afford the players a rest. Each player has to understand that his contribution in defence is vital for team success. The coach should stress the fact that he is looking for players who actively play defence with initiative, who put pressure on the ball and who are ready to help a teammate if the situation requires that. Those players who have the wrong attitude when in defence will find their place on the bench.

Man-to-Man Defence

Description and Use

When playing man-to-man defence each player is assigned an individual from the opposite team. The first aim for each defender is to stop his man from scoring, but he also needs to stay alert to help cover any attacker who becomes more dangerous than his own man. In a game situation the coach will usually determine who is guarding who, depending on the height, ability (physical and mental) and speed of the players involved. Despite this fact, when on the court some players might change their men between them, if they feel they would do a better job

guarding someone different; in this situation, it is a good idea to inform the coach.

Defence starts when possession is lost. That is the moment when the defenders should mark immediately their men – it is easier to prevent a player from receiving the ball in dangerous areas than it is to prevent him from scoring after he has received the ball in that area. The point at which an opponent takes a shot is an important moment for all five defenders. If the shot is not blocked, everybody in defence must box out his own man and then go to get the rebound. If every single player out of the five on court is doing his job, the ball will be very easily recovered.

There are several principles that good defensive teams are constantly applying:

- body posture, defensive stance – the proper defensive position is on the balls of the feet, well balanced, arms raised to prevent an easy pass or to block the shot;
- position on court – when playing man-to-man defence, the defender should stay on the imaginary line between his own basket and the attacking player he is guarding. An initial set-up for a man-to-man defence is shown in Fig 275;
- defensive footwork – as soon as the attacker moves, the defender moves too, trying to maintain the same distance between them. Using defensive footwork (sideways, backward or forward movement, step and slide) the defender will be able to keep pace with his man;
- always be aware of the position of your man and the ball – the defender should always place himself in relation to his man and the ball. He must also keep track of the position of his teammates. His peripheral view

must be used as much as possible – turning the head right or left for a split second can cause the player to lose his man or the ball;
- discourage attackers from cutting into the danger area – defenders should make every effort not to allow a free opponent under the basket or inside the 3-seconds space. A passive defence will permit moves and passes to players who will then score easy points. This is not what the defence should be about. By closing off the key area, anticipating and closing the passing lanes, and applying constant pressure on the ball to make the attackers' passing and shooting really difficult, defenders will greatly reduce the number of close-in shots and offensive rebounds and second-shot opportunities;
- communication – always talk to each other in defence to encourage, to warn teammates about opponents' moves and to discourage attackers. Use expressions such as 'I've got the ball!', 'John, screen left!', 'Watch the overload!'; and so on;
- work hard – be mentally and physically alert to prevent any scoring opportunities. Keep working hard until possession of the ball is gained.

Fig 275 Man-to-man defence – the defenders are positioned on the imaginary line between their own basket and their direct opponent.

Advantages of Man-to-Man Defence

- It allows individual match-ups of opponents based on size, height, quickness, strength.
- It allows the coach to define clear defensive responsibilities to each individual in the team.
- It places the defenders in the best defensive rebounding positions (mainly because the defender is playing inside his attacking opponent most of the time).
- It permits better preparation of each individual – the coach can scout and inform his players about opponents' strengths and weaknesses.
- It can be adapted to any opponent's offence and can be used full-court (to increase the tempo) or half-court for the duration of the whole game regardless of the score.
- It allows the coach to see immediately good individual defensive play.
- Pressure man-to-man is efficient (when done properly) and leads to interceptions, steals and other fast-break opportunities.
- It enables defenders who are guarding a weaker scoring player to help in guarding the top players in the opposite team.
- Fundamental defensive skills are fully used.

Disadvantages of Man-to-Man Defence

- It is physically demanding, requiring better condition and stamina from all players.
- It requires very good knowledge of defensive fundamentals and combinations between two or three players (for example, switching men after screens). Players also need to be able to defend anywhere on the court.
- It can be rather ineffective against a team that uses screens and cuts well.
- It can lead to mismatches in size during play.
- There is a high probability of making more personal fouls – defenders with three to four personal fouls will be the target of attackers.
- A weak defensive player is difficult to hide and this fact could be exploited by the opposition.
- Apart from individual responsibility, players also have a team responsibility.

Common Mistakes

- Two players guarding the same attacker.
- Defenders committing fouls very easily and early in the game because

of poor defensive stance and slow movements.

- Defenders playing too far away from (or too close to) their man.
- Defenders reacting to the fakes used by attackers.

Coaching Points

Most of the principles described above can be applied as coaching points. However, there are a number of other important factors to consider:

- always position yourself on the imaginary line between the attacker and your own basket;
- make sure you can see the direct man and the ball at all times;
- be ready to switch man if a screen is set by the offensive players;
- be ready to help out when necessary;
- always communicate with teammates and inform or warn them about opposite team moves.

Drills

Tag in Pairs

In pairs, players number themselves 1 and 2. Number 1 chases 2 all over the court trying to 'tag' him; once he has caught him, they change roles, and so on. It is a very good drill to teach the basic principles of man-to-man defence. Each player is responsible for guarding a man wherever he goes on the court.

1 vs. 1 Leading to 5 vs. 5 Play

This is an ideal drill for ten players, split into 2 teams. Each player receives a number from 1 to 5 (from guards to pivots). The drill starts with the number 1s in each team playing 1 vs. 1 on the full court. After 2 to 3 minutes, the number 2s join in, so that it becomes 2 vs. 2 on the full court; then the number 3s join in for a 3 vs. 3, then the 4s. Finally, the 5s join in for a 5 vs. 5 on the full court with man-to-man defence. After 2–3 minutes, the number 1s leave the court

so that it becomes 4 vs. 4. After another 2–3 minutes, the number 2s leave, and it becomes a 3 vs. 3 match. The pattern continues until the number 5s are left on the court playing 1 vs. 1. The winning team is the one that leads when the drill is over.

2 vs. 2 (3 vs. 3) at One Basket

This is a very good drill at the learning stages of man-to-man principles. Two attackers against two defenders at one basket – first team to score 11 points (or 21) wins.

Progression: the 3 vs. 3 drill can be performed as a full-court game – initially as a normal game, then with all players being allowed one dribble only and then with no dribble.

Types of Man-to-Man Defence

A number of variations of man-to-man defence may be encountered in a game situation. The following types are the most common.

Normal Man-to-Man on Half-Court

After losing the ball the players run quickly on defence to get ready to guard their opponents on the half-court.

Full-Court Man-to-Man

Also called press defence (or pressing or tight man-to-man), this is a very proactive defence. Rather than waiting for their men to come, the defenders sprint to mark their man as soon as the possession is lost.

The different types can have a tactical use – for example, the pressure man-to-man defence is used for increasing the tempo and for adding pressure on the attacking team. The hope is that they will be forced to commit basic errors such as wrong passes or shots that are not properly set, or lose control of the ball while dribbling, or to force 8 seconds, 24 seconds, 5 seconds, which will lead to turnovers. Extreme pressure is placed on the ball and the defenders contest every single pass. It is a defence that is on the attack at all times and can be very effective when the opposite team have poor ball handling;

when they do not run fastbreaks; or when they are not very organized or disciplined tactically on offence.

Zone Defence

Description and Use

The second most common type of defence is the zone defence. When using this playing system the coach will assign each player a defensive responsibility for a certain area or zone, rather than asking him to mark one individual attacking player, as in man-to-man defence. Each defender must face the ball and synchronize his moves with the movement of the ball, continuously adjusting his position in relation to it. The position of the attacking players must also be taken into account.

A zone defence will work as a team unit; all individual defenders will adopt a basic formation for the whole team from which all movements result. The name given to this formation will be the name given to various types of zones – most commonly, 2-1-2; 2-3; 3-2; 1-2-2; 1-3-1; 2-2-1. Zone defences are usually numbered from the half-way line towards the end line of court and the number indicates how many defenders are on a line on the initial set-up.

There are several reasons for using zone defence:

- the opposing team's shooters are poor from long-distance range (outside the key); this fact needs to be exploited;
- the playing area is small, which would make passing more difficult;
- the team has a player with three to four personal fouls and he needs to be protected;
- zone defence may be the only defensive system learned by a team.

2-1-2 Zone

2-1-2 zone is one of the most frequently used types of zone defence. The alignment of players is as follows: two defenders (usually the small and quick players) on the free-throw line, one player in the middle of the key right in front of the basket

Fig 276 2-1-2 zone defence.

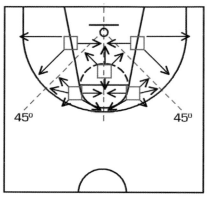

Fig 277 Areas of responsibility for 2-1-2 zone defence.

(half-way between his own basket and the free-throws line) and two defenders under the basket (one at each end of the board), as illustrated in Fig 276.

This is a flexible arrangement that is very strong under the basket area with the three players at the back in a defensive triangle formation, giving good rebound coverage.

There are very good possibilities for a fastbreak – the two players at the top are ready to receive an outlet pass and/ or to sprint on the fastbreak. One of the weaknesses of this arrangement is the fact that it is fairly difficult to cover good outside- and corner-shooting teams. Another important weakness is repre-

sented by the 'gaps' or the points where the areas (zones) of responsibility of two or three defenders meet (see Fig 206 for gaps/weaknesses and Fig 277 for areas of responsibility in the 2-1-2 formation).

2-3 Zone
By placing three men on the back line, the 2-3 zone (Fig 278) is an excellent rebounding defence that also presents fastbreak opportunities – the two players at the front are usually the fast ones.

This type of zone can be easily transformed into a 2-1-2 zone by moving forward the middle man from the back line so that he covers the area in front of the basket. Some of the main strengths of this

formation are the very good coverage of the corners and of baseline penetrations, and also the fact that it is very strong in defending the low-post men on either side of the key (see Fig 279 for areas of responsibility).

The system is quite weak against good outside shooting and the front areas are easily overloaded. Also, the spaces between the two lines of defence are usually exploited by attacking teams (see Fig 209 for gaps in the 2-3 set-up).

3-2 Zone
The 3-2 zone is very strong against outside shooting and guards who have poor ball handling because of the three defenders (the quickest players) who are covering

Fig 278 Players' positioning for 2-3 zone defence.

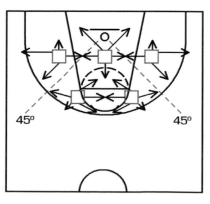

Fig 279 Areas of responsibility for 2-3 zone defence.

Fig 280 3-2 zone initial set-up.

the front area of the defence (see Fig 280 for 3-2 initial set-up).

The drives from the top of the key are discouraged by these three men, who also play a vital role in initiating the fastbreak. This zone has the main disadvantage that it is vulnerable in the corners (see Fig 281 for areas of responsibilities) and in the middle of the key once the front line is penetrated (see Fig 207 for gaps/danger areas). It can be overloaded easily in the

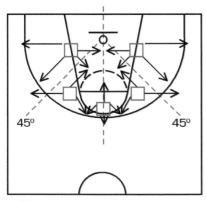

Fig 281 Areas of responsibilities in 3-2 zone.

area of the pivots and does not present good rebound coverage.

1-2-2 Zone

This zone keeps one man at the top of the key in front of the four people in a box or 2-2 formation (see Fig 282 for 1-2-2 zone initial set-up). Its main strength is the area in the middle of the key and the pivots' zone of action.

The fact that it could be easily over-loaded by playing in the corners and later-ally is clearly one of the weaknesses. The areas of responsibility are shown in Fig 283 and the main gaps/weaknesses in Fig 210.

1-3-1 Zone

Keeping three defenders in line (just inside the free-throw line) makes this zone very strong in the foul line and in the pivot area (when playing high), and effective against jump shots from the front (see Fig 284 on page 132 for initial 1-3-1 set-up).

Because of the fact that there is only one defender playing close to the basket there are rebounding difficulties in this zone. Also, it is very vulnerable to corner shooting and baseline drives. The areas of

responsibility are illustrated in Fig 285 on page 132 and the weaknesses in Fig 208.

2-2-1 Zone

Four men in a box formation (or 2-2) play quite advanced in front of the man underneath or in front of the basket area (who is usually a big center and a good rebounder) (see Fig 286 on page 133 for 2-2-1 zone initial set-up).

Despite the fact that it is efficient against close jump shots and it provides very good fastbreak opportunities, this zone is very vulnerable to playing options (drives, jump shots) from the corners of the court and baseline. Fig 287 on page 133 illustrates areas of responsibility while the gaps and weaknesses are shown in Fig 288 on page 133.

Advantages of Playing Zone Defence

- It has an impact on the number of personal fouls (lowering it) and it contributes to conserving the players' energy.

Fig 282 Players display for 1-2-2 zone.

- It offers a chance to individuals to concentrate on fewer fundamentals necessary for guarding a limited area.
- The players are well positioned to get defensive rebounds and to start fastbreak situations.
- Weak defenders and players in fouls trouble are usually protected/ covered.

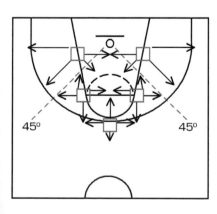

Fig 283 Areas of responsibility in 1-2-2 zone defence.

- It is very useful against teams that have poor outside shooting and poor ball handling. It can aso be effective against teams with a very good driver (usually restricting his moves).
- It is a good type of defence to use if the court space is restricted.
- It is very effective against teams using a set pattern offence that involves screening.
- It will slow down a quick-shooting attacking team and force them to shoot from long distance (3-pointers).
- A zone can ensure that your big men will always be near the basket (even if the opposition's big man decides to go outside).

Disadvantages of Playing Zone Defence

- It is not effective against teams that use the fastbreak well.
- It is weak against good outside-shooting teams.

- It is vulnerable to overloading one side of the zone.
- It is fairly difficult to cover all areas on a large court.
- There is weak defensive coverage where the areas of responsibility of two or three defenders meet.
- It requires good teamwork, cooperation and synchronized moves from all five players.
- It tends to weaken individual responsibility as there is no match-up of men according to height, size and ability.
- A good passing team can find its way past the first line of defence and create close-shooting opportunities.

Common Mistakes

- Players being slow in getting back in defence and setting up the zone.
- Defenders keeping their arms low instead of keeping them up to close a passing lane or to attempt to block a shot.

Fig 284 Initial players display for 1-3-1 zone.

- Defenders not boxing out after a shot is taken.
- Defenders arguing with each other with regard to 'whose fault it is' after allowing a basket from an area with shared responsibility.

Coaching Points

- Move the zone as a unit and synchronize your moves with your colleagues depending on where the ball and offensive players are.
- Make sure you can see the ball and that you are aware who is in your area of responsibility.
- Keep the arms up – especially players in the front line.
- Use double team as frequently as possible.
- Communicate with teammates and let them know what is happening on the court.
- Be ready to double-team opponents.

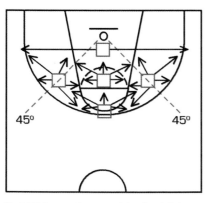

Fig 285 Areas of responsibility for 1-3-1 zone.

Drills

Zone Movements Rehearsal (5 vs. 5)

From the initial set-up for a 2-1-2 zone (or any type of preferred zone defence), five attackers pass the ball only outside the 3-points semicircle. After each pass is made the attackers are waiting for the defenders to 'move the zone' (to move their position within the zone) depending where the ball is – as in Fig 289. After the ball goes a couple of times from one corner to the other, teams switch roles.

Later on, after passing from corner to corner, attackers will pass to the pivot who is in the low post. Defenders need to learn to react to such passes too.

4 vs. 4 – Four Defenders in a Box Formation (2-2)

4 vs. 4 play at one basket with the defenders playing zone in a box formation (2-2 zone).

Later, five attackers play against four defenders on the half-court.

2 vs. 2 and 3 vs. 3 on Half-Court

2 vs. 2 play on the half-court. The main task for the defenders is to play help-defence and double team whenever their man has does not have possession of the ball.

Combined Defence

Description and Use

Most teams prefer to play the two best-known types of defence: either man-to-man or zone. However, players should be aware of another type of defence – which could be very efficient in particular

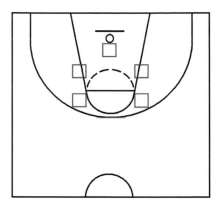

Fig 286 2-2-1 zone initial set-up.

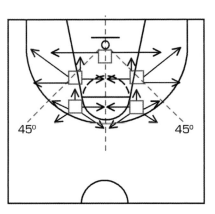

Fig 287 Areas of responsibility in 2-2-1 zone defence.

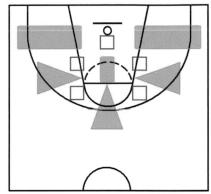

Fig 288 Gaps and weaknesses in 2-2-1 zone defence.

situations – known as combined defence (or combination defence). This type of defence makes use of the strengths of both man-to-man and zone defences. It is a very efficient defensive system, especially against an attacking team that has only one very good player (and a 3-points shooter in particular). The two classical types of combined defence are 4 plus 1 (box and one) and 3 plus 2 (triangle and two).

4 Plus 1 (Box and One)

The 'box and one' defence has four players who play in a 2-2 zone forma-tion (box) while the fifth defender plays man-to-man defence, usually against the best-scoring player from the opposition (see Fig 290).

The main purpose of this type of defence is to limit the shooting opportuni-ties of this best-scoring opponent. The fifth man can move freely around the 3-points semicircle instead of guarding one player only. The four players in a zone formation can change their position into a diamond shape – for this reason, this type of defence is also called 'diamond and one' (see Fig 291) – and the same principles are applicable (four players playing zone with the fifth one either playing man-to-man or moving/floating freely).

3 Plus 2 (Triangle and Two)

As in the 4 plus 1 defence, three defenders play in a triangle-shaped formation, applying zone defence principles, with the remaining

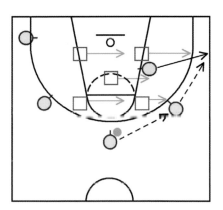

Fig 289 Zone movements rehearsal (5 vs. 5) drill.

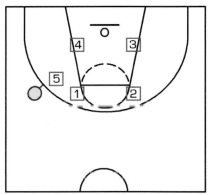

Fig 290 Initial set-up for 4 plus 1 (box and one) combined defence.

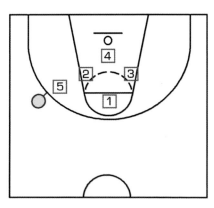

Fig 291 Initial set-up for diamond and one combined defence.

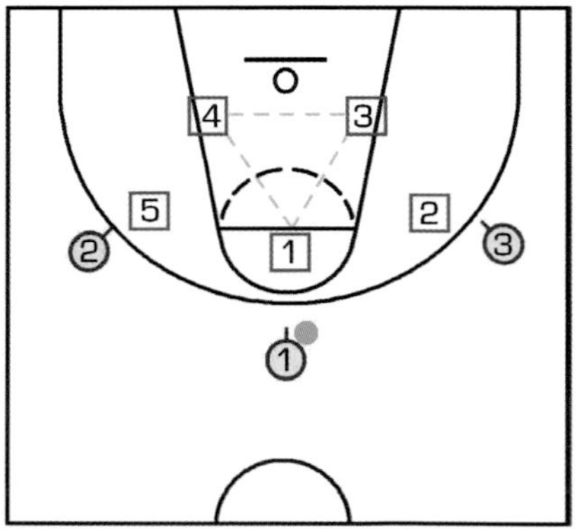

Fig 292 Initial set-up for 3 plus 2 (triangle and two) combined defence.

two closely guarding the best two players from the opposition (see Fig 292).

The triangle men usually double-team the two man-to-man defenders when they are coming into their zones. This type of defence is efficient if the opposite team relies on two players only (if it only has two good shooters) and it provides good fastbreak opportunities when gaining the possession. However, it is a weak defence against more than two good shooters and against well-prepared and patient offensive teams that use penetration and pass the ball well. This 3 plus 2 combination defence can be modified during the game and transformed into a 2 players in zone and 3 playing man-to-man defence – it depends on the coaches to read the game and the type of team and offence they are playing against.

Advantages of Using a Combined Defence

- The main advantage is the surprise factor. The other team might not be prepared to play against such defence and, by the time they have adapted, their offence will already have been disrupted, causing them to lose important possessions.
- It is efficient and good to use against teams with a very good scorer.
- It places the defenders in their most effective areas.
- It provides good fastbreak opportunities.

- It employs the strengths of both man-to-man and zone defences.
- It is very good against teams that shoot poorly from the outside.

Disadvantages of Using a Combined Defence

- Attacking players can overload the defence very easily.
- Vulnerable against good outside shooting and against good ball handlers.
- It needs to be set up immediately after losing possession otherwise it is beaten by the opponent's fastbreak.
- It necessitates a significant amount of practice time.
- Defenders (both those playing man-to-man and in zone) might get confused when it comes to exchanging men following offensive cuts.

Common Mistakes

- Two defenders (or more) failing to change men properly and both remaining and guarding the same man.
- Defenders playing man-to-man being too slow in playing defence and allowing the opponents to shoot or to dribble towards the basket.
- Defenders going and boxing out the same attacker.

Coaching Points

- Always communicate with your teammates about what is happening on the court – players cutting, setting screens, overloading one side, and so on.
- If playing man-to-man, stick to and follow that player all over the court and box him out when a shot is taken.

Drills

In order to be able to play this type of defence, it is recommended that all players first master the basic principles of the fundamental types of defence – man-to-man and zone. After this, the coach can experiment with it in training sessions and in friendly matches. Once they can demonstrate a reasonable understanding of combination defence in friendlies, the team can then use it in official matches. All the team defence drills given here are useful and will lead to an efficient use of combination defence.

PART IV

THE 'TOTAL TRAINING' CONCEPT

CHAPTER 11

TECHNICAL TRAINING

'Technique' as a notion encompasses all the technical structures and elements through which an athlete performs an athletic task, or, in other words, the specific manner in which an athlete performs a physical activity. It represents the ensemble of procedures that, through their form and content, ensure and facilitate movement. To be successful, an athlete needs perfect technique, in order to perform a certain type of exercise in the most efficient, economical and rational way. Basketball is a sport with a rich technical content, and the nearer the athlete is to perfecting his technique, the less energy he will require to achieve a given result; good technique leads to high efficiency.

When discussing technical training, two concepts are important: technique and style. As in every other sport, in basketball there is an accepted standard of the perfect technique that every coach and athlete should aim to achieve. If it is to be widely accepted, that model must be biomechanically sound and physiologically efficient. This model is not a rigid structure, but rather a flexible one, able to incorporate recent findings. No matter how perfect a model may be, athletes will not all perform it in the same way. The individual will impose his personal characteristics (his style) on the basic technique. Therefore, the model to follow is the *technique* and the individual pattern of performing a skill represents the *style*. The main structure of the model is not changed, although the athlete and coach add their personality, character and anatomical and physiological traits.

Style results from an individual's imagination in solving a technical problem or his manner of performing a motor act. In basketball (and in team sports in general), a certain approach or style may be attributed to a particular team. For example, the Russians are known for their very good defence. The term 'style', therefore, has tactical implications as well as application to technical preparations.

The term 'technique' also incorporates *technical elements* and *technical procedures*. Technical elements are the fundamentals that constitute the whole technique of a sport; technical procedures are the various ways in which to perform a technical element. For example, a technical element in basketball – shooting, for example – may have several technical procedures: one-hand shot, two-hand shot, lay-up shot, jump shot, slam-dunk shot, and so on. The technical element of passing has a number of technical procedures including the chest pass, bounce pass, javelin pass, overhead pass, and so on.

When teaching a technical element or the whole technique, the coach should always take into account the player's level of physical training; inadequate physical training will limit acquisition of a skill. Acquiring a skill occurs in three phases: the cognitive phase, the associative phase and the autonomous phase.

Cognitive Phase

During the first (cognitive) phase, useless movements occur because of poor neuromuscular coordination. The coach should judge the lack of neuromuscular coordination not as insufficient talent potential, but as a physiological reality. The beginner is trying to 'get to grips' with the basics whilst dealing with lots of visual, verbal and kinaesthetic information in the form of demonstrations from the coach or other players (visual guidance), instructions and explanations (verbal guidance), and initial trials/practice in the form of basic trial/error. Beginners are directed towards the most important aspects of the new skill and any initial success should be enthusiastically reinforced.

This phase is generally a short phase and depends on the ability and previous sporting experiences of the player and on the strategies that the coach has in place to facilitate learning.

Associative Phase

The second (associative) phase is that of tensed movements. The fundamental basics of the skill have generally been mastered and are being performed more consistently. The mental or early cognitive images of the skill have been associated with the relevant movements, enabling the coordination of the various parts of the skill to become smoother and more in line with expectations. During this stage the skills are practised and refined under a wide variety of conditions and, whilst the skills are not yet automatic or consistently correct, there is an obvious change in the performance characteristics.

Autonomous Phase

The third (autonomous) phase establishes a motor skill through adequate coordination of the nervous processes – the athlete forms the skill or the dynamic stereotype. The skill is performed relatively easily, effectively and without stress. The performance is consistent, with highly skilled movement characteristics and has become almost automatic. The player is now able to process information easily and to concentrate on additional higher-level strategies, tactics and options; he can now detect and correct errors without help.

Mastery

Once a player has reached this phase, the learning is not over. Although the performer is now very capable, improvements can still be made in terms of style and form. This is when the performer enters into what some consider to be a fourth phase of motor-skill learning: the phase of *mastery*, characterized by a highly efficient performance of the fine movements, and by an ability to adapt the performance to any changes that might occur.

Skill acquisition is based on repetition, which helps the athlete automate the skill and reach a high level of technical stability. Once learned, any technique has to become competitional: it must be modelled permanently to the specifics of the competition. Because competitive rhythm, characteristics and intensity vary with the opponent's level of preparedness and the environment, the athlete must be able to adjust the technical model, the competitional technique. Improving and perfecting technique must also be dynamically linked to physical and psychological traits because improvements in speed or perseverance may lead to slight technical modifications.

GB forward Nick George (number 6 white jersey) dribbles without looking at the ball — a characteristic of a highly efficient performance.

CHAPTER 12

PHYSICAL TRAINING

Physical training is one of the most important ingredients in training to achieve high performance; it is the foundation of a pyramid that incorporates all other components of training (technical, tactical, psychological, theoretic-methodical), and is the base on which performance is built. The stronger the foundation, the greater the potential for technical, tactical and psychological heights.

The main objectives of physical training are to increase the athlete's physiological potential and to develop biomotor abilities to the highest standards. A good level of physical conditioning will also minimize the risk of injury. Players must be in the top physical condition at the start of the season. Using conditioning programmes, the player will be able to make all the movements of the game easily – stopping, starting, sprinting, jumping, and so on. Physical training encompasses all measures and exercises that help the body to work at highly demanding levels of volume and intensity – in other words, the body is trained to produce muscular strength, power and endurance, so that the player can use his skills and employ the right tactics effectively.

In the framework of training, *exercise* is a motor act repeated systematically. Exercise represents the main training method used to increase performance. High levels of fitness cannot be achieved simply by playing the game, and coaches need to incorporate specific exercises in training with the aim of developing and enhancing the biomotor abilities of strength, speed, power, endurance, flexibility, agility, balance and coordination.

Strength and Power

Strength and power are two components of fitness that are very important when playing basketball. Many of the technical elements (such as jumping to get a rebound or sending a long-distance pass) require a muscular, powerful player.

Strength is the maximum force that can be developed in a muscle or group of muscles during a single maximal contraction.

Power is the amount of work done per unit of time and represents the product of strength and speed (a combination of the strength of the muscle and the speed with which it can contract – for example, the explosive lift from the legs when dunking).

Two of the best ways of developing strength and power are weight training and plyometrics, and basketball coaches should incorporate these into their coaching. Players should be encouraged to carry out a good warm-up before any weight training, taught how to carry out the exercises correctly and safely before beginning a specific training programme, and should build up the programme steadily over a couple of weeks.

The term *plyometrics* is used to describe any training that improves explosive force production through powerful contractions of a muscle group immediately following a stretching or lengthening phase (for example, jumping from a box and then jumping up in the air). This type of training is based on the concept that, if a muscle is pre-stretched before contraction, it will contract more forcefully. Apart from a proper warm-up, another safety consideration for coaches is to use plyometric training only with players who are not injured and who have a reasonably high level of leg strength.

Drills

All the drills relating to jumping (see pages 74–75) are suitable. There are a number of other options.

TOP TIP

When incorporating strength training for junior players it is advisable initially to include exercises that require them to use their own body weight (press-ups, pull-ups, jumps with knees up, and so on). As players grow older, free weights and work on machines can be introduced. The target muscles for weight training in basketball include the biceps, triceps, deltoids, abdominals, latissimus dorsi, quadriceps, hamstrings, gastrocnemius and soleus.

Stairs Hop

Start at the bottom of a flight of stairs. Do ten jumps up the stairs (jumping two steps at a time), making the landings quick and light. The jumps should be done continuously, without pause. Emphasis should be placed on the speed of ascent (see Fig 293).

As a progression, jumps can be performed on one foot only.

Cone (Barrier) Hop

Start with feet shoulder-width apart. Using a small degree of knee flexion, jump over

Fig 293 Stairs hop drill.

Fig 294 Cone (barrier) hop drill.

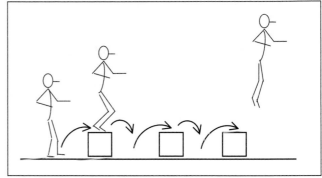

Fig 295 Continuous box jump drill.

a set of cones (five or six, or more) bringing the knees up over the barrier (see Fig 294). Contact with the ground should be kept as short and explosive as possible and the player should be on his toes. Recovery between sets of jumps should be adjusted using the 1:5 work–rest ratio.

As a progression, the same drill can be performed by jumping sideways (laterally).

Continuous Box Jump
Start with feet shoulder-width apart in front of a set of boxes spread out equally. Jump on to the first box, then down between the first and second box, then on to the second box, and so on (see Fig 295). Continue for six to eight maximal jumps, concentrating on the speed of movement. Use your arms and be on your toes.

The jumps may also be done laterally.

Speed

The important biomotor ability of speed can be defined as the capacity to put body parts or an external object into motion quickly, or the maximum rate at which a person can move over a specific distance. There are four types of running speed: maximum speed (the highest speed an athlete can reach), acceleration speed (ability to increase speed rapidly), speed endurance (ability to sustain maximum or near-maximum speed and withstand the effects of fatigue) and change-of-direction speed (also known as agility or the

ability to change direction at high speed). A coach can use several effective methods to develop speed:

- **Repetition** – the basic method used in speed training repeats a set distance several times at a given speed. Although the desired result is an improvement in speed, this method may also lead to an improvement in a skill or technical element, because a movement can become a dynamic stereotype only through repetition.
- **Alternative method** – rhythmically alternating movements (repetitions) with high and low intensities. The athlete increases and reduces speed progressively, while maintaining the phase of maximum speed. The method leads to an increase in speed and develops an ability to perform with ease and relaxation.
- **Handicap method** – allows athletes with different abilities to work together, provided that all have equal motivation. When a repetition is performed, each individual is placed (either ahead or back depending on his speed potential) so that all should reach the finish line or the end of acceleration phase at the same time.
- **Relays and games** – because of their emotional aspect, relays and games can be extensively used to improve speed, especially with beginners or top athletes during the preparatory phase. The main advantage of this

method is the fact that it also provides enjoyment and fun.

Drills

Most of the drills relating to the fastbreak and to passing (see pages 84 and 37, respectively) can be used to develop speed. In addition, the following drills could be effective.

Sprints
Sprints (six to eight maximal sprints over 20 or 30m) can be performed on a flat surface (the basketball court), or uphill or downhill. Athletes must remember to concentrate on good running technique (correct arm, leg and knee action) and work as explosively as possible. The start may be from a standing position, alternating with other positions: lying down on the floor (on the back or

> **TOP TIP**
>
> When using exercises to develop and improve speed for your basketball players remember that speed training requires 100 per cent effort and should only be done when players are fresh. Speed drills should be integrated into the early part of sessions and enough recovery time between bursts should be given. Most of the techniques/skills in basketball can be repeated with or without the ball, contributing to speed development.

front), while doing press-ups, while dribbling a ball, and so on. Sprints on sand or snow are also very efficient.

Shuttle Running

This develops acceleration and the ability to change direction quickly. Players can sprint in a straight line and quickly get back to the start, or they can perform a zig-zag run. This drill can also be performed using defensive slides (lateral movement).

Two-Pass Break Drill

In pairs – one ball per pair. Player 1 passes to his teammate and then sprints power-fully on the fastbreak to receive the pass somewhere on the opposite court so that he will catch the ball, dribble it once or twice before taking a lay-up (see Fig 296). Player 2 will sprint after he passes the ball to collect the rebound.

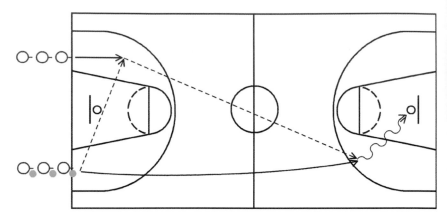

Fig 296 Two-pass break drill.

Developing Aerobic and Anaerobic Endurance

Endurance refers to the length of time during which an individual can perform work of a given intensity (during which he has the ability to repeat muscle contractions or movements without loss of performance). The main factor that limits and at the same time affects performance is fatigue. An athlete has good endurance when he does not fatigue easily, or can work efficiently in a state of fatigue.

During a game basketball players need to perform repeated bursts of high-intensity exercise and be able to recover quickly. *Anaerobic endurance training* (or speed endurance training) is vital as it accurately replicates the physical demands of basketball. It is essential to train players to cope with the varied duration and intensity of the effort so a mixture of training is needed, and this might include the following:

- *On-court interval session* – physical training can be incorporated into a squad training session or carried out individually by a player. The chosen drills need to replicate the type of movement patterns, number of repetitions, work–rest ratio and intensity found in the game of basketball.
- *Fartlek run* – Fartlek running (from the Swedish for 'speed play') involves steady jogging combined with bursts of faster running (which can vary from 2 to 90 seconds).
- *Off-court interval training* – interval training involves efforts of varying intensity interspersed with recovery periods of different lengths. Training on a running track (or grass area) can be a convenient way of developing pace judgement, as the prescribed duration can be converted to a required distance. The way athletes use their energy systems can be manipulated by varying the length and intensity of the effort, the length of recovery time, the type of recovery, the number of repetitions, the number of sets of repetitions and the frequency of these sessions per week.

Aerobic endurance training (also referred to as cardiovascular endurance or stamina) describes the ability of the heart, lungs and blood vessels to deliver oxygen to the muscles, and the ability of the muscles to use that oxygen to produce energy. Aerobic endurance is needed to ensure players can work hard in offence and defence, maintain that level of work even when recovering from periods of intense play, and delay the onset of fatigue. A well-developed aerobic system is essential for clearing the oxygen debt built up during periods of intense play. Players need to be able to maintain their work rate for at least 90 minutes, or approximately the duration of a match or club training session.

For developing aerobic endurance, work should be carried out at a moderate intensity of effort (60–70 per cent max effort) for 20 to 25 minutes, or more, at least three times a week. Suitable training includes running, skipping, rowing, cycling (either in a gym or outdoors), swimming and circuit training (which involves exercising at different work stations, each involving different parts of the body and/or different technical skills – dribbling, passing, and so on).

Flexibility and Stretching

Flexibility (or mobility) is the range of motion at a joint or series of joints. It is a prerequisite to performing skills with high amplitude and increases the ease with which the athlete can perform fast movements. Flexibility may be restricted by the structure of the joint and the soft tissues that surround it. As the bone structure of the joint cannot be altered, the key to flexibility is maintaining the range of motion permitted by the soft tissues (muscles and ligaments). To achieve optimum performance and to prevent injury, athletes should develop a range of motion that is sufficient to accommodate all the static and dynamic positions associated with their sport.

Athletes must stretch in order to be flexible. The basic principle of *stretching* means taking the structure to the end of its current range of motion and then taking it a little further. The body's soft tissue structures are pliable and, if a stretch stimulus is applied long enough and often enough, the range of motion will be increased.

A number of principles of muscle stretching should be observed:

- stretching appears to be more effective if it is done after general physical activity or an increase in body temperature;
- to increase flexibility, athletes should do three to five stretching sessions per week;
- athletes should try to avoid pain while stretching, especially if they are untrained.

Types of Stretching

There are a number of types of stretching:

- **Static stretching** takes a structure to the end of its range of motion and holds it there for a period of time, varying from 8 to 12 seconds to 30 seconds to 1 minute.
- **Ballistic stretching** is repeated swinging or bouncing into the end of the range of a movement. Connective tissue and tendons are stretched this way, as ballistic movements initiate the stretch reflex in a muscle, causing the contractile part of the muscle to be activated. This type of stretching carries a greater risk of injury than static stretching because it is less

controlled – it should be done at the end of a warm-up.
- **Dynamic stretching** refers to a combination of movement and static holds, where the athlete reaches the end of range of a movement deliberately and slowly, holds it briefly and then releases it.
- **Proprioceptive neuromuscular facilitation (PNF) stretching** refers to a group of techniques that use neuromuscular mechanisms to improve the range of motion. Techniques for PNF stretching use reflexes or responses that affect muscle tone.

During a training session, stretching should be included as part of the warm-up and of the cool-down. Some stretches may also be performed as active break/active rest between different drills and exercises during the main part of a session. The younger people are when they start flexibility training, the easier it is for them to achieve and maintain flexibility.

Stretching Exercises

The following examples of stretching exercises are relevant to basketball players.

When carrying out stretching exercises, you should start at the top of your body and work downwards to stretch major muscle groups and joints (or start at the ankles and work up).

Arms, Shoulders and Whole Body Stretch
From a standing position, extend the arms upwards and link the fingers above the head, with palms facing upwards, and arch your back – as if someone is pulling you upwards by your hands. Hold for 8–10 seconds (see Fig 297).

Next, extend your body towards one side; bring one arm close to your ear and press on your hip with the other arm (see Fig 298).

Triceps Stretch
In a standing position, move one arm behind your head, bending the arm at the elbow. Place the opposite hand on your elbow as in Fig 299 overleaf and gently pull downwards. Hold for 8–10 seconds.

The same type of stretch may be performed with one arm in front and across your chest (see Fig 300 overleaf). Apply pressure on this arm towards your chest (from behind your elbow/triceps) and hold for 8–10 seconds.

Fig 297 Arm, shoulder and whole-body stretch.

Fig 298 Whole body lateral stretch.

Fig 299 Triceps stretch with one arm behind the head.

Fig 300 Triceps stretch with one arm across the body.

Fig 301 Whole body flex with feet wide.

Fig 302 Whole body flex with feet together.

Fig 303 Hip flexor stretch.

Fig 304 Quadriceps stretch while standing.

Whole Body Flex

With feet shoulder-width apart (or wider) try to touch your toes by gradually lowering your body in a flexing position (see Fig 301), without bending the knees. Hold for 8–10 seconds.

A more difficult option is to have your feet together and try to touch your shoes or to place your palms on the floor (see Fig 302).

Hip Flexor Stretch

Take a big step forwards and bend the front knee so that it makes a 90-degree angle at knee level (see Fig 303). Keep the upper body in an upright position and gently push the hips forwards and downwards.

Quadriceps Stretch

Standing on one leg, hold the other foot behind you. Maintain your balance and pull the foot up towards the bottom (see Fig 304). Hold the stretch for 8–10 seconds and then repeat with the other leg.

A similar effect can be achieved while seated on the floor. Have one leg extended to the front while the other one is flexed to the side at a 90-degree angle. Try to touch the shoe of the extended foot (see Fig 305). Hold for 8-10 seconds, and then lie down on your back without changing the position of your feet and extend your arms on the floor (see Fig 306). Do the same for the other foot.

Hamstring Stretch

With one foot in front of the other, flex your back foot (which is flat on the ground), while keeping the front leg straight (the toes of this foot should be lifted upwards) (see Fig 307 overleaf).

Calf-Muscle Stretch

Lean forwards as in Fig 308 overleaf and bend the front leg. The leg behind needs to be straight with the heel on the ground – the stretch should be felt in the Achilles tendon and the calf muscle. Hold for 8–10 seconds and then change legs.

Groin Stretch

Sit on the floor, feet together with soles touching. Bring the feet in towards the body (holding them at shoelace level), and apply pressure with the elbows on the knees (see Fig 309 overleaf). Hold for 8–10 seconds.

Buttocks Stretch and Upper-Body Stretch

Sit on the floor with one leg straight and the other one bent over the straight leg as in Fig 310 overleaf. Lean across and put the opposite elbow on the knee – press with your elbow towards the outside (laterally). Hold for 8–10 seconds.

Lower-Back Stretch

Lie on your back with shoulders and head on the floor, and arms stretched out to the side. Bring one knee up towards your chest, then roll the knee across the body (towards the opposite arm), and touch the floor on the opposite side with the foot (see Fig 311 overleaf). Hold for 8–10 seconds.

Alternatively, in the same position, extend one leg and move it to touch the opposite hand (see Fig 312 overleaf). Hold for 8–10 seconds and then perform the same action with the other leg.

Knee and Hip Stretch

Lying on the floor, bring one knee to your chest while trying to extend your knee at the same time (see Fig 313 overleaf). Repeat with the other leg. Hold for 8–10 seconds.

Stabilization Exercises

As well as stretching moves, stabilization exercises are also very useful. Their main aim is to strengthen the muscle of different parts of the body and generally to enhance the posture.

Fig 305 Quadriceps stretch and body flex while seated.

Fig 306 Quadriceps stretch while lying on the back.

Fig 307 Hamstring stretch.

Fig 308 Calf-muscle stretch.

Fig 309 GB international Luol Deng demonstrates the groin stretch.

Fig 310 Buttock stretch and upper-body stretch.

Fig 311 GB centre Pops Mensah-Bonsu warms up with a lower-back stretch.

Fig 312 Lower-back stretch with leg extended.

Fig 313 Knee and hip stretch.

Fig 314 Stabilization exercise for abdominals and quadriceps.

Fig 315 Stabilization exercise for one arm and side muscles of the upper body.

Fig 316 Stabilization exercise for quadriceps, arms and abdominals.

Fig 317 Stabilization exercise for quadriceps, arms and abdominals with one foot extended.

Stabilization Exercise for Abdominals and Quadriceps

Adopt the position in Fig 314, forearms and toes supporting the whole body. Try to keep your legs and upper body in a flat line and maintain this position for 10–15 seconds.

Stabilization Exercise for One Arm and Side Muscles of the Upper Body

Support your body on one arm and on your foot as in Fig 315. Try to keep the feet and upper body in the same line and hold the position for 10–15 seconds then change for the other arm.

Stabilization Exercise for Quadriceps, Arms and Abdominals

Lie on the floor with your body supported by your arms (and shoulders) and your feet as in Fig 316. Lift your hips off the floor so that your body is in the same line as your feet (as your quadriceps) and hold for 10–15 seconds.

Alternatively, in the same position have one foot extended (so that the body is supported by the arms, shoulders and one foot only, as in Fig 317).

Stabilization Exercise for Shoulders and Quadriceps Muscles (Plus Arms and Abdominals)

Support your body on the forearms and feet, as in Fig 318 overleaf. Try to keep your body flat (in line with the quadriceps), so that it makes a 90-degree angle at the knee and shoulder level, and hold for 10–15 seconds.

Alternatively, perform the same exercise but with one leg extended, as in Fig 319 overleaf. Hold 10–15 seconds and then change legs.

Coordination

Coordination is a complex biomotor ability closely interrelated with speed, strength, endurance and flexibility. It is of determinant importance for acquiring and perfecting technique and tactics, as well as for applying them in unfamiliar circumstances (different opponents, a different type of ring and backboard, light, type of floor, and so on). Coordination is also solicited in space orientation, either when the body is in unfamiliar conditions (such as jumping for a rebound or to take a shot), or when there is a loss of balance (landing, quick stops and changes of direction).

Fig 318 Stabilization exercise for shoulders and quadriceps muscles (plus arms and abdominals).

Fig 319 Stabilization exercise for quadriceps, arms and abdominals with one leg extended.

A successful programme for developing coordination should rely heavily on acquiring a high variety of skills. All young athletes involved in basketball should also experience the skills of other sports, as this will ultimately improve their coordination. Apart from this, a number of other methods will prove to be efficient:

- an unusual starting position when performing an exercise;
- performing skills with the opposite limb or in an unusual position (dribbling while lying on the floor, for example);
- altering the speed or tempo/rhythm of performing a movement;
- changing technical elements or skills;
- increasing the difficulty of exercises through supplementary movements;
- combining known skills with newly formed skills; and
- creating unusual performance conditions.

A coach should include exercises for coordination in the first part of the training session, when the player is rested and has a high concentration capacity. Athletes acquire coordination most successfully at an early age, when the plasticity (the ability to alter and adapt in conformity to the environment) of the nervous system is much higher than in adulthood.

Warm-Up and Warm-Down

Before undertaking any physical training, it is important to carry out a thorough *warm-up*. The warm-up is a physiological and psychological preparation for the training tasks to come. A warm-up that increases the temperature of the muscles and increases the blood flow will prepare a player's body for optimal physical performance by doing the following:

- increasing the speed of contraction of the muscles;
- optimizing the efficiency of muscle contraction;
- helping the body to produce more energy in the muscles during activity due to greater oxygen extraction from the blood;
- increasing the stretch of the muscle and connective tissue;
- reducing the risk of injury (muscle strains and pulls).

An effective warm-up will cover an initial activity to raise body heat and increase respiratory and metabolic processes; stretching exercises of the muscle groups that are used in basketball; and rehearsal and practice of some of the activities that will be used in training (or a game). The objective of this last part of the warm-up is to tune the athlete to the type of work that will be done during the session. Exercises should involve the same movements as those that he will be required to perform in the training or the game (for example, backward and forward running, lateral movement, jumps, and so on). This type of warm-up will help prepare players both physically and mentally for the activity to follow (whether it is training or a game).

The *cool-down* (or *warm-down*) helps recovery by returning the blood from the exercised muscles to the central circulation and by rapidly decreasing accumulated lactic acid in the blood. An effective cool-down involves activity of a light intensity (jogging slowly, then walking, for example) for approximately 3 to 5 minutes. This will reduce the body temperature gradually and help the player wind down both physically and mentally. Some stretches could also be performed while the players are still warm.

CHAPTER 13

TACTICAL TRAINING

Tactics and *strategy* are words that are generally present in every coach's vocabulary. Despite the fact that they mean the same thing (more or less) – the art of performing a skill in a competition with direct or indirect opponents – they signify slightly different concepts. *Strategy* is the art of projecting and directing the plans for a team (or athlete) for a whole season or longer. *Tactics* refer to the attribute of organizing the plans of a team (or athlete) for a particular game or competition.

Tactical training is the means via which athletes absorb methods and possible ways of preparing and organizing offensive and defensive actions to fulfil an objective (in other words, to score, to achieve a certain performance, to win a match). During competition, an athlete applies all his biomotor abilities and skills according to the real, practical conditions in a confrontation with an opponent. The basis of a successful tactical plan for any sport is a high level of technique, and is strictly interrelated with (and sometimes depends on) the physical training, psychological training and theoretic-methodical training that has taken place.

Tactical training includes the following tasks:

* study and be familiar with the competition rules and regulations;
* investigate and be aware of the tactical abilities of the best players in the game;
* develop individual tactics for the upcoming competition based on personal strengths and weaknesses;
* develop a tactical model with variations;
* learn and repeat this tactical model until it becomes a dynamic stereotype.

Tactical discipline is a vital requirement of training and very important in the game of basketball. However, quite often players are exposed to tactical problems that the coach has not foreseen. In this situation, the player(s) must solve the problem instantly, based on personal experience, imagination and creativity. It is a good idea to expose your players to various situations (in training as well as in friendly matches) that demand tactical solutions from each player, to give them the chance to solve problems using their creative potential.

Another concept with which coaches need to be familiar is the *game plan*. This plan, which is a result of anticipation and mental preparation based on previous information and predictions, needs to be drawn up, applied in the game (or competition) situation and then analysed. The creation of such a plan will rely on the following:

* a realistic evaluation of the opposition (qualitative and quantitative data) as well as your own potential and preparation level;
* an awareness of the specifics of the facilities and environment of future competition;
* a knowledge of future opponents' strategy as well as their physical and psychological potential;
* clear tasks for individuals and a coordination of individual actions with team tactics (tactical skills and combinations to be used under specific game situations).

The game plan needs to include every tactic that the coach intends to teach and use during the season: man-to-man offence; zone offence; man-to-man defence; zone defence; jump ball alignment; side-line possessions and set plays to inbound the ball; free-throw alignment; fastbreak scenarios; procedures for before (travel, warming-up), during (time-out procedures, half-time) and after the game; codes and signals between coach and players, and so on. Obviously, the coach should not ask players to experiment in a game situation with something that they have not covered in training, and should avoid changing players' habits during the last few days before the competition. He must also acknowledge good performance of a skill or tactical manoeuvre, to build the athletes' confidence, create motivation and increase the desire to start the competition under optimal conditions.

CHAPTER 14

PSYCHOLOGICAL TRAINING

In basketball today, winning matches, especially at the top level of the game, depends to a significant extent on the concentration levels of the players. It is therefore essential for a coach to recognize the importance of training the mind of his athlete as well as the body. Without the correct mental approach to sport, an athlete's performances will always be below his best. Psychological training is aimed at knowing the sportsperson (his personality, motivation levels, intellectual level, aspirations, and so on) in order to maximize his physical, technical and tactical skills and abilities. Performance profiling, goal setting, concentration, arousal and anxiety management and imagery are just some of the tools available to coaches looking to include psychological training in their coaching programmes.

Performance Profiling

Performance profiling is a procedure that coaches can use both to identify the objectives of mental skills training for athletes, and to make it easier for athletes to keep to that training. Coaches who use performance profiling benefit in several ways:

- it creates a visual display of the athletes' evaluations of their specific mental skills (strengths and weaknesses);
- athletes, as well as coaches, are able to identify the qualities required for consistent performance;
- athlete self-assessments can be matched with those of the coach at different times in a season;
- priorities for mental skills training can be established.

The mental skills that are needed in basketball include (but are not limited to) concentration, confidence, dealing with errors, injury management, visualization, arousal management, ability to relax, ideal performance state, and goal setting. Mental skills training is a developmental process that begins with simple familiar examples and gradually develops, with practice and good instruction, to apply to complex and unfamiliar situations (such as those that are encountered in game conditions). A good and clear explanation can often set up an effective practice and learning experience. Key teaching points should be presented to athletes, and coaches should segment the activities they will use to make them easier to absorb.

Before the athletes move on to another part of the coaching session, it is critical that they summarize what they have practised and learned. They should be left in no doubt as to what the objective was, why it was relevant, what they can practise on their own and when the next session will take place.

Goal Setting

Goal setting is a planning, organizational and evaluative tool that helps players of different ages and ability levels to perform better. It has a direct influence on performance by focusing athletes' attention on important elements of the skill they are performing, mobilizing their efforts, prolonging their persistence and fostering the development of new learning techniques. A training programme that contains goal setting helps athletes to make training more challenging, foster pride, self-satisfaction and self-confidence, become more committed and motivated, develop psychological maturity, and cope better.

Goal setting involves a step-by-step process of achievement, starting from a baseline level of performance in one of the following goal areas: physical, technical, tactical, mental and behavioural. Goals can be set using several principles. Individual goals must be identified, records should be kept, and ways to evaluate goals should be provided. In the case of team goals, they are established, all team members are involved, progress is monitored, and progress towards goals is rewarded. Despite all this, a coach might encounter problems in goal setting:

- when there are too many goals too soon;
- if athletes need to be convinced actually to set goals;
- if the coach fails to adjust goals when they have or have not been achieved;
- when the coach fails to arrange goal-setting evaluation and follow-up procedures.

The 'Three Cs' of Peak Performance

Concentration

Concentration, together with composure and confidence (the 'Three Cs' of peak performance) are experienced quite vividly during the best game an athlete plays. Playing up to your potential involves these three essential ingredients; to play your best, you must concentrate, keep your emotions under control and believe in your ability.

Concentration is the ability to pay attention to the right things at the right time (see Fig 320) and includes three aspects: focusing on relevant clues; staying focused; and being aware of changes as they happen. Like any other technical, tactical or physical skill, concentration can be learned and developed with practice, patience and persistence.

Often, the mark of fully prepared athletes and teams is their ability to bounce back and refocus during periods of distraction. Sources of distraction may not be related to the game (for example, problems at home or interpersonal problems with other players), or they may be game-related (for example, pain, fatigue, mistakes made, the score or the stage in the game). By preparing refocusing plans to deal with distraction and difficult periods, athletes are not thinking negatively, they are thinking ahead.

Composure

Composure – controlling the emotions and remaining calm in stressful situations – is another feeling that is experienced during peak performance. Being 'mentally relaxed', the peak performer feels highly energized. His intensity and involvement in the game do not relate to the negative emotions of fear, anger and anxiety, but rather to the positive feelings associated with high energy – the joy of success (the elation experienced when a goal has been achieved, which always comes with a

Fig 320 GB forward Luol Deng is fully concentrated before shooting a free throw in the game against Israel.

reduction of the tensions that accompany the goal, such as the desire to win); power (the thrill of victory); and the constant search for a challenge are often used to describe these feelings.

Confidence

Peak performers are confident and optimistic, with a generally positive outlook, and they usually feel 'in control'. A lack of self-confidence influences performance in two ways. First, negative thinking can become a self-fulfilling prophecy. Athletes who do not believe in their abilities expend less effort. They hold back so that they can use lack of effort as an excuse for not being successful. Second, a player's thoughts direct his body. Any player who holds negative images about his ability to dribble, for example, cannot help but dribble poorly because the mental pictures show vague or uncoordinated movements. The positive thinker does not let his mind dwell on negative thoughts. The mind only accepts and acts according to what it truly believes to be real. Believing in yourself and your skills comes from experience. For example, if you have been successful in the past at some skill, such as shooting, you may be truly confident in performing that skill in the future – you are confident because you have clear mental images of performing that skill well in the past.

Confidence in any skill is largely a matter of learning, practice and having had prior successful experience. According to John Wooden, one of the greatest basketball coaches, 'Confidence comes from being prepared.' If you want to develop total confidence in your game, you must totally prepare yourself for competition – physically, mentally and emotionally.

Arousal and Anxiety Management

While arousal refers to the general physiological and psychological activity of athletes at a particular moment, ranging from when they wake in the morning (low arousal) to

when they compete (high arousal), anxiety refers to a negative emotional reaction to arousal at that time, and feelings of nervousness, worry and apprehension. *Cognitive anxiety* is the degree to which athletes ruminate, worry or have negative thoughts about an event. *Somatic anxiety* concerns the moment-to-moment changes in physiological activity during an event, for example, sweating, and increases in heart rate, breathing and muscular tension.

An enhancement of the self-awareness of arousal and coping skills can be achieved by asking athletes to identify their ideal performance state. Coaches can simply ask their players to identify a 'best-ever performance' and to recall how they felt, and what they did on the day, night, morning or afternoon before the game.

Imagery

Imagery (mental rehearsal or visualization) simply involves creating or re-creating an experience in the mind. There are both physiological and psychological reasons for its effectiveness in sport and both beginners and skilled players benefit from its use.

In learning an athletic skill, the athlete must have a clear mental picture of the correct technique or form before he can do it successfully. This is where mental rehearsal comes in. Mental rehearsal is the creation of a mental picture or a series of mental pictures illustrating a proper technique or movement and the goal to be accomplished. Through mental pictures the athlete instructs his body and mind on what he hopes to achieve and how to carry out the necessary skills and movements. The more vivid and detailed the image, the better the mind and body can understand what they must do. For example, using mental rehearsal to develop shooting concentration involves developing a clear picture of the target (the centre of the basket) and the goal (putting the ball in the basket). It also involves developing a clear picture of when to focus on the target during the shooting movement – in this case, the player should centre on the target when he is bringing the ball up over his head, just before releasing.

CHAPTER 15

THEORETIC-METHODICAL TRAINING

Theoretic-methodical training refers to the process of transmitting current theoretical knowledge from coaches to performers with the main aim of optimizing performance during training and competitions. The acquistion and application of such knowledge is important in the development of athletes' skills and abilities, as well as finding the right motivation for their involvement in sport. At the same time as developing their skills and abilities, coaches must introduce athletes progressively to notions, terminology, concepts, principles, and rules about basketball in particular and sport in general, extending their athletes' general and sport-specific education.

Obviously, the coach must possess this knowledge himself – the only way to be one step ahead of his players in this respect is for the coach to be concerned with his own education and to be prepared to share this information. Athletes should always have access to a coach's expertise. The knowledge areas from which athletes will benefit include the following:

- the rules of the game and the latest changes to these rules and their interpretation by the referees;

- the governing bodies of basketball on a national, European and international level;
- the teams, leagues, and existing competition systems;
- sports training performance factors (the components of sport training) and the principles of training;
- the causes, prevention and cure of injuries;
- planning and periodization concepts and their use in training;
- basic sports psychology notions, including communication skills, behaviour modification, stress and coping with it, concentration, and so on;
- nutrition, hydration and their relationship and importance to performance (before, during and after the competition);
- anatomical and physiological adaptation following training and basic hygiene notions related to participation in sport;
- knowledge about significant historical dates relating to basketball on a national and international level;
- great basketball players and great club and national teams.

The coach has several means at his disposal for the theoretical training of his athletes: attendance at coaching and refereeing clinics and dissemination of findings; discussions between the coach and athletes about the results of major basketball competitions (Olympics, World Championships, Eurobasket, and so on); video analysis; distribution of basketball magazines and periodicals; a survey of his players regarding different aspects of organizing training sessions and their content; presentation of case studies highlighting examples of positive and negative behaviour on and off the court (both basketball-specific and in other sports). The coach's explanation and knowledge-sharing process during training sessions, pre- and post-training discussions and conversations while travelling to away matches or during camps are all important to theoretical preparation of the players.

The content of the theoretical knowledge that is shared by the coach needs to to be adapted to suit the age and gender of the players, their performance and ability level and their experience in the sport.

CHAPTER 16

BIOLOGICAL TRAINING

Biological training is represented by the physiological, natural or artificial measures – nutrition, hydration and means of recovery – applied in the training process. The main aim is to increase the capacity of the body to perform at high levels of volume and intensity.

Nutrition

It is now well accepted that nutrition plays a vital role in sporting performance. Ongoing sports nutrition research continues to make it clear that an athlete's dietary requirements are different from those of the normally active population. As well as being important to athletic performance, a nutritionally sound diet is essential to both the immediate and future health of the athlete.

The training diet should aim to do the following:

- provide athletes with enough fuel and fluid to meet the demands of training;
- provide all the nutrients essential for good health and in the right balance;
- trial various eating strategies for competition.

In order to meet the demands of training, athletes need more energy than the normally active population. If an athlete is unable to meet these demands by consuming the right amounts and types of food and fluid, he will be more easily fatigued and his performance will be impaired.

The nutritional components of which the coach and athlete should be aware are the carbohydrates, fats and proteins, while the protective elements include water, vitamins and mineral salts.

Carbohydrate

The main role of carbohydrate in the body is as an energy source. Intensive training makes heavy demands of muscle glycogen and its depletion is thought to be a major cause of fatigue. Carbohydrate also has a 'protein sparing' effect: if an athlete has an adequate intake of carbohydrate, then the body will use it in preference to protein (or muscle), thus preventing muscle depletion.

To help meet their carbohydrate needs, basketball players should eat carbohydrate-rich snacks throughout the day, such as fruit, yogurt and fruit, and grain-based bars. They should also eat carbohydrate-rich meals during the day based on breads, cereals, rice, pasta and other grains and starchy vegetables. In addition, carbohydrate-rich meals, snacks or fluids should be consumed as soon as possible after exercise. Their daily carbohydrate intake should be 5–6 grams/kg body weight for light training (below 60 minutes per day training), and up to 8–10 grams/kg body weight (and more than 10) for endurance training (more than 120 minutes per day of intensive training).

Fats

Fat plays many important roles in the body: it is an energy source, it plays a part in hormone production and the structure of the body cells, and it provides fat-soluble vitamins A, D, E and K and essential fatty acids. For athletes, the main disadvantages of a high total fat intake are an increase in body weight and levels of body fat, which can be detrimental to performance and can affect the athlete's intake of vital carbohydrate-rich foods. Basketball players should consume around 20 to 30 per cent of their dietary energy intake in the form of fat (ideally coming from fish, whole grains, nuts and seeds).

Protein

Protein is essential in the diet for building and maintaining body tissue. It forms the structure of components such as muscles, skin, blood and antibodies. Protein comes from two main dietary sources: animal foods (meat, eggs, dairy products, fish, poultry) and plant foods (nuts, legumes, dried beans, cereal products). The diet of basketball players must include 250 to 300 grams of protein per 24 hours.

Vitamins and Minerals

Vitamins and minerals are essential for health and desirable for optimal physical performance. The most important vitamins are vitamin A (contributes to improvement of eyesight and accelerates healing of skin wounds), B1 (a lack of which leads to more rapid fatigue), B2 and PP (influences the proper work of digestive organs), C (refreshes the body, strengthens the resistance of the body to infection), D (a lack of which affects the skeletal system), and E (contributes to the muscle metabolism).

Poor mineral status is also known to affect athletic performance. Most minerals occur in a wide variety of foods and are essential for nerve transmission, muscle contraction, fluid and electrolyte balance, energy production pathways and bone, muscle, skin and blood structure. The most important minerals are the following:

- iron (main function: haemoglobin production; oxygen carrier; energy production; helps learning and memory). It is available in liver,

kidney, green leafy vegetables and breakfast cereals;
- calcium (bone formation and maintenance, nerve and muscle function). Milk, cheese, yogurt and fish are important food sources of calcium;
- zinc (immune function; wound healing; energy production). Zinc is available in oysters, red meat, liver, nuts and seeds.

Hydration

Meeting the body's need for water is essential for both health and physical performance because water is the most important constituent of the human body. Deficiency of water causes various pathologic conditions, which are manifested in the form of a disturbed metabolism, heavier heartbeat, fatigue, and so on. As a consequence it is vital not to allow the body to dehydrate – coaches should ensure that athletes are well hydrated before training (or matches), as well as during (in the time-outs, for example) and after the sessions. Coaches should encourage players not to rely on thirst to prompt them to drink and should provide cool (not cold) fluids where possible, as these are emptied faster from the stomach and are more palatable.

Medication

Athletes striving to be the best are always looking for that extra edge. Often they are tempted to take ergogenic aids, substances that they believe will enhance their performance. If they are considering this (or thinking about using any other medical and biological means to help the recovery process, or to support the protein synthesis process or the optimization of the balance of vitamins and acids and bases), coaches and players should consult the team doctor or other qualified health professional (sport physician, dietician, physiologist). They must take seriously any short- or long-term health risks associated with their actions.

In the case of an injury, the team doctor must have the final say as to whether a player is to compete or not.

Fatigue, Rest and Means of Recovery

Players are fatigued after training and the greater the fatigue, the greater the after-effects, such as slow recovery rate, poor coordination and decreased speed and power of muscle contractions. Strong emotional fatigue often accentuates normal physiological fatigue, especially following competitions, from which it takes longer to recover.

Fatigue

'Fatigue' is a rather generic term, which is used to explain feelings of muscular tiredness or perhaps laboured breathing during exercise. The overload that determines the effectiveness of a training stimulus is linked closely to the allowances made for recovery between training efforts, sessions or cycles (periods) of training. Hard intense training without sufficient recovery produces fatigue rather than optimum performance. Athletes need recovery time to adapt to the stress of training, so the coach must plan recovery time and recovery activities.

Recovery

Recovery (or regeneration) is a multi-dimensional process that depends on intrinsic and extrinsic factors:

- the athlete's age, experience and gender will all affect recovery rates;
- environmental factors (for example, competing at high altitudes or training in cold weather);
- the types of muscle fibre;
- the type of exercise and type of energy system;
- psychological factors;
- availability and replenishment of micronutrients (vitamins and minerals).

There are several ways in which recovery is achieved and they include natural, physio-therapeutic and psychological means.

Natural Means of Recovery

Natural means of recovery do not require any special devices or modalities. These means can be divided into active rest and passive rest. Active rest (or kinotherapy) refers to rapidly eliminating waste products (lactic acid, for example) during moderate aerobic exercise or stretching. Passive rest (or complete rest) is the main physiological means of restoring working capacity. Athletes require 8 to 10 hours of sleep (80 to 90 per cent of it during the night). An athlete can use a number of methods to promote relaxed sleep, and relaxation techniques, a massage or warm bath before bedtime are all helpful.

Physiotherapeutic Means of Recovery

These means of recovery have special modalities and include massage, the use of heat (thermotherapy) or cold (cryotherapy), contrast baths, oxygenotherapy, aerotherapy, altitude training, reflexotherapy (acupuncture, acupressure) and chemotherapy (taking vitamins to supplement the energy needs).

Psychological Means of Recovery

These means of recovery can provide benefits such as increased self-awareness, improved motivation and decreased reactions to stress. A strong relationship exists between physical and mental relaxation – they produce a similar response (lower heart rates and blood pressure, and improved mood states). Some of the techniques used include meditation, imagery and visualization, directing the thought processes of athletes towards calmness and relaxation. Listening to music, watching a movie, reading a book or visiting a park or an art gallery can also provide a relaxing diversion from hard training, and thus facilitate recovery.

Recovery techniques must become habitual and be synchronized with the biological adaptation to a training demand and the correct alternation of work with regeneration. Recovery must be a daily concern and not follow only isolated training lessons and main competitions. In this way, players regenerate following the training session and prevent acute exhaustion and overtraining.

CHAPTER 17

ARTISTICAL TRAINING

Artistical training is another component of the sports training process. It is more obvious in those sports (such as gymnastics, synchronized swimming and aerobics) in which success is determined by the technical content (difficulty, originality and risk elements), as well as by the artistic and aesthetic presentation of the performance.

In basketball, artistical elements come into play when players execute technical elements in a special way, contributing greatly to the beauty of the game. These might include passes behind the back, or players running at high speed and dribbling behind the back, between their legs or performing 360-degree turns. Slam-dunks are the most spectacular element in the game of basketball, and blocked shots performed in a powerful and vigorous way are also impressive. Spectators also enjoy the highest jumps and a player's ability to perform moves while in the air, as well as shots scored from a distance, and court-length passes that lead to easy points being scored.

GB forward Nick George in full action.

APPENDIX

FIBA (the world governing body of basketball) have decided that new court markings will be in place from 1 October 2010 for all international level competitions. In England this change will be phased over the next five years – see the England Basketball website for more details.

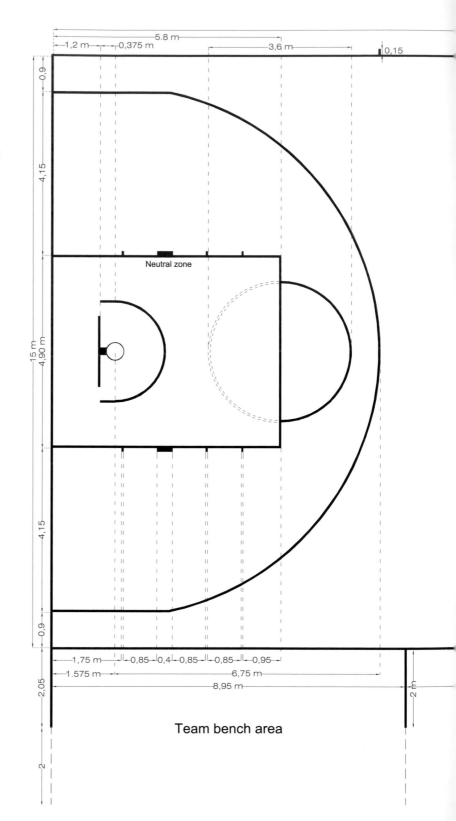

Neutral zone

Team bench area

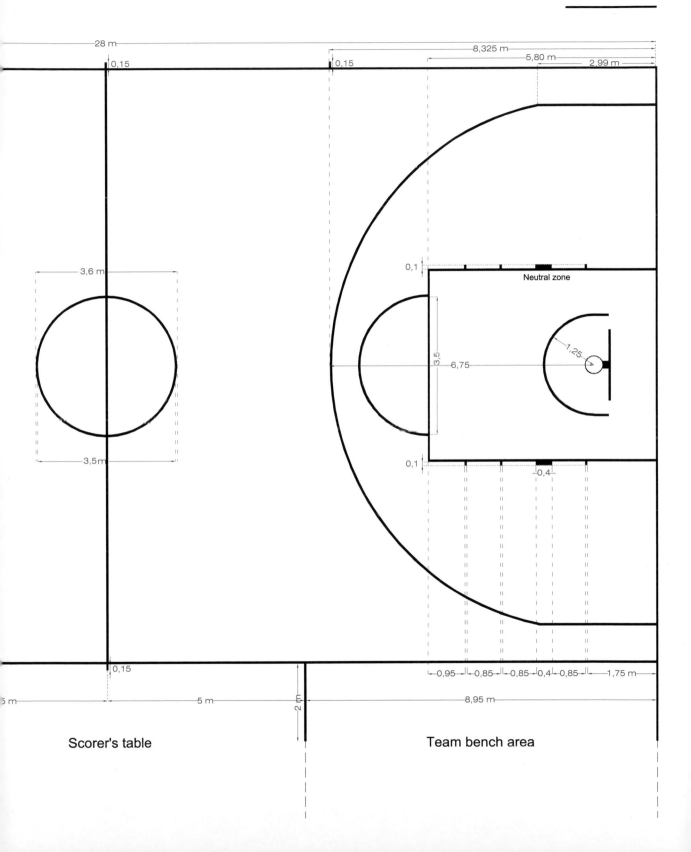

GLOSSARY

Assist   An excellent pass that enables a teammate to score easily.

Back court   The half of the court containing a team's own basket (the basket they are defending). A 'back-court violation' occurs when the team in possession of the ball passes the ball back to someone in their own half of the court.

Backboard   The flat, often transparent board supporting the basket.

Back-door   A term used to describe a cut by an attacker towards the basket to the side of the defensive player away from the ball. It is mainly used when the attacking player is being overplayed.

Bank shot   A shot where the ball bounces into the net off the backboard.

Baseball pass   One-hand pass, usually used for long passes. Also called javelin pass or shoulder pass.

Baseline   The end line of the court (behind the backboard).

Baseline drive   A powerful run along the baseline to attack the basket.

Basket   The target and also the name for a score; a field basket is worth two points.

Box and one   A type of defence with four players playing in a 2-2 zone formation (box) while the fifth player is playing man-to-man.

Boxing out   The positioning of a defensive player to prevent an attacker from moving to the basket to gain a rebound.

Break   The rapid movement of a player to a space where they hope to receive a pass.

Center   The tallest player in a team (also known as the pivot or post player), who plays around the key. Also, the name of a playing position.

Charging foul   A personal foul committed by an attacking player charging into a stationary defender.

Combination defence   A type of defence where some players play in a zone formation and others play man-to-man.

Controlling the boards   Gaining the majority of the rebounds.

Cut   A quick movement (usually towards the basket) by an attacker without the ball to gain an advantage over the defence.

Cutter   A player who cuts (or breaks).

'D'   Abbreviation for defence. 'Tough D' means playing a determined defensive game.

Diamond and one   A combined defence with four defenders playing zone in a diamond formation (1-2-1) and the fifth defender playing man-to-man.

Double foul   Simultaneous foul by opposing players.

Double team   Two players defending one attacker with the ball (also called 'trap').

Drill   A practice/exercise performed during a training session.

Drive   The movement of an attacking player who is dribbling towards the basket in an attempt to score.

Dunk   One- or two-handed spectacular shot when the player takes the ball above the level of the ring and thrusts it down through the hoop.

Fake   A feint or a dummy made with the aim of deceiving an opponent into making a wrong move.

Fastbreak   A fast attack that attempts to create an easy scoring opportunity before the defence is organized; the main aim is to achieve numerical superiority or a position for a good shot.

Field-goal attempt   A shot taken in an attempt to score two or three points.

Fouled out   After committing five personal fouls, a player is fouled out, and is required to leave the game.

Foul line   The free-throw line.

Forward   One of the positions in the team. Forwards are taller than guards and shorter than centers; they usually play on the sides of the court between the side lines and the restricted area.

Free throw   A penalty shot from the free-throw line, taken unopposed and worth one point.

Front court   The half of the court in which the basket that a team is attacking is located.

Full-court press   A hustling pressure defence covering the full court and not just the defending team's half.

Fundamentals   The basic skills of the game, necessary as a background for all individual and team play.

Gap   In zone defence, 'gap' refers to the area of court where the zones of responsibility of two defenders meet.

'Give and go'   An attacking combination between two teammates in which a player passes the ball and then cuts towards the basket for a return pass.

Guard   One of the positions in the team. Guards are usually the shorter players and they usually play between the centre line and the free-throw line extended to the side lines.

Half-court press   A pressing defence that operates in the team's back court.

Held ball   When two players from different teams have their hands firmly on the ball (the referee will call 'jump ball', which is decided by the arrow possession).

High post   The position occupied by an attacking player at the top of the key area (near the free-throw line).

Hook shot   One-handed shot with a swinging motion side-on to the basket.

Jump ball The method of starting the game, with the referee throwing the ball up between two opposing players in the central circle of the court.

Jump shot One-handed shot released at the top of a jump.

Jump stop A stop with the ball when the player lands on both feet simultaneously.

Key The keyhole-shaped area extending from the baseline under the basket.

Lay up A shot delivered at the end of a run at the basket (usually with one hand against the backboard and into the basket).

Low post A position filled by an attacking player (usually the tallest) at the bottom of the key area, close to the basket.

Man-to-man defence A defensive system in which each player is assigned to guard a specific opponent rather than covering an area of court.

Motion offence A style of attacking play in which players follow a set of rules to all move at the same time in an attempt to create a shooting opportunity.

Offence Attack.

One-on-one A situation in which an attacker plays against one defender.

Out of bounds The area outside the legal playing court.

Outlet pass A pass that initiates the fast-break to either side line from a defensive rebound.

Overload Outnumbering the defence.

Overtime Extra 5-minute periods that are played in case the score has been tied.

Pass and cut Also called 'give and go' – a combination between two players.

Playmaker The guard who is handling the ball and is announcing the set plays to be followed.

Pick and roll A side screen followed by a pivot towards the basket by the player who has set the screen, useful against a switching man-to-man defence.

Pivot Another name for a center (or post player).

Pivot foot The foot that is in contact with the floor during a pivoting action. This action is aimed at protecting the ball and performed by a player who has finished dribbling and who steps more than once in any direction with the other foot (called the stepping foot).

Point guard The guard whose responsibility is to bring the ball up the court and to control the attack.

Post Another name for a center (or pivot). Also, the term describes the position close to the basket where the pivots play.

Press A defensive attempt to force the opponents into making some kind of error and, thus, to lose possession of the ball (usually by aggressive defence, double-teaming or harassing the ball). The press can be applied full-court or half-court.

Rebound Retrieval of the ball as it bounces off the ring or off the backboard after an unsuccessful shot.

Safety man An attacking player who plays with the aim of defending against possible fastbreaks or loss of possession.

Screen Occurs when an attacking player attempts to prevent a defender from reaching a desired position or maintaining his defensive position.

Screen and roll A side screen followed by a pivot towards the basket by the player who has set the screen.

Scrimmage A practice game.

Set play A pre-arranged form of attack.

Skip pass A pass made in an attack that misses out one or two players in the attacking formation.

Steal Taking the ball from an opponent against his will or intercepting a pass.

Stride stop A stop with the ball, performed using a 'one-two' rhythm.

Strong side The side of the key area into which the attacking team has passed the ball.

Switch A combination between two defenders in which they exchange defensive responsibilities by changing the player they are guarding. It occurs usually during a screen situation.

Three-point shot A basket scored from outside the 3-points semicircle (6.25m from the basket).

Tip-off The centre jump ball at the start of play.

Trailer An attacking player who follows behind the ball handler.

Transition A team moving from attack to defence, and vice-versa, after a change of possession.

Travelling The attacker stepping more than twice when holding the ball – an illegal move.

Triple threat A position in which an attacker has the ball and has not dribbled. He has three options: shoot, pass or dribble.

Turnover Loss of ball possession without a shot being taken.

Weak side The side of the key area where the attacking team does not have the ball.

Wing A position on the court between the end of the free-throw line and the side line.

Zone defence A defensive playing system in which the players cover areas of the court rather than marking individual players.

WHO'S WHO IN BASKETBALL

FIBA (Fédération Internationale de Basketball)

Founded: 18 June 1932
Address: Av. Louis-Casaï 53, 1216
Cointrin/Geneva, Switzerland
Tel: +41 22 545 00 00
Fax +41 22 545 00 99
E-mail: info@fiba.com
Website: www.fiba.com
President: Mr Bob Elphinston (AUS)
Secretary General: Mr Patrick Baumann (SUI)
Secretary General Emeritus: Mr Borislav Stankovic (SRB)
Affiliated National Federations: 213

FIBA EUROPE

Founded as an independent FIBA Zone Commission in 2001.
Address: Widenmayerstrasse 18, 80538
Munich, Germany
Tel: +49 89 78 06 08 0
Fax +49 89 78 06 08 27
E-mail: info@europe.fiba.com
Website: www.fibaeurope.com
President: Mr George Vassilakopoulos (GRE)
Secretary General: Mr Nar Zanolin (CAN)
51 federations are members of FIBA Europe.

England Basketball

Address: England Basketball, PO Box 3971, Sheffield, S9 9AZ
Tel: 0114 284 1060
Fax: 0114 284 1061
E-mail: info@englandbasketball.co.uk
Website: www.englandbasketball.co.uk
Chief Executive: Keith Mair

REFERENCES

Books

Bazany, B., Coleman, B., Ransom, D. (1993) *Attacking a Zone Defence*, English Basketball Association

Bompa, T. (1999) *Periodization. Theory and Methodology of Training* (4th Edition), Human Kinetics

Coleman, B. (1993) *Coaching Basketball. Individual and Team Fundamentals*, English Basketball Association

Cousy, B., Power, F. (1970) *Basketball. Concepts and Techniques*, Boston: Allyn and Bacon

Dragnea, A. (1996) *Sports Training*, Bucharest: Pedagogical Printing Press (Antrenamentul Sportiv, Bucuresti: Editura Didactica si Pedagogica)

England Basketball (2001) *Basketball Level 1 Coach Award. Candidate Manual*

England Basketball (2001) *Basketball Level 1 Coach Award. Candidate Resource Manual*

England Basketball (2007) *Basketball. Manual for Table Officials*

Harley, R., Doust, J. (1997) *Strength and Fitness Training for Basketball. A Sports Science Manual*. NCF Publications

Marcus, H. (1991) *Basketball Basics. Drills, Techniques and Strategies for Coaches*, Chicago: Contemporary Books

Mikes, J. (1987) *Basketball FundaMENTALS. A Complete Mental Training Guide*, Champaign: Leisure Press

Pyke, F. (2001) *Better Coaching. Advanced Coach's Manual* (2nd Edition), Australian Sports Commission, Human Kinetics

Sports Coach UK (2007) *Planning and Periodisation*, Coachwise Business Solutions

Stimpson, P. (1984) *Basketball. The Skills of the Game*, Crowood

Wooden, J. (1980) *Practical Modern Basketball* (2nd Edition), New York: John Wiley

Wootten, M. (2003) *Coaching Basketball Successfully* (2nd Edition), Human Kinetics

Online Resources

englandbasketball.co.uk
fiba.com
fibaeurope.com

INDEX